"There are many pretenders to the crown of Patricia Highsmith, but Mathilde Merlot's *Death at Vassar* is the real thing, a direct line in the Highsmith lineage. The description of the repressed and thus sexually-boiling-over 1950s, the deliciously coy and intelligent quality of the heroine, and the spot-on recreation of sometimes deadly emotions circulating on that era's college campuses all confirm this conviction. A revelation."

Dennis Broe,
author of *Calamitous Corruption*,
the Harry Palmer 1940s LA trilogy

"This book owns all the qualities you look for when you drown in a novel: moving, thrilling, profound and funny; extraordinarily psychological and entertaining."

Emmanuelle de Villepin,
author of *The Devil's Reward*

"High in characters and insightful of the dreams and desires of young women, this amoral and suspenseful tale also paints a beautifully bleak picture of the human condition."

Lars Bill Lundholm,
best-selling author of
the Stockholm Murder Series

DEATH AT VASSAR

A Madeleine Rousseau Mystery

MATHILDE MERLOT

To L.B. Lundholm, godfather of my writing.

"All sins are attempts to fill voids."
Simone Weil

Chapter 1

A heavy wind blew through the small opening in the window, scattering loose papers across the floor. The skirt's light fabric played quietly around her knees. On the floor lay a left shoe, black with a small leather bow. The other one, she still wore. Soft strands of hair danced across her face as her head hung heavily. A beautiful silk scarf encircled her delicate neck so tightly her eyes bulged as she dangled, lifeless, from the pipe.

The spring of 1959 saw too many young women dying of "sadness and broken hearts." The socially permissible blanket terms for suicide made it gentler on the ears yet the issue continued to plague the female population in their twenties and had certainly not spared Vassar College. In the last year, three students had ended their lives, one of them on campus. The administration held high hopes the fall semester might bring a wave of peace and tranquility back to the student body, sparing any more damage to the school's reputation. They prayed the picturesque campus, with the last warm rays of sun, might erase the previous term's ghastly events.

Suicide was the very last thing on Madeleine's mind as she casually strolled across the freshly mowed lawn toward her new home for the year. On the contrary, wearing her Christian Dior black and white polka-dotted dress from a last trip to Paris and her favorite Hermès purse in hand, she was overwhelmed by a beaming sensation of happiness. Her heart swelled as she took in the particular smell of New England's dry earth, which this late in the summer, desperately craved next season's rain. With birds chirping in the trees across campus, all the girls smiling at the freedom provided by the university for the semester, nothing could possibly ruffle Madeleine's feathers or so she thought.

The weekend before classes started, Strong House, where most returning students were assigned, appeared busier than an ant farm. In front of the three-story red brick dormitory, clusters of young women formed, sharing tales of brief estival romances and comparing class schedules. Madeleine waved to a few familiar faces without stopping. In a determined demeanor, she walked into the building, oozing an effortless and enviable confidence. As this was her third year, Madeleine knew exactly where she was going. On the last floor, the hallway was filled with the brouhaha of more enthusiastic students carrying bags and suitcases, excitedly searching for their designated rooms. Madeleine had low expectations with whom she was to be paired with. During her freshman and sophomore years at Vassar, she had not veritably liked her roommates. Sure she'd made do but had not bonded the way she had last year with Phyllis and Joanie. They were a class below her but nonetheless the three girls had formed a nice trio. Hopefully they would all be on the same floor. Snapping out of her thoughts and before anyone saw, Madeleine quickly and quietly entered her room, relishing in solitude. A little time alone was necessary before slipping into her social persona.

On the bed furthest from the door, Madeleine unpacked the leather suitcase, setting aside the carefully wrapped gift she'd brought back for Phyllis. The box had traveled across the Atlantic, arriving at its final destination unscathed. Phyllis would definitely be impressed, appreciating its true value. She was not one of those girls who had come for a "M.R.S." degree, hoping to snatch a husband. She was genuinely interested in expanding her mind and had earned herself Madeleine's respect and friendship. Joanie, on the other hand, had no other aspiration than to wed an Ivy League boy to start life. Ultimately, if it was her only route to achieve happiness, so be it, Madeleine thought, but it certainly did not merit a reward. She turned to the empty side of the room, the bare blue and white striped mattress, an invitation for the mystery resident for the next nine months. Whose body would lay in that bed, friend or foe? Madeleine brushed the thought out of her mind. It was useless pondering.

While traveling in Europe, Aunt Evelyn and Madeleine had been strolling along the Boulevard Saint-Germain in Paris one afternoon while Uncle Pierre tended to some business. They had initially stopped at Deyrolles on rue du Bac. The store was extraordinary, filled with taxidermied birds, mammals, and exotic creatures; a fantastic zoo of stillness. In the innumerable drawers of the tall armoires, lay hundreds of incredibly colored butterflies and beetles, all delicately impaled by needles plunged into the soft, silk cushioning of each case. Uncle Pierre had long been a supporter of the Deyrolles institution, both for the pedagogical role it played and also to rub shoulders with artists like Dalì who often frequented the place. The staff had immediately recognized Aunt Evelyn when she came in and catered to her every need. With Madeleine's help, they had decided on the most fantastic six-foot male peacock in all of its multi-colored splendor to be shipped to their New York residence. While no one saw, Madeleine had touched the feathers of the stiffened animal. She thought it might be a strange sensation to touch death. It really wasn't.

Further down the Parisian boulevard, on the left-hand side, in a quaint boutique was an array of wonderful accessories for women gauchely displayed in the window. The expertly hand-crafted parasols, umbrellas, and gloves were all more refined in detail and finish than the next. The small and cramped store smelt of old wood and leather. A short French man had come out from the back atelier when the single bell above the door had signaled customers. Madeleine had immediately noticed his hands: despite the swollen knuckles, they looked strong from years of manual labor. His disheveled wispy white hair gave him an air of a mad scientist but when he spoke, a fondness poured out as he had detailed each piece the way he might have described an adored grandchild. Charmed by it all, Aunt Evelyn had insisted Madeleine get two pairs of the expensive leather gloves; one navy blue and one light rose. Both were made from buttery, supple lambskin with tiny holes perforated throughout the top in the design of a daisy. Madeleine loved her beautiful gloves so much, she had impulsively thrown her arms around her aunt's neck to thank her. Occasionally she let the thrill of receiving what she wanted completely overtake proper etiquette and behavior. It was limited to her aunt and uncle really as they were the only ones who gave her anything. Madeleine often wished they were her own parents and with the sudden death of their daughter, her cousin Margot two years ago, they practically were.

Madeleine and Margot had become like sisters since the age of twelve, when they had spent the entire summer together. Nearly inseparable, they were almost like twins were it not for their physical differences. Margot had thin, straw-colored hair and light eyes, with an elegance to her demeanor she was too young to grasp. Instead, she found her features to be all too small and delicate, especially her chest. On the other hand, Madeleine's shapely figure developing in early adolescence, was the absolute envy of her cousin, particularly because it did not go unnoticed amongst boys and men alike. With beautiful dark chestnut hair, she looked more like an Italian actress while Margot resembled a frail, romantic artist from the previous century.

Since one of Uncle Pierre's greatest joys was pleasing his daughter, seeing the bond they'd formed that summer, he had offered to pay his niece's tuition for the all-girls' Catholic school Margot attended in New York City. She loved her cousin dearly and being an only child was lonely. Likewise, Madeleine was all but too happy about the proposal, stepping into a life of luxury, leaving the suburban tranquility where she had long been ignored. She lived with her aunt and uncle, in their New York penthouse only to return to her parents' home in New Jersey at the end of the week. Madeleine was one of the rare children who hated weekends.

Returning to New Jersey was the perpetual reminder of her insignificance. After her brother Philip's death, her parents had lost all interest in life, and in her. To this day, Mother was void of any sort of curiosity when it came to Madeleine, who harbored a secret disdain for her mother's person mixed with an eternal desire to be held by her. Father had buried his ambition along with his son and solely took comfort in the repetition of his days. He thought of nothing, performing the same daily actions, in hopes of finding a sliver of solace in routine since the accident. Some eighteen years ago, Father had decided to take his seven-year old son to town to choose a present for Madeleine's fifth birthday. Philip had been promised a toy too. But before they had reached their destination, another vehicle had come speeding down the windy road from the east, over by where the highway ran. The driver had failed to stop at the intersection and had violently struck the passenger's side, killing Philip on impact. Father, having suffered only minor injuries, had pulled his son from the mangled pieces of metal that had stolen his life. Without a word, he had carried the body along the road, in the direction of the town, until the police had stopped him. When they took the child's corpse away, Father fell to his knees. Ever since, he was but a shadow of himself, living an automated life of mere survival. Mother had been understandably shattered as well, finding her comfort in a numbed illusion of normalcy, supplied by her doctor in the form of pills. From her fifth birthday on, no one bothered to pick up or hold the remaining living child in the house.

With time, Madeleine learnt to live with being ignored. Father forgot his dreams and continued working the mundane life of an accountant, never trying his hand at the ventures he'd once dreamt of. Meanwhile Mother solely cared for her husband and the house. It was all she could accomplish, finding her life's purpose in being at her vapid husband's beck and call. Her maternal instincts had all but disappeared and she was only capable of teaching her daughter how to be the perfect homemaker. At times Mother would attempt an exchange and pass on "nuggets of life advice" as she called them: best to starch a man's shirt by starting with the collar, the extra dash of nutmeg to make the mashed potatoes exquisite. But Madeleine did not relish the inconsequential information given to better please a future husband.

All she longed for was the love she was being deprived of. By the time Madeleine was nine years old, she'd succeeded in emotionally isolating herself completely from her parents. She had knew to seek out care, parental figures, and an entire other life elsewhere.

Psychologically ousted from her birth family, Madeleine regularly conjured up excuses to spend the least amount of time in their presence. The closest replacement figures made the transference easy. She had long admired her father's graceful sister, Aunt Evelyn, who lived with her husband, Uncle Pierre, on the Upper East Side in New York City. She was kind, intelligent, and spent afternoons donating time and money to several charities and museums. Often stroking Madeleine's hair while speaking, she asked questions always giving her full, undivided attention. Lately, she was participating in the organization of the opening of her dear friend Peggy Guggenheim's permanent space for modern and contemporary art and had snuck Madeleine in for an exclusive visit. Her aunt and uncle traveled, hosted parties, and dinners filled with both American and international intellectuals, artists, and elites. With a taste of this life of ease thanks to her cousin's affection, Madeleine had easily adapted and taken more than a liking to it.

Understandably, as spring semester came to an end, Madeleine had been prepared to do anything if it kept her from spending time in the New Jersey parental shrine dedicated to a dead son. Though her parents and her aunt and uncle had both lost children, they had had handled the situations completely differently. While the Rivers plunged into an abyss of pain, never to seek the surface again, Uncle Pierre and Aunt Evelyn had doubled their love and affection for their niece, whose emotional craving was bottomless. And this year, they had surprised her with an invitation to Europe, allowing an escape from the banal months of watching her mother bake her famous peach cobbler and listening to her "nuggets." This European trip had been planned for years as a high school graduation gift for Margot. After her untimely death senior year, Uncle Pierre and Aunt Evelyn couldn't bear the thought of going on their own. Two years later, they had wanted to honor the memory of Margot and take their niece instead. The vacation was spent traveling from one sumptuous hotel to the next, eating exclusively in Michelin-starred restaurants, and following private tours of museum collections normally closed to the public. From the southern coast of the Riviera, driving through Cannes, Nice, a short stop in Antibes at the Eden Roc before heading into the Principality of Monaco for a charity evening. In the grand reception hall, cascades of exotic flower compositions poured out of antique vases intoxicating guests with their perfume while champagne continuously flowed in crystal glasses. After the dinner and auction, Madeleine had been invited to dance by a number of notable Italian, French, and Spanish aristocrats. As she was expertly spun around the room while maintaining intelligent conversation, she maneuvered closer to the royal table where Princess Grace sat in all her regal elegance. Before her partner sent her in the other direction, Madeleine' eyes met the Princess's, taking her breath away. At that very instant she seared the moment into her memory: this is the life she wanted.

On their last night in Paris, after having dined on foie gras and the renowned hare "a la royale" at the historic Grand Véfour, the three opted to walk back as it was only dusk, despite the late hour. While strolling under the limestone arcs of the rue de Rivoli, heading toward the Hotel de Crillon, Madeleine had turned to Uncle Pierre and Aunt Evelyn.

"I couldn't have spent a lovelier evening. Thank you for such a wondrous gift. This trip has been truly magical. The only thing . . ." Madeleine's voice trailed.

"What is it, darling," Aunt Evelyn asked, concerned at the sadness veiling her niece's face suddenly.

"I very much wish I was crawling into bed with Margot tonight, the way we used to when we were little; giggling under the covers," Madeleine said.

Her aunt and uncle had reached out, each taking Madeleine by the hand. Their eyes wet, linked by a profound pain, they walked in silence into the Parisian night with their "other" daughter, as they liked to call her. That's exactly who Madeleine wanted to be.

Chapter 2

"Madeleine Rivers? Or is there a Madeleine Rousseau here," Janet, the Resident Assistant, called out from the hall. Clipboard in hand, she was verifying a list while slowly pacing down the hallway. Although the girl's hair was brushed, it was not properly groomed, and no care had been given to styling. She wore thick black-rimmed glasses, which regularly slipped down the slope of her nose. Definitely a sheep; one who followed all of the rules, especially if it was on a list. Madeleine shuddered and put on the kindest smile before responding.

"Yes, hello. I'm Madeleine Rousseau," she said, waving Janet over. Relieved, the girl dressed with a skirt fit for a peasant, headed down, flipping back and forth between two sheets of paper with an air of confusion.

"I don't understand on this list there is a Madeleine Rivers and on this one a Madeleine Rousseau. Or is there another Madeleine here," she asked, her eyes darting back and forth.

"No, they are both me. I now go by Madeleine Rousseau," she answered with an assurance meant to end the conversation.

Feeling privy to an unaccustomed level of intimacy, Janet excitedly reached out for Madeleine."Oh! Don't tell me: you got married and he is letting you finish your degree?"

Madeleine winked and Janet smiled back. She didn't care to share any details of her life with this girl. There was no need for her to know she had arbitrarily opted to adopt her uncle's last name instead of her father's. Slowly but surely, she was erasing the existence of Madeleine Rivers.

"Oh goodness. I am going to have to redo the entire floor. I'm not sure who your roommate will end up being because I thought you were two separate people," she replied, staring at the list again.

"Don't worry, I'm sure you'll make a perfect match," Madeleine said as she patted Janet on the back and walked away, wanting to isolate herself. The R.A. watched her and felt lucky to have such lovely girls to watch over.

Not two minutes had passed when a knock was heard at the door. Madeleine took a deep breath to present herself to her newly assigned roommate. As she opened the door, a large smile spread across her face as Phyllis appeared.

"Since when do you knock," she asked jokingly, before hugging her friend.

Madeleine approved of Phyllis all across the board. She was smart, neat, and calm. All important attributes. Though her clothes weren't always fashionable, they had a simple style which corresponded to who she was, one of the most intelligent women Madeleine knew. She was doing a double major in Political Science and Diplomacy. Her dream was to become a United States diplomat like Eugenie Anderson. Phyllis would never be so average as to collect pictures of actors and singers like James Dean or Marilyn Monroe. She dreamt of being an actor on the international political scene and proudly representing her country in negotiations and agreements. The faculty recognized her intelligence and talent and had sent Phyllis as the youngest woman to represent Vassar at the 1958 Model United Nation at Wilkes College in Pennsylvania. She had given an incredible speech on the assigned theme of strengthening the United Nations, which had then been printed in the school paper. Phyllis hadn't even been affected by the temporary gain in popularity. All she was interested in was politics and her own future in it. She had even tried to entice Madeleine to join the Diplomacy Club but that's where the line was drawn. Madeleine wanted no part in activities where she would be asked to comply to ridiculous rules that brought nothing to her future.

"Come in, come in," she said, moving out of the way. Phyllis entered waving *The Washington Post* in her hand. Since last year, Phyllis and Joanie had gotten into the habit of bringing up Madeleine's newspaper along with their own mail. The newspapers and any oversized packages were left in a wicker basket on the counter, beside the wall of individually assigned locked metal mailboxes. Uncle Pierre insisted Madeleine subscribe to *The Post* to keep up with current events. There was nothing he despised more than ignorance. Besides, anything he or Aunt Evelyn asked, Madeleine accepted. They were the ones paying for her four-year degree at Vassar. Of course, they had originally intended to do so for Margot therefore it seemed all but too natural for them to offer their niece what they could no longer give their daughter. At least Madeleine saw it that way.

In return for the love, attention, and financial comfort, she was prepared to do everything they asked. Every two weeks since she was away at college, she sent a letter to keep them in the know or *au courant* as Uncle Pierre liked to say, about what was happening on campus, in her classes, with Phyllis and Joanie. She wrote with her favorite fountain pen on thick, off-white paper which thirstily drank the ink. At the top of the stationery the monogram "MR" was embossed. The stationery had been Margot's. As they shared the same initials, she had strangely inherited it after her death. Did Uncle Pierre and Aunt Evelyn ever open the envelope and indulge for an instant in the fantasy of their own child writing from college instead of their niece, she wondered. Perhaps. And Madeleine saw nothing wrong with that. On the contrary, she felt rather righteous. She had finally found a family in which she had a role to play: bringing solace to mourning parents.

Phyllis placed the newspaper on the bare bed and stood awkwardly, not knowing what to do with her hands.

"Tell me about your trip Madeleine! I read all of your letters at least twice, but I want to know more. How tall was the Eiffel Tower, how impressive was the Louvre, how blue was the Mediterranean," she asked nearly breathless with excitement to hear firsthand impressions of places she'd only read about.

"Oh Phyllis, it was wonderful. I took some pictures with a camera Uncle Pierre bought me. I will show you when I bring them back next time. You would have adored it. And Paris! It is the most magical place on Earth. Wait."

Madeleine jumped to shut the door, ensuring no one would interrupt them. She opened the desk drawer and took out the deep wine-colored box wrapped with a delicate cream satin bow. She handed it to Phyllis with satisfaction.

"This my friend, comes from Paris, France, *pour toi.*"

Phyllis's face flushed. She wasn't often embarrassed. She rationalized all feelings and was usually able to get herself out of any situation using her intellect. Except with emotional intimacy. This included friendships, which was why she kept so few. And although Madeleine often made her feel uncomfortable, she was still very much drawn to her, sometimes inexplicably so.

As Phyllis untied the bow and opened the box, Madeleine was hanging the custom-made dresses bought in Paris, along the rue Saint-Honoré. They deserved an audience going from her trunk to the closet, she believed. Phyllis gasped as she saw the navy gloves and brought them to her cheek, feeling the buttery softness of the young lamb's skin, sacrificed for human pleasure.

"I thought of you immediately when I saw them. Look I got a pair of pink ones! Oh but don't tell Joanie, I didn't get her anything," Madeleine confided.

This was exactly the type of comment from Madeleine which made Phyllis feel both special and slightly guilty.

"Oh, I won't, I wouldn't want her to feel left out. But Madeleine these are beautiful. Are you sure? Thank you so much. You shouldn't have. I can't imagine what these may have cost you."

Madeleine shrugged her shoulders.

"Beautiful things in life are meant to be enjoyed. You have such delicate small hands, it seemed like these gloves were made for you," she twirled with a dress on a hanger pressed up against her body. "What do you think of this one?"

"The green color looks absolutely fantastic on you," Phyllis kept pulling her new gloves through her hands as if contemplating a seventeenth-century duel.

At the sound of a knock, Phyllis quickly hid the gloves under her dress as she sat down on the chair by the unclaimed desk. The door opened just enough for the R.A. to poke her head in.

"Hello again," Madeleine prompted.

"So, no one has come in here yet," asked Janet.

Madeleine glanced around the room. "Not yet! Now if you don't want to put anyone in here, I'm fine with having the room to myself," Madeleine winked at Phyllis.

Janet, already distraught by the situation, did not understand Madeleine's humor. She immediately went into a complex explanation concerning the system of how everyone was assigned a specific room but Madeleine's two last names had wreaked havoc.

Madeleine had stopped listening and continued putting her shoes and fine sweaters away.

"I trust you will do your best and I will be more than content with your decision," she coaxed, tilting her head like a submissive puppy, in hopes she would leave.

Janet returned a half smile and turned questioningly to Phyllis, who hadn't budged.

"I already have my room, it's number 19," she replied to the inquisitive look. Checking the list, she nodded and left to putter about her business elsewhere.

"So, you don't know who your roommate is? You'll surely be assigned a girl from your class," Phyllis pondered.

"I don't know and to be honest, I don't really care. I'm not looking to make friends. If she's nice, fine; if not, as long as she doesn't get in my way. We'll have a great year and then, I'll be off to Paris for the summer," Madeleine confided, putting a finger to her sealed lips. "But that is our little secret."

Although they did not spend summers visiting one another, the thought of her friend's departure immediately tainted Phyllis's mood, like a dark cloud creeping into her soul. They had barely gotten back to school and she was already thinking about leaving. But she brushed it off; Madeleine didn't like sentimentality. Changing the subject, Phyllis blurted:

"I'm thrilled about my classes this semester. Also there is a chance that I may be able to work at the State Department next summer for almost month. Can you imagine all I could learn?"

"Oh Phyllis that would be fantastic, as long as you aren't relegated to menial administrative desk work," Madeleine replied, placing a pile of perfectly ironed collared shirts in the cupboard.

Madeleine had a way of encouraging and undermining a person in one fell swoop. She considered it helpful and honest, so as to prevent disappointment. Phyllis had gotten used to the delicate blows received from her friend, unaware it slowly chipped away at her confidence. Pulling out the navy gloves from under her dress, she caressed them once more, reassuring herself.

"I guess I'll go and put these away before Joanie gets back. I do love them Madeleine. Thank you again. I shall wear them only on special occasions."

Madeleine was content with Phyllis's response to the gift. She was grateful and even a bit awestruck, it seemed. Aunt Evelyn would never notice if she didn't wear the navy gloves. She still had the pink ones and had left them in New York for an appropriate occasion. Madeleine was going to visit them the third weekend in September. Her own parents, on the other hand, had not even asked if she was returning home at all. Instead, she would go to New York for Margot's birthday. Every year since her death, she had made it a point to be with her aunt and uncle to celebrate the day her cousin was born. To this day, no one knew Madeleine had been present the tragic day Margot fell out of the attic window to her death.

Chapter 3

For the first encounter of the semester with Professor Beardsmith, Madeleine wanted to make an entrance. The emerald dress had a very flattering square neckline, showing off her graceful collarbones. She liked that part of her body, and most of the rest as well. Inheriting her features from her mother, the two looked nearly like sisters, especially with their matching dark chestnut hair. What really set Madeleine apart from her mother and anyone else for that matter, were her eyes. She had developed heterochromia after Philip's death. The weeks following his passing had been a blur for both Mother and Father. Still young and reeling from the trauma, Madeleine only had brief sensorial snapshots of the period: her favorite pink bunny which faintly smelled like her mother's perfume, the bedroom wallpaper with miniature bouquets of white lilies tied with rose-colored bows. It was only after a few weeks that Aunt Evelyn, while paying a visit to her brother and his family, saw her niece's different colored eyes. Neither parent had noticed the change in little Madeleine. After multiple doctor's visits, the heterochromia was inexplicable and remained. When asked if she'd suffered an injury, Mother couldn't recall anything particular about Madeleine in the past few months. She couldn't remember anything else but the void, the hollow, the wretched pain eating away at her heart. So Madeleine was left with one amber eye while the other one had turned dark green. Unfortunately, it hadn't been sufficient to remind them *she* wasn't dead yet.

The professor would be in his office in the Hughes Building before heading to the lecture hall. Although Madeleine didn't have any classes to take with him for her degree in French Literature, she wanted him to be her advisor for the paper on Rimbaud. She would use it as an added justification to obtain the summer scholarship at the Sorbonne in Paris. It was the second year Vassar and the French university were having an exchange. Two seniors and one junior would be chosen to spend June and July of the new decade in Paris; Madeleine was determined to be one of them.

Once she procured the sole junior slot on the exchange program, she wanted to finish her senior year there. The idea had been for Uncle Pierre to extend his generosity and pay for Madeleine's life abroad. Yet after what she had witnessed in his native country over the summer, it would be challenging. Uncle Pierre still held a lot of anger against his fellow countrymen for having conceded to the Germans during the war. While having lunch at the Brasserie Lipp, Uncle Pierre had overheard Parisian socialites and known *collabos*, or Nazis collaborators, boast about their fictitious role in the resistance. Her uncle's anger had brewed and grown until he could no longer hold back. The waiter had just placed their appetizers on the white-clothed table. Six *escargot* shells lay glistening with buttery garlic drenching the baked mollusks. As Madeleine tentatively began to chew the delicacy, Uncle Pierre stood from the table to address the men to his left. What ensued was a loud discussion where he shamed even the restaurant for hosting such infamous commoners. He took Aunt Evelyn's arm and dropped several bills on the table. Madeleine had hurriedly grabbed her purse while still chewing on the escargot. It had become a tasteless piece of rubber she could no longer swallow. She repressed the urge to vomit and discreetly spat it into her hand and dropped it, making a dark stain on the Parisian sidewalk as she ran after them. Aunt Evelyn took Madeleine across the street to the Café de Flore, as Uncle Pierre went walking along the Seine to calm down. At the café, served in a small carafe on a silver tray, was the most exquisite hot chocolate in the world. The sweet, dense, liquid erased both the memory of the mollusk and the fight. This kind of incident was why Uncle Pierre kept his trips to France to a minimum. So a temporary, let alone permanent, move there would not be well received.

"I'm sorry you had to see all of that, sweetheart," her aunt had said, pushing a strand of Madeleine's hair behind her ear. "It is difficult for your uncle to be here. Next summer we'll be going to Egypt depending on the situation. Maybe a few other places. You will come with us. Won't that be exciting?"

"Oh certainly! But you know, Aunt Evelyn, I do love being here in Paris. I . . . I may even want to live here one day."

"Oh now, stop with this nonsense, you could never live here. We love you too much and want you close. What would your parents say?"

Nothing, they would say nothing. But Aunt Evelyn always kept up appearances as if Madeleine was not aware of her own familial situation.

"Don't even dream of mentioning anything about that to your uncle, he'd get furious all over again. Here he comes!"

She waved her gloved hand to catch his eye and like that, she had hoped to sweep Madeleine's dream under the rug and let it die. But both France and her uncle had always fascinated her. Over the years she had learnt the language and become fluent, studied the literature; as if she too had wanted to be absorbed by the exoticism of being foreign.

The summer exchange was the best means to an end and with the handsome Professor Beardsmith on the selection committee, it wasn't too taxing to give it her all.

As Madeleine walked down the hallway, she carefully avoided slipping on the wet floor the janitor was wiping with a mop, methodically, from side to side. She knew Beardsmith's schedule, usually better than the secretary of the department did. Madeleine knocked on the wooden frame of the opaque-paned glass door. In black letters, the inscription read "Professor Andrew Beardsmith, Chair of English Department and Modern Literature."

"Come in," said a voice from inside the office.

Madeleine turned the knob and entered the familiar office. Pressing her back against the door to close it, she stood there, staring. Andrew Beardsmith hid the fact he was dazzled by this student's demeanor. Her dark hair grazed her shoulders in tightly bound curls. She always looked prepared, with an assurance bidding the question of whether she'd ever known self-doubt. He was attracted by confidence and therefore by Madeleine.

The professor had not landed at an all-women's college by chance. Yes, he had an excellent reputation and his teachings and publications were respected in the world of academia. But he also harbored a profound need for love and reassurance he nursed with attention from the female attendees of his lectures. Seducing women had always been child's play. But this particular student had done more than amuse Andrew Beardsmith.

"Hello, professor. Did you have a nice summer," Madeleine asked.

Beardsmith looked up, a coy smile stretching across his face. He removed his reading glasses and laid them on top of the papers he'd been browsing while daydreaming.

"Summer's not over yet, Miss Rousseau."

And with that he got up from behind his large desk covered in books, left there more for show than anything and headed toward her. His jacket remained hanging on the back of his chair, leaving him with only a light blue shirt, the top buttons left undone. His chest hair peered out casually, unlike his strict coat-and-tie classroom attire. Madeleine felt a warmth spreading inside at the thought of what was about to occur. As the professor came closer, she naturally leaned her hips forward. His hands wrapped easily around her small waist and as he inhaled deeply, he pressed against his former student. Opening her mouth with his lips, he allowed his thumb to graze her breast through the green raw silk of the dress, sending a rush throughout her body.

As their two bodies formed one, Madeleine relished not only in the physical pleasure but at the excitement of seducing a university professor who could lose his job. He had sex with other women but that wasn't so much of a concern, just as long as it wasn't with other students. She had refused his repeated advances to sleep together and had not given in, saving it until she obtained what she wanted. And maybe even then, she wasn't sure yet. It was last year during the fall semester she had overheard two professors discussing the fact Beardsmith was choosing the lucky junior attending the Paris summer exchange. Madeleine had promptly devised a scheme. Throughout the spring semester, she had led a subtle yet intense cat and mouse game with the professor. He was her ticket to Paris.

Andrew Beardsmith was titillated by the situation. Madeleine was both smart and attractive. The coloring and features of her face had a brooding quality, harboring a sort of endless depth he'd never come across. Her green and amber eyes were unsettling yet enticing, drawing you in unwillingly. Though he would never admit it, he asked himself how at his age and with his status, he could be intimidated by a twenty-one-year-old. It was as ridiculous as if men were walking on the moon. A thirty-four-year old professor at an all-women's college should not be mesmerized by a student, but he had never met anyone quite like her. There was something he couldn't put his finger on; a certain detachment was it? Holding her complete attention was like trying to hold water, only a few drops were ever left in your palm. Beardsmith never slept with students, well, for the most part. It had happened on a couple of very rare occasions over his six years here at Vassar. He did not want to get trapped by some undergraduate wanting to wed and have children. Not yet at least. Now that he had been offered tenure, there was more to lose. He did not want to encumber himself with a relationship for the time being. The only person in a rush for him to get married was his mother, constantly pestering about grandchildren. Watching the new students squirm and elbow, literally and figuratively, for his attention was incredibly pleasurable. Although he often gave in to some harmless flirtatiousness, satisfaction had mainly been procured outside of the confines of the college campus.

Until Madeleine had come along. It was dangerous but he was careful, always calculating to be sure he had the upper hand. Being the big forbidden fish in a small pond stroked his ego perfectly.

The professor wanted to slip his hand into her panties but she grabbed his wrist firmly. He had not expected a visit today and could hardly contain his excitement. Despite Madeleine's back arching at the contact of his warm wet lips on her skin, she stopped before going too far.

Unlike most women her age, Madeleine's healthy sexual appetite did not necessitate emotional connection. This was but one of the multiple consequences of her parents' abandonment: an easy disassociation between how she felt versus how she acted. As a little girl, she had neatly packed away feelings and learnt to use her mind to provoke sensations. Uninterested in usual seductive masculine factors of intelligence, money or popularity, she was only aroused by the forbidden. She knew how to trick herself into desire, using jealousy as a form of lust. It was her way of making do with the mediocrity she found in the majority of men, and also women for that matter. This anger was one of the many well-kept secrets Madeleine tucked away. She tamed this unladylike trait but occasionally it reared its ugly head. Her fists tightened, her knuckles went white, and her jaw clenched. She'd lash out at an unsuspecting soul, striking with a humiliating comment. Only once, had she gotten so angry she'd lost complete control. But no one had ever discovered her secret.

Their passionate embrace finished, Madeleine, in a rare act of what could be interpreted as tenderness, brushed a strand of hair away from the professor's eyes.

"I do hope you'll have time to help me with my paper this semester, professor," she said flirtatiously.

"I believe I'll be able to make time for you, Miss Rousseau, though we may have to work late," he said following the curves of her silhouette with his finger.

Now the professor was getting cocky, she could not wait to get out of the muggy office with its uninviting, cheap grey wool sofa, a skin-chafer for sure. Madeleine disliked not being taken seriously. The idea of being touched anymore made her shudder. Glancing at her watch, she excused herself hurriedly, leaving with the assurance he would help with the paper and ultimately, Paris. She had to finish her letter to Uncle Pierre and Aunt Evelyn to be sure it went out with the morning mail.

Chapter 4

The last floor of Strong House was warm and a gentle breeze came in from the window on the opposite side of the stairs. Madeleine was appreciating the perfectly agreeable temperature when she saw the door to her room was open. She remembered closing it when leaving to meet with Beardsmith. Had she been assigned a roommate after all? It would have been preferable to be in the room when the new girl came in; a basic animal instinct of territoriality. Setting the tone without saying a word. The new girl would then know she was walking into an area that already had been claimed. Madeleine mindlessly tucked her brown locks behind both ears and smoothed her dress before entering her room.

There she stood, right in front of her. Taller than average, she had mid-length blonde hair and immediately turned when she heard Madeleine. One couldn't say her face was generically attractive: her nose was too big, her eyes further apart than one would draw, her mouth too wide. She looked like a gathering of exaggerated features so Madeleine let out a sigh of relief. There was no threat.

"Oh hello! My name is Rose. Rose Suggs," the girl said in a charming southern drawl, extending her hand.

"Hello. I'm Madeleine. Madeleine Rousseau," she answered, taking the offered hand and shaking it firmly. But it was Rose's aura that caught Madeleine off guard. Holding her hand for a few seconds too long, a rush came over her. This new girl was ethereal, on another plane where nothing bad happens and if it did, it would quickly be replaced by another pleasant moment.

"Oh. The R.A. told me your name was Madeleine Rivers. She must have you confused with someone else," Rose explained, her mouth stretching into a wide grin. Even her eyes seemed to smile.

"Perhaps. Where are you from Rose Suggs with that lovely accent of yours," asked Madeleine, eyeing what Rose had unpacked on her bed: a few well-starched shirts, two pairs of pants, and some neatly wrapped shoes.

"I'm from Atlanta, Georgia. I grew up there and this was my break to leave the south and migrate north for the winter," she said, laughing at her own joke.

How light-hearted, thought Madeleine. This was a trait which usually made her doubtful of people's intelligence. But not today. Today, all she wanted was to keep listening to Rose speak, inexplicably enthralled with her entire being. She appeared so unafflicted by life. And if she had made it to Vassar, it certainly vouched for some scholastic achievement.

"Where are you from Madeleine," Rose returned the question as she continued floating around the room gracefully and giving all of her captivating attention.

"From New York," she lied. With a girl from Georgia, it was best not to go into the details of her parents in New Jersey. Besides, it wasn't a complete lie. She had spent practically all of her teenage years in New York with Margot.

"New York City," Rose interrupted enthusiastically. "Oh, I've only but dreamt of going but Mommy won't allow it. She is afraid of the big city, but I think she's actually afraid I may get big ideas of becoming a star or singer. Instead, I should find a nice husband like she did!"

"You also sing?" Madeleine asked enviously as she remained standing, hand on her hip.

Rose had approached and suddenly a sweet scent filled the air; a melange of vanilla and a more masculine note, perhaps musk or sandalwood. Madeleine found it difficult to concentrate on the conversation.

"Well, I did in a few talent shows at school and fairs. Nothing professional of course but I am signing up to Choral Club. You know just to keep the old muscle working! You should join too," she said excitedly, putting her hands together in a prayer-like fashion, practically pleading Madeleine.

Singing had always been her secret passion although she wasn't much good at it. She and Margot used to sing Peggy Lee's songs together. Margot had the clearest voice and perfect pitch. While Madeleine could follow a lead, her timbre was utterly indistinct in comparison and she knew it. Madeleine pointed to the Firestone phonograph Uncle Pierre had insisted she take with her this year along with a selection of his favorite jazz records.

"Feel free to put on a record if you ever want to. I usually tune into the radio to know what is happening in the world but it's nice to be able to listen to these. But if it disturbs you, do let me know," Madeleine said showing off.

"Thank you! How wonderful! We're so lucky to have one of these in the room," Rose answered, admiring the device and flipping through the records, her eyes widening with each new cover. "Was it a gift from your parents," Rose wondered aloud.

"How did you guess? For my good grades," Madeleine easily lied again. Technically, Aunt Evelyn and Uncle Pierre were her chosen parents. A good liar left not an inkling of hesitation to modify reality.

Rose continued examining the small collection of records until she pulled one out.

"This one is wonderful. May I?"

Rose's choice of Sarah Vaughn stirred something inside of Madeleine. When she still lived in Millburn with her parents, she remembered singing to "Thinking of You" on the radio. She'd open the window of the living room, turn up the transistor and sit on the front steps, letting the music find her. Madeleine watched the coming and goings of the neighborhood, curious if everyone was living the exact same life. All of the homes on the street were the same. The parents all dressed the same. The kids had the same toys. They all had similar cars. Theirs was a Chevrolet Bel Air 150. Occasionally, it had trouble starting but Father refused to have it fixed. After the accident, he had never wanted to set foot in Dixon's garage ever again. The contorted leftovers of the vehicles involved in the accident had been towed there. His presence was required when the pictures of the burnt cars were taken for insurance purposes and it had been understandably overwhelming. The remaining evidence of his son's death were safely tucked away in a brown attaché case, hidden under Madeleine's bed. Mother had given it to her daughter discreetly, asking her to keep it in a safe place, away from Father. For years she had locked her bedroom door to let all of the documents "breathe". On the carpeted floor she would carefully lay out the police report, the newspaper clipping, and all of the photographs. Madeleine constructed the ephemeral shrine to her deceased brother every twenty-third of the month. The ritual was performed in hopes of grasping a semblance of an explanation as to why her sibling's disappearance had caused her own. No answer ever came.

"Mommy seems to think any music outside of the church is the devil's work but Papa knows better than that. He's taken me to concerts while she was away visiting Aunt Vera in Savannah," Rose commented as she removed the record from its slip, interrupting Madeleine's recollection.

"I'm not entirely sure how to work this," she said with a doe-eyed stare.

Madeleine was desperately trying to resist the spell this woman was casting. Was she really so helpless, wondered Madeleine. Taking the record from Rose, she accidentally grazed her fingers. They were soft like satin.

As the music filled the air, Rose twirled like a graceful ballerina atop a music box. And when Sarah Vaughan began to sing, she accompanied her in a low-toned voice, sending chills down Madeleine's back.

She dropped her eyes, not wanting to reveal an overly admirative gaze. Rose continued unpacking and galavanting around, personalizing her side with small knick-knacks from home. All of them visibly expensive, especially the porcelain magnolia flower with gold leaves she placed on the nightstand. Madeleine turned the volume up before sitting down at her desk. Rose seemed interesting and talented and that was fine. Would they be friends? Pen in hand, she needed to finish the letter but thoughts swirled in her mind. Madeleine shook the strange sensation looming and decided Rose would fit nicely into the trio with Phyllis and Joanie. At first for such casual things, like eating. That way Joanie would have someone to sit in front of. Taking a deep breath and speaking over the music, interrupting Rose's fabulous singing, Madeleine offered:

"My friends and I usually walk over to the dining hall together around 5:30 if you care to join us for dinner."

"Yes, I'd love to! I'm happy to meet your friends. Besides I can always finish unpacking later. Let me go freshen up," Rose exclaimed grabbing her toiletries from the drawer before heading to the bathroom. "This is going to be a fantastic year, I can just feel it Maddie!"

Madeleine dropped her pen, stricken. Only Margot had ever called her Maddie. No one else was allowed, especially since her cousin's death.

"Is it all right if I call you Maddie," she asked, stopping in her tracks.

"Absolutely."

Chapter 5

As fall approached, fires were lit in the grand stone chimneys across campus and the choice spots, the couches and plush armchairs closest to the flames, were rare. The cozy foyer was ideal once the cold settled. But until then, Madeleine and her friends enjoyed eating early to linger outside before the days shortened and the nights got too chilly.

Inside, the high ceilings of the main dining hall were filled with chatter. Even when few women congregated, the room sounded full as the echoes bounced from one wall to the next, all the way to the top. There was no assigned seating in the dining hall but like everywhere, social confines broadly defined where one might be included, popular or permitted. At Vassar, certain of these rules were respected: one of them was seniors got the tables by the windows.

Phyllis, Joanie, and Rose followed Madeleine's lead to the next best seats, the ones by the radiators and with only partially blocked views. As they passed the empty tables next to the windows leading to the quad with the last glittering rays of sunlight, Rose paused.

"Why don't we sit here? It's lovely to look out, don't you think," Rose asked.

"Oh those are reserved for seniors actually. See all the seats by the windows are," Joanie chirped like a helpful Jiminy Cricket. She was always wanting to be the most helpful and agreeable. It was a self-appointed role. Judging herself harshly, she wasn't as unattractive as she imagined. Joanie was the definition of grey mouse. Her hair was neither light or dark, her eyes either. She was neither thin nor plump, simply average. She did have freckles across her nose she was told to be ashamed of, but in fact she thought they made her look sweet. But how could one count on her physique when there were Madeleines and Roses in the world? So Joanie was the nice one, hoping that would be enough to secure the right place in society.

"I'm a senior. Let's sit here," Rose exclaimed and put her tray down in front of the seat closest to the window. The other three looked at each other. Joanie shrugged her shoulders and kept standing. Already Rose was swarming everyone with her seductive lightness, her naiveté, and now, access to better seats. Madeleine hadn't realized her roommate was a senior and it stung for some reason, but if only for a second.

"Are you sure it's ok for us to sit here," Joanie asked nervously. "We're not in your class and I don't care to be humiliated in front of everyone."

"Oh Joanie, you come let them say something. We'll see how that ends," Madeleine stepped in to reassure her and regain some form of authority over the group.

Joanie had seen Madeleine get mad before. Last year in the dormitory, Alice Hauser had accused her of stealing a gold chain bracelet. Alice had left it on the ledge of one of the six sinks. When she had finished bathing, it had disappeared. Joanie had come in right after and Alice accused her. Hearing the yelling, Madeleine had come to her friend's rescue and defense. Alice would hear nothing of it and kept accusing Joanie loudly, drawing a crowd. Madeleine had gotten very close to Alice, forcefully grabbing her arm, and had whispered through clenched teeth. Alice had stopped talking and by the time the R.A. had come to break up the dispute, Madeleine was already leading Joanie out of the bathroom, pushing past the gathering of curious girls. When the R.A. had asked what happened, Alice had said it was a misunderstanding, rubbing the bruise already forming on her arm. Madeleine would never tell Joanie she'd sworn to sneak into Alice's room in the night and break the delicate fingers she used to incessantly practice playing Chopin's Nocturnes in Skinner Hall.

It wouldn't be the first time Madeleine purposely hurt someone. After her brother's accident, Madeleine had had several incidents, including breaking a classmate's arm. It was when Ben, her elementary school crush, had stopped paying attention to her and only had eyes for Mary Combes. No Rice Krispy treats from home or the promise of a new set of jacks could get Ben to leave Mary's side. Every single one of their laughs had made Madeleine's blood boil. She'd swing from the jungle gym's cold metal bars, flying across with such agility, anyone would have been impressed. But Ben hadn't even noticed. So as the teacher had called everyone in, Madeleine challenged Mary to compete one last time, promising her the set of jacks Ben had disdained.

At the halfway point, when Mary's arms had grown tired, Madeleine purposely threw a knee against her back, knocking Mary into the damp, hard sand. A loud snap was heard as Mary began to cry, her wrist broken. Everyone consoled Madeleine's crocodile tears, including Ben, while Mary was carted away to the infirmary by Mrs. Futrell and eventually to the hospital. It had been a small price to pay to get back into Ben's good graces.

Though Alice had no knowledge of this story, a shudder had gone down her spine as Madeleine painted a vivid and horrid picture of fingers bent in the wrong direction. In an instant, her ruined future had flashed before her eyes and she'd retracted the accusation. Joanie regretted such a scene had been made. She'd wanted to keep the bracelet safely tucked away and give it to Madeleine for her birthday, right before school let out. She couldn't afford to purchase a gift she believed her friend might like.

"Would the girls here really do that," Rose asked smiling and looking around. "Everyone seems so nice and civilized."

"Don't be fooled, Rose. Those well-coiffed dos and pretty dresses can hide some vicious creatures," answered Madeleine without looking up.

"Well, I'll happily explain to any girl who wishes to make a remark," replied Rose, digging forcefully into the juicy meatloaf.

How had she not realized Rose was older, Madeleine wondered. Why hadn't she said so when they first met? Madeleine's sense of superiority had been perturbed. Stifling the sentimental commotion Rose's arrival had ensued, she had to reclaim control of the situation.

Perhaps by making herself essential to Rose, the way she had with Margot? She had already introduced her to the tight-knit brigade. All she had to do was gain her trust and secrets.

Walking alongside the main building and then down one of the paths to the water, the four girls approached the bench closest to the soft bank. The sun had set but an unusual warmth trapped in the depths of the ground was emanating. These last summer evenings reminded Madeleine of the house in Sandspoint with Margot, running carefree on the estate. At dusk they were called in for dinner and they knew better than to be late. With barely enough time to shower and change, the two would race each other up the wide wooden staircase. Breathless, they hurried to be back down to slide into their seats in the dining room at eight-thirty on the dot. Uncle Pierre detested tardiness and Madeleine never wanted to be the source of his disapproval. Varying guests and cocktails hosted by the Rousseaus altered the backdrop but for the cousins, all that mattered was being together in their adventures. From running down to the beach as soon as the sun came up to hiding in the sand dunes, laying on their backs, holding hands, and making wishes on the first star appearing in the evening sky. Spending every waking moment together was essential for more and more minutes of sunlight were lost as the days went on, meaning the time for Margot to return to New York and Madeleine to her parents in New Jersey approached rapidly, leaving a pit in the latter's stomach. Her entire being would ache at the thought of heading back to that transparent existence. At the age of eleven, she was resolute about never returning home. Despite her young age, Madeleine had made up her mind and nothing could change it. By that time, she'd learnt to puppeteer like a master, grooming her aunt and uncle at every family reunion and weekend she was able to see them. She had made herself essential to Margot, catering to her every need, manipulating and nurturing all of her pre-adolescent insecurities. By the end of the following school year, Margot had begged her parents for her cousin to live with them and attend the exclusive and expensive Brearley School too. Much to their dismay, Uncle Pierre and Aunt Evelyn had never been able to have other children than Margot. They constantly doted on her, giving in to every capricious demand, rarely denying the latest whims or desires of their only child. The summer of 1950 had been pivotal in Madeleine's pursuit of a better life. From that point on, she was the piece of the puzzle the Rousseau family never knew they were missing. She had in turn abandoned her own parents without a trace of remorse or guilt, feelings she had never known. And to say they noticed nor cared would be a lie.

Rose and Madeleine sat on the bench while Joanie spread the plaid blanket she'd brought from her room. It was cheap rough wool making her legs itch, but she thought it was more chic to bring it along than to sit in the grass. Her parents were modest people and had made significant financial efforts to send their daughter to Vassar, but had raised a proper young lady. She'd sooner die than have the others think she didn't know any better.

"So Rose, tell us more about yourself," Joanie enthusiastically questioned. "You are from Georgia . . ."

"What is it that you want to know Joanie? I grew up in Atlanta. I have two older brothers and a younger sister. I was at Agnes Scott but then decided to transfer here," explained Rose. Her face had changed ever so slightly and before Madeleine could dig a little deeper about the reasons why, Phyllis interrupted.

"Agnes Scott! One of the Seven Sisters of the South. Makes sense that you would come to Vassar. What are you studying?"

"English Lit."

"What do you intend to do after you graduate," inquired Madeleine. She was curious to see if Rose, like Joanie, was here patiently awaiting to snatch a Yale or other Ivy League graduate.

"I'm not sure. I definitely don't want to go back to Georgia. Maybe go to New York City. Can you imagine? If I could, I'd love to sing onstage in front of an audience . . . ," Rose interrupted her own musings. "That's nothing more than a hobby, of course. My mother always says that I don't want to be with the kind of man who would want to marry a singer . . ."

Joanie put her hand on Rose's knee. She was trying to contain her excitement, but although she'd never heard her sing, it felt incredibly natural to imagine Rose on a stage. As she spoke of her experience in various talent shows in the south, Joanie was glued to every word coming out of her mouth, interrupting to ask for more details about what she had worn, which song she had sung, and of course, would she ever sing for them.

"I'd love to sing for you, maybe not right this moment. I feel like we've been hearing the sound of my voice all evening. Anyhow, it's silly I know; a little girl's dream. I used to think it would be the only thing that might make me happy in life," snapping out of her reverie she turned to the others. "What does the future hold for you?"

"I am going to go and work for the Department of State to eventually become a diplomat," Phyllis answered, having perfectly mapped out her life. "And then become an ambassador."

"That's absolutely incredible! I admire your determination to enter such a world," Rose exclaimed.

"Yes, nothing is stopping our darling Phyllis from fixing every international political situation on behalf of our great country. We are faithful supporters of your endeavors, Ms. Burrows!" Madeleine stood and gave a military salute. They all laughed.

"What about you Joanie? You've also got a couple of years left but what will you do when you are done here," asked Rose.

Joanie smiled sheepishly and stroked the bristly fibers of the throw.

"I don't have much talent I can contribute to the world so I look forward to being a nice housewife and a good mother to my children," Joanie answered, self-conscious in a group who seemed to want more out of life than she did. She wanted to have grand dreams as well but she simply did not. Perhaps to do better than her parents and climb the social ladder would allow to consider her life a success? A modest background hung above her head like the sword of Damocles. The goal was to find a smart and ambitious man willing to marry and care for her. Wild insecurities even had her wondering how any man might be interested in her to begin with. So by keeping perfect hair, flattering dresses, and playing the role of the docile woman, she hoped to eventually strike someone's fancy. Joanie had vowed to herself to marry the first man who asked just so she, too, could start to exist.

"Listening to her, you would think that she was the most uninteresting girl to walk this campus! Come on now Joanie, we wouldn't be friends with you if that were the case. Joanie belongs to a bunch of clubs, is extremely active on campus, always has the greatest advice and the best ear. Joanie, you're just a naturally good woman and that my friend, *is* a talent, not bestowed on many," Madeleine finished, touching Joanie's face.

Rose wondered if she would fit into this trio with its obvious leader. Madeleine defended her friends tooth and nail, even from themselves. She wasn't sure she would ever get to that level with the girls nor if she wanted to. Rose liked to be free and not necessarily be associated with a group. In high school, she had belonged to the singing group and had ended with a tainted reputation when two of the other girls had been caught drinking and misbehaving with boys. Her parents had been appalled, taking her out of school, and getting a tutor for the rest of the year. Her mother was extremely concerned about gossip and how that would affect the rest of her life, meaning her marriage. James Boudereaux had been the hopeful candidate since they were teenagers. From an old southern family too, he would inherit his family's estate in Garden Hills. As the eldest son, he would also eventually take over his father's law firm. The best of both worlds. Rose didn't doubt her mother's love but it seemed a vital need for her daughter to become someone else's responsibility. Was that what motherhood was about? Handing off a package you had carefully prepared for another to handle? For the moment her mother was far and Rose wanted a chance to live life unhindered, at least during her time at Vassar.

"Let's head back," Madeleine declared authoritatively. Joanie and

Phyllis got up and folded the blanket together. The girls moseyed slowly along the lake, back toward Strong House as Rose paused.

"I'm going to keep walking for a bit. I need time to take in all of this. It was absolutely lovely having dinner with you," Rose said excusing herself.

"Are you sure? We can wait for you if you like," offered Madeleine insincerely. The air was getting damp and she hated getting chilled to the bone.

"Aren't you the sweetest? I'm fine, thank you, Maddie," Rose replied, smiling but her eyes told a different story.

Phyllis and Joanie waved to Rose as they headed in the opposite direction. Madeleine wondered why she wanted to be alone. Was she sad? Did she not like them? Who was this strange girl? She didn't trust her completely, that was for sure. There was something about her . . .

"By the way, girls, I'm actually a junior! But wasn't it fun to sit at the best table," Rose winked at them.

Chapter 6

Madeleine walked silently, taking in what had happened. She had been fooled so easily.

"I didn't doubt Rose for a minute," Phyllis said, surprised at her own gullibility.

"I thought it was grand! Rose is incredible," exclaimed Joanie, still laughing at the trick they'd played on everyone in the dining hall.

"Did she call you Maddie," Phyllis asked with a twinge of jealousy.

"I told her not to but she keeps doing it. Maybe she's just trying to fit in. But don't go getting any ideas. I'm giving her a pass because she's new," replied Madeleine, giving Phyllis's shoulder a squeeze. She wondered if Madeleine might be subjugated by Rose and like her better in the end. They did run in similar social circles, creating a bond Phyllis couldn't replicate.

As the three girls walked back toward Strong House, Joanie's eyes dropped down to the ground where she noticed the grass was damp. She'd forgotten to protect her shoes with the Esquire polish her mother had packed in her bag. Apparently the lanolin softened the leather but also kept water stains from showing. With no discretionary fund, she cared greatly for her belongings, always creatively mixing and matching her entire wardrobe so it gave the illusion of a fuller one.

"My shoes," Joanie exclaimed.

As droplets gathered on the tip of the shoes received for her birthday, she sped up the pace. She intended on using them next spring as well. The two others followed suit until they were bolting across the quad and racing up the stairs of the front of the building, laughing whole heartedly. Joanie turned to look at her friends, conscious of this perfect moment of sorority. The three of them, about to embark on another journey together, standing on the cusp of a new school year.

"Tell me your shoes are safe," Madeleine joked, catching her breath.

Her maternal concern and the way she held their little trio together reassured Phyllis and Joanie, who felt safe in the dynamic. Rose would surely not break such a bond, simply add to it. Reaching the front doors of the building, the three girls stopped to compose themselves. Linking arms, with one girl on either side of Madeleine, they stepped through, as if they owned the place.

When a sliver of morning light peered through the curtains. Madeleine did not open her eyes, as if she were still asleep, peering through half-closed lids without a flutter. Rose was not awake yet. She could finally stare at her roommate undisturbed. Her nose was definitely too big for her face, looking like what Uncle Pierre would refer to as a "potato" nose. Madeleine wasn't sure if it was a French expression or his own but understood what it meant and Rose had one. Also her lips were so full and wide. Nearly vulgar. But that radiance. As if someone had packed up pure sunshine and poured it into her being. Perhaps it was her skin, Madeleine reasoned. It was unblemished and uniform, smooth and milky like a bar of white soap. She had that going for her.

Satisfied with her analysis of Rose's unusual features, Madeleine turned over to face the wall. She was not yet ready to get out of bed and slip on her robe. She loved being in her bed, or any bed for that matter. She could lay there and contemplate the day, prepare the future all the while remaining in the warmth and protection supplied by a down duvet and plush pillow. The day didn't truly begin until she arose. Last night, she'd purposely steered the conversation to what the girls were going to do after graduation. People loved to talk about themselves and Madeleine listened. She, on the other hand, rarely revealed anything. No one needed to know much about her, leaving her less predictable. And the last thing Madeleine ever wanted to be was predictable. Expertly circumventing questions without arousing suspicion was one of her favorite past times. Life was a mental chess game, where every move deserved contemplation. How else would one control the outcome? What Madeleine hadn't understood was an unassuming opponent had stepped in to checkmate the game.

Procuring the junior slot for the summer exchange in Paris was the objective, although Madeleine had shared it neither with friends nor family, except Phyllis. The time had not come yet. In Paris this summer, she had been filled with the confirmation she wanted to live in the city of lights as they'd walked the cobblestone streets heavy with history. The French were chic and interesting; their lifestyle resonated more with her than an American one. Madeleine was craving an adventure in the depths of her core. Hearing of the program last semester, a sense of urgency had come over her. She was a good candidate for the exchange, but her lack of involvement in extracurricular activities played against her. Hence the affair with Professor Beardsmith being necessary. All she had to do was keep him interested until he made the announcement. Despite Uncle Pierre's possible initial reluctance of his niece living in Paris, Madeleine was convinced he would be so proud if she got there by her own means. Perhaps he and Aunt Evelyn might show their enthusiasm by renting a nicer apartment than she would be given by the school or even buying one once she made it clear she had no intention of returning.

Madeleine imagined herself in the Saint-Germain neighborhood, walking through massive double wooden doors into a courtyard with a grand tree at its center. Two flights of stairs lined with carpet would take her to the noble floor of the traditional Haussman-type building. With high ceilings, large double windows, antique oak hardwood floors, the marble fireplace and its moldings, Madeleine imagined every last detail. While she was deep in thought about decorating the Parisian living quarters, Joanie burst into the room holding *The Washington Post*. The stir awakened Rose, who immediately smiled at the intruder through half-opened eyes.

"Oh I'm sorry, Rose, I thought you would be up by now," Joanie gushed.

It was better when Phyllis brought *The Post*. Joanie only liked to read the obituaries and it annoyed Madeleine to have sift through the paper and give Joanie the section before she was done reading. Also, she hadn't even said hello before apologizing to Rose, who'd sat up in bed.

"What a beautiful nightgown," Joanie complimented.

"You're so sweet, Joanie," Rose replied. Joanie rushed to grab the matching pale pink satin robe hanging on the back of the closet door and handed it to her.

"Thank you! This is the nicest way to start the day, don't you agree, Maddie," Rose continued.

"Absolutely. Good morning Joanie," Madeleine said in a reprimanding tone. "What an entrance."

"Oh hi, Madeleine. Yes here's your paper. I got up early and had time to run down to the mailroom and make a cup of coffee."

"It seems like all of that caffeine is pumping through your veins and straight to your head. Why don't you give our new friend Rose a little space to breathe before she starts her day," Madeleine insisted.

"I don't mind," Rose intervene. "It's lovely to see a friendly face!"

"Rose, would you like me to walk you to your first class," offered Joanie, desperately wanting to be helpful.

"That would be fabulous. Let me get dressed and freshen up. I'd love for you to show me around," Rose said as she began laying out her clothes for the day.

Madeleine watched from bed. She too had admired the quality of Rose's night set, though she would never admit it to anyone, including herself. Her own was a lovely lavender robe but it was a few years old and now she regretted saying she hadn't needed anything extra at the Bon Marché, when Aunt Evelyn was buying all of her undergarments and sleepwear. Imagine if Madeleine's nightgown was from Paris, it would have made Rose beyond envious, outdoing her petal pink set. It was probably chosen in a banal attempt to match her name. Slipping into a pale yellow dress matching the color of her hair, Rose interrupted Madeleine's thoughts.

"Joanie told me you speak French?"

"I do. You see my uncle is from France and he taught me along with my cousin."

"*Alors nous pouvons parler en français?*"[1]

Madeleine couldn't believe the perfection of Rose's accent, nearly that of a native speaker.

"Are you French?" she asked, incredulous.

Rose's laugh bounced off the walls and she struck a very stylish pose.

"*Merci beaucoup,*[2] but sadly no. I am but a Georgia girl with a good ear, my dear!"

She grabbed a few books from the desk and placed her purse on her forearm.

"At least we'll be able to have our own secret language, *n'est-ce pas mon amie*?"[3]

She winked at Madeleine, paralyzed on the bed, drowned by a wave of yet more fascinating details about her roommate. An interwoven sense of admiration and envy overcame her as she watched Rose leave the room, prepared to dazzle the rest of the world.

---

1   "So we may speak in French?"

2   Thank you very much

3   Isn't that right, my friend?

Chapter 7

Once Rose had left with Joanie, Madeleine opened her closet to pick a dress. It was the first week of school and no longer having classes with Professor Beardsmith meant chance encounters on and off campus had to be strategically plotted. She had to focus on the priority at hand. The crimson one might trigger his sensorial memory as she had worn it on her first visit to his house.

Madeleine would drop by at the end of his two o'clock class to instigate an invitation for drinks or dinner later this week. Soon the selection of the lucky three students headed to Paris was to be made. She had already inquired about transferring her credits to the Sorbonne and graduating from there. Madeleine wanted this more than anything; getting as far away from her own past, and especially her parents, as possible. In Paris, reinvention was possible, removing herself from the mediocrity which had seized her parents' life. She surprised herself how easily their existence slipped her mind and spoke of her aunt and uncle as her true genitors. She didn't wish any ill on her parents but their existence left her completely unfazed. If she never saw them again, her life wouldn't be altered in the slightest. Detachment was healthy. In fact, when people spoke with awe of their parents, she thought them lacking maturity. Only children were blinded by unconditional love for their mothers and fathers. She had no recollection of feeling like this, of ever having felt like a child really.

The hundred-year-old oak tree cast a wide shadow on the lawn, where Madeleine took refuge, awaiting for Professor Beardsmith's lecture to finish. The grass had been mowed earlier in the day and the scent from the fresh green piles of cut blades immediately transported her to the backyard of the house in New Jersey. Shortly before the accident, Father had purchased a Lawn Boy resembling a small tractor. Philip's excitement was grand as Father would sit him on his lap and the two spent hours together riding around the yard. The lawn had never received so much care and attention. Observing from afar moments of familial bonding, Madeleine too had wanted to be invited on her father's lap. But it wasn't an activity for little girls. And after the accident, the Lawn Boy was retired to the garage, forever. Madeleine shook off the memory, annoyed.

A crowd of young women exited the front doors of Rockefeller Hall. From across the quad, Madeleine watched them; a myriad of colored dots trickling down the stairs and dispersing onto the grass. The day was unseasonably hot for September and Madeleine had cautiously waited under the oak tree so as to not overheat and leave perspiration stains on her dress. Women had to think of everything. She wanted to stroll past and strike up a seemingly innocent conversation with the Professor that, from afar, could resemble any other student-teacher exchange. In fact, she would be letting him know her availabilities for their next encounter. Perhaps they could have dinner at his house. On campus, they had to be extremely careful about how often they were seen together. This was why Madeleine had waited months before revealing their affair to Phyllis. Eventually it had reached a point of needing an accomplice to avoid getting caught. Imagine if Uncle Pierre and Aunt Evelyn ever found out! The disappointment could force them to cut her off completely. Her perfectly arranged life would be over, as would her future, therefore she tread very carefully.

Heading toward the building, Madeleine admired and respected the camaraderie brought on by an all-women's institution like Vassar. She very much valued the benefits of spending the majority of her time with people of her own sex. Nurturing the feminine bond was important. As a few girls brushed past her, she noted how awfully giggly they were, probably chatting about the handsome professor who taught 19th century English literature. It was Beardsmith's least favorite class but when it came to handling new students, he gave them sufficient attention and compliments to stir girlish excitement. Madeleine admired how put together women were on campus.

Surely with attractive professors and being the feeding ground for the Yale boys to take their pick, appearances ranked high on the list of priorities. But whether pursuing an education or a future as a finely educated housewife, the women looked good doing it. Inevitably it occasionally gave way to some feminine rivalry and jealousy, but the sisterhood provided by such an institution rapidly dissolved these temporary scuffles.

The flow of girls had nearly finished as she approached, slowing her pace to cross paths with the professor somewhere between the exterior stone stairs and the end of the hallway, leading to the second floor. Madeleine leaned on the railing for a few moments pretending to fix her shoe, buying herself a few extra seconds. As she reached for the handle, the door pushed open from the other side and as if by magic, there he appeared. Beardsmith was holding the door open and before Madeleine could utter a word, Rose stepped through.

"Thank you, professor," Rose said smiling back to him. Was she purposely holding her books tight to her chest so her neckline was agape? Everyone knew the trick. From the professor's angle, he could easily see down the front of her dress to reveal more cleavage. As she turned and saw Madeleine, her face lit up. "Maddie! Hi there!"

Rose had to know what she was doing, Madeleine thought. Behind the fake innocent sweetness, she was just another girl looking to seduce. How had she not seen it? Her heart was racing but had to regain her composure quickly.

"Hello, dear Rose! And hello Professor Beardsmith," Madeleine said as she desperately searched the professor's face for any indication of an emotion, betraying his intentions with the new student.

"Miss Rousseau, how do you do," asked the professor, stoically. Perhaps his face wasn't as stoic as Madeleine perceived it but she could find no indication of sentiment, of regret, or, for that matter, of affection. She only wanted a minute acknowledgement of the intimate link between them; she was the chosen one.

But he let nothing transpire. Nothing at all. There were no classes in the building for another couple of hours and if she didn't come up with an excuse as to her presence here, it would be obvious why she had shown up at the end of his class.

"I'm divine Professor Beardsmith! I see you've met my lovely roommate," she said gesturing towards Rose, wanting to establish the dynamic in this unexpected trio. Would that be enough to keep him from pursuing anything with Rose? Madeleine had to up her game.

"I did. Miss Suggs was just telling me about her move from Atlanta. I got my PhD at Emory so we've had lots to discuss," he said.

"I remember you mentioning that," Madeleine said, needing to assert her relationship with the professor in front of Rose without being explicit. Hopefully Rose would pick up on it, although Madeleine was no longer sure she could predict anything about her roommate.

"Well, I must run. I've misplaced my favorite gold pen and I am hoping to have accidentally dropped it here the other day," Madeleine fumbled. Why would she have been here before classes began? Luckily neither one seemed to question it.

"Oh I saw a beautiful gold pen on your desk this morning," Rose replied.

"That's an old one. My aunt bought another one for me while we were in Paris this summer, so I'm desperate to find it," Madeleine blurted. Of course she only had the one gold pen and now she had had to lie again to cover her tracks because Rose volunteered information without being asked.

"I can come help you look if you like," offered Rose.

"No, thank you Rose. You go on ahead. I'm sure the professor has terrific Atlanta stories to share! I'll see you back at the room later," Madeleine responded as her annoyance grew. Things had gone awry. When would she next see the professor alone?

Disappointment was particularly hard for Madeleine to handle.

The R.A. was going to question why her aunt and uncle repeatedly changed the date of their fictitious visit, the excuse for missing curfew one night this week. As if her family didn't have better things to do than venture up to Poughkeepsie in the middle of the week. She would have to invent another pretext.

As Madeleine walked past the imaginary couple, the professor reached out for her and said: "You may want to ask Marion, the janitor. His office is in the basement."

He had touched her arm. That was the sign. It revealed an intimacy that anyone with half a brain would notice. So Rose probably hadn't. There should never be any bodily contact between student and teacher, let alone between a man and a woman. Madeleine immediately felt relieved and decided to follow through with her lie and pay the janitor a visit, looking for a pen, which had never been lost.

"I'll do just that. Also professor, I may need to come by your office later today to show you my outline for the Rimbaud paper," Madeleine again lied.

"I'll be happy to go over with you. Good luck finding your pen," he responded as he turned away.

Madeleine walked through the doors and paused. She thought she saw the professor putting his hand on Rose's back to guide her toward the right, the pathway leading to the building where the offices of the English department were, including his own. Madeleine's mind raced as her heels clicked on the perfectly polished floor. At the top of the stairs leading to the basement, she heard a faint sound of music coming up. Would the professor bring Rose to his office? Would he try and seduce her? She had noticed a glimmer in his eye; perhaps the attraction of an additional prey? Rose was pretending to be naive, playing the damsel in distress. What profoundly detestable behavior, Madeleine thought. It reminded her of Mother and the car incident.

On a sunny Saturday afternoon, Mother was to take Madeleine to have an unsightly crooked tooth removed. The Chevy wouldn't start and Father was off fishing alone for the afternoon. He had spoken multiple times about the battery's malfunction and how to fix it. A certain wire had to be moved away to keep it from short circuiting, allowing the car to start. Madeleine had fiddled with the wires to avoid the dentist, Dr. Krenson. He was an old friend of Father's from high school, and one of his arms was shorter than the other. His handicap was not the reason Madeleine despised him. It was due to the awkward stance he took to lean into her mouth making his pelvis rub against her upper arm. Between the discomfort of a man's private parts resting on her and the powdery moth ball scent emanating from his person, she would rather keep the said "ugly" tooth.

But Mother had been determined to make it to the appointment. Still in her room on the second floor of the house, Madeleine had watched the growing agitation. George, the only neighbor they weren't friendly with, had come out to mow his lawn. And there, she had watched Mother transform. Elizabeth Rivers had fixed her cleavage, slammed the door as hard as she could and kicked the side of the vehicle. She had then added her best desperate hands-in-the-face mimic and waited. Madeleine peered through the new curtains with little flowers on it, made by Mother. She had sewn them with the mint green Singer sewing machine, the way she did all of her own dresses and Madeleine's too. A very talented seamstress, her clothes were always well-made and of the latest fashion. Except Madeleine preferred expensive designer dresses or even department store dresses. While she was daydreaming about the embarrassment of admitting where her dresses came from when she was in the city with her cousin Margot, she saw the neighbor finally take notice of her mother's charade. And like a knight in shining armor, George came running over. In the silent movie unfolding before her eyes, she saw Mother had squirmed and made grimaces worthy of the comedia dell'arte. George's chest had swelled with pride and sense of masculine purpose. And off he had gone, filled with determination, to open the hood of the car. Sure enough, in no time the car roared. Mother had practically thrown herself into George's arms as if he had saved her from being kidnapped by the enemy during warfare. Madeleine would be obliged to see the short-armed dentist. Fuming and in a fit of anger, she had taken her right fist into her mouth and bit down hard. The satisfaction and release of biting overtook the pain. Madeleine had sighed heavily, pulling out the wet fist from her mouth; blood slowly coming to the surface, filling in the marks where the skin had been torn by her teeth. She had vowed never to resemble Mother or feign weakness.

Madeleine rushed down the stairs, letting her hand slide along the cool metal ramp. Right before she got to the bottom, she felt a sharp pain. She winced and saw a red droplet quickly forming from a small gash across her palm. It stung and Madeleine held her wrist tight.

"Can I help you," asked a tall Black man, standing in the hall. He was surely more than six foot four since he appeared taller than Uncle Pierre, with broad shoulders and visible definition of his strong arms through the worn beige button down shirt. He was the same age as Professor Beardsmith and the years of a harder life had only etched one deep wrinkle into his forehead, leaving the rest of his body impressive with strength. But before she could open her mouth, "Rock Around the Clock" came on from the radio in his office. She remembered listening to that song with Margot. Grabbing each other's wrists, they would spin around, going faster and faster until the two collapsed on the floor laughing. If Aunt Evelyn had been there today, she would say it was Margot's spirit letting Madeleine know she was present. Aunt Evelyn was always saying that kind of thing. She was extremely superstitious, which Madeleine didn't like. How could an intelligent person believe knocking on wood would keep the destined course of life from happening or seeing a black cat crossing the road ahead would alter the universe with bad luck. This was the kind of preposterous nonsense Madeleine expected from Mother. Madeleine forgave her aunt, assuming the loss of her own daughter was a pain so great it overtook any sort of common sense or logical reasoning. Yet Aunt Evelyn had been that way, long before Margot's passing.

"Need something for that hand," he asked pointing to the small droplets of blood pooling on the floor.

"No, that's not why I came down," Madeleine automatically replied, but her wound did need attention. "I guess if you have some gauze until I get back to my room. Or perhaps the infirmary."

The janitor retreated back into a room and Madeleine followed, curious to see the inside. There was a clean dark wood desk, resembling the one in Professor Beardsmith's office. On it were several files. On the right were buckets of various sizes, mops, rags, tools hanging on the wall. The opposite side was lined with lockers she imagined were filled with more apparatus to keep the school running.

He opened one of the lockers and took out a white metal case with a red cross on the top. Madeleine noticed his hands and nails were clean. Actually now that she looked with more detail, his office, his clothes, his entire demeanor was tidy for a person whose work required manual labor. The janitor pulled out some alcohol and gauze. As he opened the bottle and put some of the liquid onto a cotton ball, he looked at Madeleine.

"So why is it you were coming down to see me," he asked, at the same time pressing the ball into her hand. After one second came the burning sensation of the rubbing alcohol applied onto an open wound. Madeleine gasped with pain.

"I thought you might feel that. I tried to distract you," he continued.

"You didn't do a very good job," Madeleine let out a chuckle while twisting her wrist.

He removed the cotton ball. The bleeding had stopped and he expertly wrapped Madeleine's hand and wrist.

"You'd better be sure you got yourself a tetanus shot. I've seen men die of tetanus and it's a bad way to go," he reflected aloud.

"Do you also work at the infirmary," Madeleine questioned, impressed with the dressing.

"I was in the war so the basics I'll never forget. That and what I saw over there. Anyhow young lady, what may I help you with," he urged, knowing it best not to spend too much time in his office, unsupervised, with a student.

"Thank you for this," she said holding up her hand. "I came to ask if you had by chance found a gold pen I may have dropped a couple of days ago."

The janitor walked over to another locker and opened it up. He pulled out a shoe box and placed it on the desk, removing its black cover. Inside was a collection of knickknacks: brooches, pens, purse mirrors, bracelets, chains, and other small items.

He pushed the box over to Madeleine. She peered inside knowing her pen wasn't there.

"I doubt it would be here. It's a solid gold pen so anyone who might've found it would be smarter to keep it for themselves or sell it. They'd make quite a bit of money," she lamented.

The janitor wasn't sure if Madeleine was purposely trying to imply he'd steal it if he found it but suspected so. He was a Black man and suspicion always came first. Though he knew he hadn't stolen a thing, in his mind he was almost sure this wouldn't be the last time he'd hear of the stolen gold pen. Would he lose his job? Perhaps. Would he go to jail? He'd have to be extra wary of the unfolding of the events so as to not be locked up. He couldn't bear it one more time. He had paid his debt to society, given everything for his country and would not be wrongly accused. Lost in these thoughts, he had not responded to Madeleine, whose last sentence didn't necessarily require comment.

"Fine, let me know if you do. I'm hoping I'll find it before long because I don't want to make a fuss about it, except it was a gift and besides its monetary value, it is most importantly of sentimental value," she continued.

"I understand. But you lost it here in this building, before classes even started? Are you sure about that?"

Of course, her story didn't hold up. She wasn't even sure the building had been open before classes started. He had caught her in a lie and now she wasn't sure how to get out of it.

"I will let you know if I find anything at all. Here write down your name for me so I can leave a note in your mailbox if I do," he said as he pulled a piece of paper from a pile. As he did, some handwritten sheet music caught Madeleine's eye.

"Are those yours," she asked, pointing to the music as she jotted down her name, hoping to distract him.

"They are," he quickly glanced at the name on the paper. "Miss Rousseau. That's got a nice ring to it. I used to play in New York every night but around here, I gotta wait for the weekend. So during my breaks, I write what I wanna try out with the guys."

Madeleine nodded, acknowledging a sudden level of respect for the musical janitor who wrote music in the basement of Rockefeller Hall.

"Do you play anywhere around here," she pressed.

"I do. In town, off Prince Street, there's a jazz joint open on the weekends called Raymond's. There's a back room and we play until late into the night."

"I've been to The Five Spot and Birdland you know. My uncle took me there last year. It was fabulous," Madeleine responded, smiling at the memory.

"The Five Spot is incredible. You are lucky to have witnessed any sort of music being made there," he replied.

"Maybe I will go to Raymond's," she said giving him a flirtatious smile. "The only jazz I get to listen to while at school is on my records. What's your name?"

Not liking where the conversation was heading, the janitor was ready to go about his business.

"My name is Marion. Marion Ward. But I must say, I'm afraid Raymond's isn't a place for young ladies," he said putting the piece of paper with her name on it in the top right drawer.

What was she doing? After being vexed by the professor, all of the sudden she had found herself flirting with the janitor. Madeleine snapped out of the moment and the tension she had created.

"No, no of course it isn't. Nice to meet you, Mr. Ward. I'll see you around campus and thank you for my hand!" She grew hot and ran up the stairs, carefully avoiding the ramp which had torn her skin on the way down. Pushing the doors of the building, she stepped outside and inhaled deeply. The janitor had seen right through her somehow.

Before hurrying back to Strong House, she took a detour by the lake. It was inevitable. Once on the bank, behind a few overgrown bushes, she reached into her pocketbook for the gold Montblanc and dropped it into the murky water, unseen.

Chapter 8

Madeleine hurried to the dormitory building for no other reason than to check if her roommate was back. She had caught a glimpse of Rose's schedule and was fairly confident she had no classes after Professor Beardsmith today. If she was not in the room, it meant she might have gone to his office. That's how it all started last year between Madeleine and the professor.

Twenty-eight of the seventy-three faculty members at Vassar were men, so plenty of students fawned over them, scarcity playing in their favor. Deprived of sufficient male contact, the women easily swooned at each and every decent looking, and even the less than average, male professor. It was practically part of the curriculum. The weekends luckily provided relief to the sexual frustration of the Vassar girls thanks to the longstanding relationship with neighboring Yale. But the weeks were long and fantasizing about seducing an attractive teacher was as common a daily activity as brushing teeth. Madeleine knew to differentiate herself. She had done her research and had discovered Andrew Beardsmith had grown up in the cold winters of Wisconsin in a modest family but with his intelligence, had gone on to study at Yale before getting his doctorate at Emory. The key pieces of information she had obtained were that Beardsmith had spent a few years in Paris after the war, spoke French, and had a real affinity for its literature. He was the one who had established the program with his contacts at the Sorbonne, hence his decisive role in the selection committee. This was her in, the standout advantage over all of the boring and dull females populating his modern literature classes.

Her ingenious move had been to sign up to *Philatheleis*, the English department's literary society. The club met every week to exchange on the arts, recitations, music, and other aesthetic recreations. They would even write and put on plays in the college chapel, which was all too socially engaging. Although the other girls always begged her to join, she'd kindly refuse without ever seeming rude. What she had wanted was to make a notable impression on Professor Beardsmith with a poem from Baudelaire, "The Music." Uncle Pierre adored French poetry and recited for Margot and Madeleine all of what he had memorized in school. This particular one Madeleine had always loved. She had learnt it by heart years ago to impress her uncle, but its words truly captured the very notions of being transported by music.

Madeleine had worn a violet dress, the one which was particularly snug and accentuated her waistline all the while raising her bosom, making her breasts look like two soft rounded pillows, waiting to be touched. She purposely breathed so her chest would swell up and down, so more attention might be drawn to her cleavage.

The night of the reading, she had asked Beth, the club's vice-president and timekeeper, to go last, closing up the evening. Madeleine so often declined invitations to social events that her classmates felt graced with her presence when she finally decided to attend. Beth had been thrilled when Madeleine joined *Philatheleis* and was prepared to render any favors. By going last, she was hoping the professor might strike up a conversation and walk out of the gathering with him. When it came to be her turn, Madeleine had moved slowly to the front of the room. As she did, Phyllis and Joanie had clapped loudly stopping after a few moments when no one else followed suit. She had seen Professor Beardsmith check his watch in the audience. Madeleine had looked down, taken one last bosom-swelling breath in. When she had lifted her head, her expression had completely changed. She began reciting the poem with unprecedented gusto.

"Music oft seizes me and sweeps me like a sea toward where my star shines pale,

With mists for ceiling, or through an immensity of ether I set sail."

Professor Beardsmith had snapped to attention. Though not an

obscure piece, never had a student selected it from the grand reper-
toire of Baudelaire's work. Beardsmith admired the poet's description
of escapism through music and the sense of hearing, always having
found it strangely exciting, and tonight, even more so. But he wasn't
sure of the identity of the person speaking the translation of one of his
favorite French poets. She had seemed vaguely familiar, perhaps he
could have seen her on campus but didn't believe she was in his class.
Madeleine recited the poem as if the words were being wrenched from
her guts. Every breath was perfectly calculated and the audience hung
on every word. By the time she was done, the room was filled with a
tension which felt practically sexual. Upon finishing her last phrase,
Madeleine had stared at the professor, her eyes boring right through
him. Every visceral instinct indicated this student should be kept at
bay. But Professor Beardsmith had made his way to the front and
found Madeleine, standing with Joanie and Phyllis.

"What a performance," he complimented.

"Thank you professor. I'm thrilled you enjoyed it," she'd replied, not
detaching her eyes from his.

"It would have been impossible not to. May I ask why you selected
this very piece? It's one I particularly love . . . ," he'd insisted.

This was exactly where she had wanted the conversation to go.
Moving away from her friends, Madeleine told Beardsmith about
Uncle Pierre and wanting to go to France the following summer on the
exchange program. When she told him her uncle's last name she had
chosen to use at school, Rousseau, he was even more charmed. With
such a beautiful French name, it was clear she had to move to Paris
he'd said. Madeleine had cut the conversation short to intrigue him.
But before she'd excused herself to join Phyllis and Joanie who were
eagerly awaiting her by the doors, Madeleine reached out and touched
the professor's arm discreetly.

"I do hope we will get to finish discussing this; perhaps with less
people around," she'd said, flashing him the most charming of smiles.

"Oh we must," he had replied immediately.

Madeleine had transferred into his class the following week, the same one Phyllis was in. When she sat down next to Phyllis's desk, she thought she saw him flinch as he spotted her in the first row. Phyllis always liked to sit up front. She couldn't see very well despite her thick glasses and found no need to go and hide in the back rows as she was there to be educated. Madeleine had always been a quick learner, making her lazy when things didn't naturally come to her. If it wasn't organic and with minimal effort, she became impatient and lost interest. But in this class, wanting to seduce the professor made for a very serious student.

At the end of the lecture, Madeleine had taken her time packing up, all the while half-listening to Phyllis's rant about the lack of women authors on the curriculum, again this semester. As Madeleine rose to get to the center aisle and exit the class, Professor Beardsmith had called out to her.

"Miss . . . Rousseau, if I remember correctly."

A knowing smile stretched across her lips as she turned to the front of the class where he was putting the last of the lecture notes back into a brown leather briefcase.

"May I see you for just a minute," he'd asked.

Phyllis had rolled her eyes.

"Of course he wants to speak with you. I have to go study for my history quiz tomorrow. I'll see you later," she'd told her, annoyed.

Madeleine had walked down the steps of the small auditorium and leaned against the side of the desk, resting her books on her hip.

"You just transferred into my class, is that correct?"

"It is," Madeleine had replied without missing a beat.

"So you may be behind on the readings we did the first couple of weeks. Would you like to come by my office so we can be sure you have everything you need," he had suggested.

Madeleine hadn't expected it to be this easy. It almost turned her off that he was offering himself up to her in such an obvious way. Where was his sense of charm and flirtation? She'd now have to retreat if only but for the intensity to grow, yet carefully enough so he would not lose interest or get frustrated. After all she wanted him to get her to Paris. If she was agile enough now, she could tease him enough in order to arouse her own desire again.

"My friend Phyllis very kindly offered me her notes." she'd said, showing her notebook with weeks' worth of handwritten pages.

Professor Beardsmith had immediately shut down. Had he misinterpreted her longing gaze during the poetry reading? He hadn't taken her for one of those girls who only feigned interest but never took action. Irritated at the idea he'd entertained any fantasy which might risk his job and reputation had it come to fruition, he was done with this student. An animalistic attraction had made this young woman ever so appealing, but he was now mad at himself and though he'd never admit it, his ego was bruised.

"Suit yourself," he'd replied, passing in front of her to walk out of the room.

"Professor," she'd called out to him.

He'd turned back, raising one eyebrow to mark his impatience.

"I was wondering if you might be interested in finishing our conversation on French poetry."

"I think you'd find the French club might be better suited to exchange with your peers," he'd said before walking off. The seduction game was back on.

From that point forward, Madeleine had strung his interest along. She'd led impressive class discussions, handed in remarkable work and was always dressed with sufficiently revealing outfits when showing up unannounced to his office. Beardsmith's frustration had built up for weeks as she'd expertly fueled the fire. Objectively, she was irreproachable in behavior. No one could accuse her of seduction, but she was sketching an image of a student whose mind was as equally intriguing as her body was attractive. He'd been incapable of understanding how she remained at the forefront of his thoughts. He had had hundreds of female students over the years, one more beautiful than the next, all youthful, excited, enchanting little creatures. They regularly flung themselves at him and he had always known how to handle it. But in this case, things were different. Unknowingly, he'd found himself wrapped in an invisible web of desire, which he could no longer bear. Desperate for relief, he'd slept with the waitress who worked in the local café in Poughkeepsie. For the past five years, every other Saturday at ten, he went in for a cup of coffee and a peanut butter and raspberry jelly on toasted white bread. He no longer needed to order, she or any of the other waitresses would bring his sandwich along with a cup of coffee, no questions asked. The combination of salty peanut butter and the sweetness of the jelly was his Proust's madeleine. He adored it, not only for the memories it stirred of being cared for by his darling mother in the small and cozy kitchen of the house in Eau Claire after school, but also to appreciate how far he'd come. Now with a renowned reputation in academia and with an even more promising future, he toyed with the idea of going for the position of Dean of Students in a few years, even President of the college one day. His reputation needed to be impeccable. But the Rousseau girl continued trotting around in his mind, like an aftertaste he hadn't managed to get rid of.

After several weeks of playing cat and mouse and as summer approached, the tension was ripe for Madeleine to take action. She'd observed the professor's comings and goings from classes, his office hours, and his habits on campus. Researching and gathering information like a hunter with its prey, she'd even discovered his escapades at the café. On a Saturday morning, she had dragged Phyllis and Joanie into town to purchase art supplies for the dance committee. They were organizing a luau-themed dance at the end of the month and had been assigned the decoration of Main Hall's entrance. It was another one of those social activities she had forced herself to join with an ulterior motive. Madeleine had spotted the professor from afar and had wanted to interact with him alone. Only later would she describe it to Phyllis as a simple "crush." Madeleine excused herself pretexting a stop at the post office, for an imaginary package not yet received. This had begun the domino effect altering the course of her life.

Madeleine had walked into the OK Café confident, to say the least. She was going to order three muffins to go, pretending not to see the professor sitting by the window grading papers. She would speak loudly enough to be noticed and laugh so as to sound lighthearted but not stupidly so. Then, when she turned around to leave, if he hadn't said anything to her by then, she would address him.

The woman at the counter was plain but seemed kind. Her perfectly oval shaped face resembled the back of a spoon. And everything else about her appeared smooth and unremarkable, like a soft and worn favorite blanket. She had greeted Madeleine with no emotion in her voice, pen in hand, prepared. Madeleine had peered through the glass display case exposing the multitude of baked goods: moist blueberry muffins, dark-colored banana bread speckled with nuts, red cherry pies with flakey, buttery crusts. On several occasions she had seen the professor with a muffin in hand or on his desk when she purposely strolled by his office. What wasn't known was they had come from the professor's occasional lover, the spoon-faced woman standing behind the counter. Madeleine ordered three muffins to go and then dropped a few coins on the floor to give Professor Beardsmith a chance to look up from his papers.

"Oh how unfortunate! Just a minute, miss," she winced. And with the grace of a royal curtsy, she had knelt down to pick up the coins and laid them on the counter.

With her white paper bag, she'd turn to exit the coffee shop before "spotting" Professor Beardsmith by the window.

"Professor! Fancy meeting you here," she'd exclaimed, approaching his table uninvited.

Beardsmith had observed Madeleine come in, as he did with most clients of the coffee shop. He enjoyed people watching in general and definitely beautiful women. When she had entered, his interest had been piqued. Would he stop her to say hello? Probably not. He didn't want her to believe he was interested in her any longer after she'd rebuked his advances. But there she stood, right in front of him with her large smile and perfect teeth.

"Hello, Miss . . ." he'd hesitated.

"Rousseau, professor, Miss Rousseau," she'd replied, not bothered one second he had pretended to forget her name. Looking around and catching sight of the waitress at the counter staring at their interaction, her feminine instinct immediately suspected a sort of intimacy between them. The game became even more exciting, with an aroused and envious audience watching.

"Is this your usual stomping ground," she'd asked.

"It's a nice change of scenery," he'd replied curtly. Madeleine was not put off by his attitude. She had decided right then and there he'd invite her. Seeing how the conversation had started, it was an uphill battle, but she loved nothing more than a good fight.

Madeleine had glanced at back at the waitress and then to the man she was determined to seduce.

"I suppose if you aren't enjoying the scenery on campus, this one could do," she'd said not dropping his stare.

Uncomfortably, Beardsmith had grabbed his cup of coffee and taken a sip. He was dying to engage in the conversation but had placed the cup back down on the formica table without a word. A few of the crumbs populated the now empty plate where his peanut butter sandwich had been. She reached in the white paper bag and pulled one of the blueberry muffins out.

"It looks like you are done with your meal. But here," she'd said, placing the muffin in the middle of the plate, "if you want to move on to dessert, you can always nibble on this."

Madeleine had purposely brushed his hand.

"How awfully generous, Miss Rousseau," Beardsmith had said while beginning to peel back the paper cup in which the moist muffin was held. "How can I resist such a kind offer . . ."

"I wouldn't want you to miss out on dessert, professor. It really does complete a meal . . . ," she'd said flirtatiously.

"I'm not that easily satisfied young lady," he had replied while sinking his teeth into the muffin.

Yes you are professor, yes you are, Madeleine thought.

With such unequivocal talk, the professor had safely taken the bait, inviting her to come by his office in the late afternoon. With the offices closing at five o'clock, she had been asked to be there at quarter 'til, so as to avoid any disruptions. Beardsmith had struggled to concentrate, impatient for the end of the day. She was polluting nearly every one of his thoughts. Not once in his adult life did he recall having been so obfuscated by a refusal, so vexed by a rejection. He hated himself for having been too hastily suggestive.

But soon, Madeleine would reward him for his patience. The forbidden attraction elevated the stakes, therefore her interest tripled. The student handbook stipulated any student-teacher interaction outside of the academic realm was strictly prohibited. The student would be punished by permanent suspension from the college and the teacher dismissed from their position. The professor had much more to lose, so the tension had had to be sufficient to throw all caution to the wind.

The English Department hallway was littered with picture frames of classic authors, surprisingly poor in portraits of female writers for an all-women's college. Madeleine had rushed past Twain and Faulkner, to be on time for the appointment with Professor Beardsmith. The hall was busy as other teachers and administrative staff were wrapping up their day with an urgency to leave early to lengthen their weekend, even if only by a few minutes. Madeleine silently pitied them and their predictable lives. How did job security and repetitive days not render everyone insane? Was their contribution to life to be like sheep? Projecting herself into such a mundane existence was impossible. The janitor, the one who had wrapped her hand, had been meticulously mopping the floor from left to right. He, in contrast to the staff, had seemed in no hurry whatsoever to finish. His sway was like a hypnotic metronome as she approached. The motion, evenly gliding from one side to the next, was rhythmically captivating. He had looked up at her. Their eyes had locked and neither one of them smiled. He'd raised his hand and Madeleine nodded back. He'd resumed his activity, checking the time on the clock.

Madeleine had prepared a list of questions about the readings coming up in case the conversation veered unromantic and needed to extricate herself out of an unexpected situation. With a deep breath and preparing her best sultry but sweet smile, she knocked on the door, with dreams of Paris floating through her mind.

Beardsmith, on the other hand, had been tossing the idea back and forth of whether or not he might engage in any sort of extracurricular activity with the young Madeleine Rousseau. Allowing his mind to believe it was still up for discussion when it had long been made up, gave him some solace. Besides the physical and intellectual intrigue, there was a twinge of revenge eating away at him. Ever since he was young, once rebuked by a girl, he could wait years for his revenge of seducing her. The first time was in middle school when he had liked Emily Strickland. His friend Alfred had told her but she was not interested in Andrew; she liked another boy. Crushed, he'd retreated. It wasn't until his senior year of high school when he had finally had a growth spurt, played on the football team, and was one of the desirable boys in his class that things had changed. He had flirted heavily with Emily until she had finally asked him to walk her home. She had not only expected but longed to be kissed by Andrew. And he had obliged. In that kiss was the very commitment to go steady, to have and to hold her, to begin a relationship, and a date for the senior prom. There was a hunger in his embrace that was deep and powerful and could easily be mistaken for the burgeoning of love. In fact it had been a hunger for revenge, for the win. Andrew had waited four years for this kiss and it tasted sweeter than imagined. Especially when he knew it was the last time he'd ever speak to Emily, leaving her confused and saddened. A fair price for his pride.

Beardsmith opened the bottom drawer and reached all the way in the back for the emergency bottle of whiskey. The Laphroaig was dark and smokey, exactly the liquid courage needed. With two swigs straight from the bottle, the alcohol caressed his throat and began numbing his reason before he called out for Madeleine to enter.

The flirtation lasted longer than expected, though neither Madeleine nor the professor spoke of love or commitment. They resembled each other in that way, both self-serving. By not giving herself entirely to him, she maintained both tension and dominance. Every encounter was a chance to finally have her entirely. Their first meeting had been expectedly passionate. She had entered his office and sat down on the leather chair across from him, the desk separating them. Being on his turf made him even more confident than he sounded in class, which was hard to imagine. It was no secret other professors found Beardsmith to be a snob, criticizing him in the teacher's lounge which he never frequented. After a few minutes of chit-chat, the conversation had turned more suggestive as the professor had moved to sit on the couch at the back of the room.

"My office hours are nearly over, Miss Rousseau . . . ," he'd said, propping his elbow on the armrest.

She had stood facing him, while leaning on the back of the chair, pretending to be hesitant at what step to take next. She wanted to be direct about her intentions now. The build-up had lasted long enough.

"Does that mean I can have a drink too," she'd asked, having smelt a light waft of alcohol on his breath upon entering. The same faint odor chased her father around after the accident.

He'd walked back toward the desk to serve her a shot of whiskey from his secret stash. Pouring it into a small glass placed on the leather desk cover, he had invited Madeleine to drink it. She'd walked around to his side and downed it without flinching.

"And another?"

The whiskey was a token of acceptance of what was about to take

During a game of hide and seek that summer, while looking for Jamie, she'd run further out than before. Reaching the woods, Madeleine had gone too far. Leaning against the burgundy-colored shed at the corner of the property, she'd caught her breath and taken in the view of the open field splayed in front of the main house, squinting to spot any small figures making a beeline back to home base. Only the wind had moved the branches of the trees, but no human figures caught her eye. She'd pushed herself off of the wooden boards to head back when she heard panting. Excited about having found Jamie, as quietly as a mouse she had walked around the opposite side of the shed. The breathing got heavier as she approached silently, prepared to pounce on him. But when Jamie came into full view, Madeleine gasped. There on the ground, she saw him laying face down.

It took a few seconds for her brain to register the image and understand. Jamie had four legs coming out from his torso. After a moment, Madeleine had realized he was laying on top of someone else. Her heart racing and a pit forming in her stomach, she'd silently watched. Jamie was sliding his entire body up and down, like two hands being rubbed together to keep warm. The red polkadot material. The same one her ten-year old cousin Sophie's dress was made of. At that moment, the image was seared into her mind forever. She had understood what was happening: the secrecy, the heavy breathing, the motion: it resembled what she did at night, alone in her bed with Mr. Bear. Ashamed and vexed, Madeleine had gone running back to the house, tears of rage streaking down her face. She didn't speak to Sophie for the rest of the weekend, ignoring when she'd skid her knee badly on the gravel that Sunday. Madeleine had walked away smiling, convinced she had only gotten what she deserved.

When she'd returned to the reunion as a fourteen-year old, no one, including Jamie, recognized her. Madeleine had had a growth spurt and looked like a young woman, with full perky breasts, widened hips, and long legs. Sophie had not been able to come that year, therefore missing the spectacle of Jamie trying to get Madeleine's attention the entire stay. He'd offered piggy back rides during which she'd purposely press her chest on him, forcing impromptu jumps into the lake to hide visible excitement. The last night before the reunion was over, a few of the cousins had gone night swimming. In the middle of the lake was a wooden floating dock they would all use to dry off in the summer sun, sneaking adolescent glances at each others' changing bodies, hoping to remember every detail when back in one's bed. Madeleine had caught Jamie staring. Of all the cousins, her body had definitely changed the most. Margot was still her small and skinny pre-pubescent self. She still hadn't gotten her period, her breast had remained swollen nipples with no volume, though she insisted on wearing a training brassiere. That night, when they had all reached the dock, Madeleine had held on to the side and Jamie had swam up to her.

"I hate this! There are strange things touching my legs," she'd shrieked, moving around.

Jamie had laughed, wholeheartedly.

"You don't have to be scared. There's nothing dangerous in the lake. Here, you can hold on to me if you want," he'd offered.

Jamie had been facing the dock, holding on with both hands. Diving into the darkness of of the water, she'd slipped between Jamie and the floating wood, wrapping her legs around his waist.

"Is that better," he'd asked awkwardly.

"I guess so. At least your legs will get eaten before mine."

Their limbs had felt soft and slippery against one another. All of the other cousins had been laughing and jumping off the dock on the other side into the dark night, paying Jamie and Madeleine no mind.

"Can you lift yourself out of the water with me hanging on like this?"

Proud to demonstrate his strength, Jamie had pulled himself and Madeleine until their torsos were out of the water.

"Wow! I'm impressed."

As they submerged themselves into the water again, she had let her inner thighs slowly slide past Jamie's hips. She felt him hard as he drew in his breath. Her body instinctively rocked toward him as he'd remained completely immobile. Immediately she remembered that summer day and the red polka dot dress, Jamie's heavy breathing. The pang of jealousy she'd felt came rushing back and inflamed her desire. She had tightened her legs again and this time it was she who had gasped, with the familiar warm pulsation and wanting more than anything to reproduce the sensation she'd discovered on her own. But Jamie hadn't moved for fear the magic would end if he took any initiative. So Madeleine had slid herself against his body a few times, and eventually reached his open mouth with her lips to gently lick his tongue. Having been granted permission, he had grabbed her waist with one hand and guided her up and down the front of his swimming trunks. The noise from the rest of the cousins had died down as they had begun heading back to shore. But Jamie and Madeleine had been too busy to notice until Margot swam up. Jamie had quickly turned around.

"We are all heading back in. Are you com—" Margot had interrupted herself. "Why are you so out of breath?"

Madeleine hadn't skipped a beat.

"Oh Margot, you have to try this. We are holding our breath underwater to see who can go the longest!"

"Let me try!" And with that, she had disappeared under the surface. In the obscurity, Madeleine had slipped her hand down the front of Jamie's swimming trunks. His jaw dropped and his lids shut tight. So she'd counted out loud both for Margot's underwater experiment and to keep herself on rhythm. She had overheard the high school girls talk about what to do when they were touching a boy. When Margot's head had bobbed back up, Madeleine congratulated her on the longest time holding her breath as they headed back to dry land. But before she had snuck back into her bed, Jamie had found Madeleine. Taking him to the same spot behind the shed where she'd seen him with Sophie, she'd looked up at the stars, satisfied. This time, she had won.

The same summer reunion was to be held after the girls' high school graduation but Margot's death had put a grinding halt to it that year and ever since. After having lost her daughter, Aunt Evelyn had made it a point to busy Madeleine during the summers with propositions of travels, parties, and open invitations to New York at the end of every letter. Madeleine usually tried to visit her aunt and uncle a couple of times during the semester. Her own parents never asked for a visit. Last year, she'd not returned home for Christmas, pretexting research at the public library in New York. The seventeenth of September, Margot's birthday, was a couple of weeks away. Madeleine always celebrated with Aunt Evelyn and Uncle Pierre ever since she had fallen to her death. This would be the third anniversary and Madeleine had thought of an idea: inviting Phyllis, Joanie, and most importantly Rose to a weekend in New York City. If presented correctly, Madeleine knew Aunt Evelyn would agree. Deciding to phone her directly, there was no time to be wasted putting this into motion.

As she sat in the wooden calling cabin, waiting for the butler on the other end to fetch her aunt in their grandiose apartment, Madeleine watched the vaudeville in the foyer of the residence. In the corner, by the fireplace, she saw Rose's profile, deeply invested in her book. With a ribbon holding her blonde hair in a pony-tail and her honey-colored sweater, she looked like a Fragonard painting. A trip like this was a good way of getting to know her better and inquire about the budding relationship with the professor.

"Oh Madeleine, what a lovely surprise," Aunt Evelyn said as she picked up the receiver.

"Hello, dear aunt! How are you? I miss you and Uncle Pierre tremendously," she responded. The outpouring of love her aunt supplied constantly had taught Madeleine to reply by being equally as vocal, even if the feeling didn't necessarily follow.

"There isn't a day that goes by where I don't think of you! How is school? When are you coming to visit," she inquired immediately. Aunt Evelyn liked cutting to the chase. That was a part of her personality Uncle Pierre hadn't been able to soften like the rest.

Madeleine suggested a dinner be held in honor of Margot's birthday

"Phyllis! It's a fun weekend in New York, not a voyage into your future! I was thinking we could go out and listen to music, maybe take Rose to a jazz club," Madeleine nudged Phyllis.

Madeleine turned to Rose. Why was she so quiet? What if the girls were overly enthusiastic and Rose decided not to come? Then she would be alone here for the entire weekend and have plenty of time to seduce the professor while no one watched over her. The way she had wildly flirted with the boy in the red convertible, Beardsmith didn't stand a chance if he struck her fancy. And now it was impossible to cancel the weekend if Rose stayed, Aunt Evelyn and Uncle Pierre would simply be too disappointed.

"Oh Maddie, I don't know if I can go. My mother would lose her mind, but that's every other day with her. I'm absolutely dying to see the city and be with you, but I also have a lot of work," Rose said, perplexed.

The parental situation was easily circumvented as Janet's R.A. questions were textbook predictable. But what project necessitated so much attention at the beginning of the semester?

"Oh Rose, it really wouldn't be the same without you. Your mother will never find out, I can promise you. And for the work, is it something we can help you with? I'm not overloaded right now and amongst the three of us, I'm sure we could help you get enough done. Right girls," Madeleine turned to Phyllis and Joanie who were eagerly nodding. The two always loved a group effort, instilling a sense of solidarity neither of them had ever truly felt. Here at Vassar, they had finally found their people.

Rose smiled kindly at her new friends, desperate for a positive answer to the tempting invitation.

"What are you working on that is making you hesitate about going," Joanie asked.

"Professor Beardsmith asked me to do a presentation on Thoreau and the Transcendental Club," Rose replied.

Madeleine's heart dropped as her facial muscles tightened ever so slightly. It WAS for the professor's assignment that she was thinking of staying. If Madeleine had to do the entire presentation herself, she would not leave Rose to stay on campus over the weekend.

"Piece of cake," said Phyllis, capable of writing the entire presentation on her own. With an incredible gift for public speaking, she often presented without notes, only a few talking points she might jot down. Phyllis enticed the listener as if in an intimate conversation. Madeleine had a certain ease when presenting, but not to that extent. She meticulously wrote out everything, should she lose her train of thought.

"It will be my first presentation here and Professor Beardsmith wanted to check it before I give it."

The plot was thickening. Beardsmith was seeing her over the weekend then. Madeleine didn't feel jealous. She wasn't, she convinced herself. But she very well couldn't have Rose swoop in to reap the seeds so carefully sown, and it seemed she was well on her way to doing so.

"We're more than happy to help but if you need to stay, we don't want to force you. My uncle is an avid jazz fan so I thought we'd go to Birdland. It could have been fun. But another time," Madeleine said, as if going into New York was as easy as going into Poughkeepsie to buy a comb at the drugstore. It wasn't and they all were very appreciative of the prospect. Rose, having never been to New York and with friends volunteering to help, was torn. Madeleine put the final nail in the coffin by reaching out and saying:

"If it were any other time, I would reschedule for you but, you understand, with my cousin's anniversary and all . . ."

"Oh Maddie, of course. I'd love to go! I want to be you girls and go to the jazz club and meet your aunt and uncle," Rose said sheepishly. "Are you sure you don't mind helping me?"

"Anything for a friend," Madeleine answered.

The weekend to New York was sealed. Departure was set for after lunch on Friday to catch the train in town. Until then, every spare moment was dedicated to helping Rose with the presentation. The quartet functioned as one unit around campus for the entire week prior. They dined together, worked together, walked together, laughed together. The bonds of their friendship were intensely solidifying as they moved toward a common goal.

Meanwhile, Madeleine was also strategizing on her approach with Beardsmith. Perhaps he was getting bored with her or an easy prey like Rose was more than he could resist. He was an intelligent man and the risk of seducing another student seemed grand. Sure, he was a great professor but he wasn't irreplaceable either. Vassar College chose from a pool of elite applicants for their faculty. Why double the odds of endangering his future? Madeleine's desire dwindled at the thought of how very average his behavior was. She flipped through the pages of her planner to count the weeks before the announcement of the internship to Paris would be made. Seven. Seven weeks for a ticket to Paris.

Chapter 10

An ongoing source of envy had been cousin Margot's French heritage. Traveling to her father's country several times, she spoke the language and had a natural elegance, surely gifted by her genes from the old continent. Madeleine, thirsty for belonging, had read every book she could get her hands on about the land of philosophers and baguettes. She'd pored over Uncle's Pierre's family photo albums wishing the same blue blood pumped through her veins.

As children, she asked Margot to read the tales from the Comtesse de Ségur, repeating the words silently to better her French accent. By the time they were teenagers, Madeleine's French was nearly impeccable, but her American pronunciation gave her away. She would never be mistaken for a native. Regardless, the two cousins used their second language to share answers on tests and gossip about classmates directly under their noses. It had been after school one day when Margot had suggested the craziest of ideas. What if they went to live in Paris together after high school? The girls spent weeks daydreaming of their life abroad: should they go to the Deux Magots or Café de Flore to sit and wait for inspiration to strike; would they buy dresses at Christian Dior or Yves Saint-Laurent; where would they find the best eclairs or the most buttery croissants on the Left Bank. For Madeleine, the perspective of moving came like a crucial breath of fresh air she hadn't known she'd been craving. A sense of ultimate freedom, a liberation from ever returning home. Madeleine held on to their secret like a lifeline. It was senior year when everything changed.

The Rousseau country residence stood on a large property delineated on one side by a wide creek, which in the fall and winter often overflowed. As children, Madeleine and Margot had been forewarned not to play there during the wetter months as the gorged banks grew soft with the rain. But the two secretly enjoyed running down and dropping sticks, paper boats, and flowers into the stream, watching them disappear into what they imagined was another world.

Aunt Evelyn had chosen this house in New Jersey despite it not being the prime real estate she and her husband could afford. They had a magnificent residence in Sands Point, which everyone preferred, but she found it important to not always distance herself from her sole brother and his family. It was good for Madeleine and Margot to stay together in her native New Jersey, not forgetting the commonality of their roots.

One January afternoon, Uncle Pierre and Aunt Evelyn had left to visit an old friend of the family's for a late lunch. The girls had not joined, preoccupied by the refurbishing of Margot's new room. She had managed to claim the entire third story of the house, formerly the attic, as her domain. The space felt as wide as a tennis court, with a grand vaulted roof and thick wooden beams supporting the structure like the massive muscles of a strong man. They had spent the Christmas holidays ordering furniture, carpets, bedding, pillows to be displayed according to a very specific floor plan. Gifted with exquisite taste like her mother, Margot had designed and organized the room herself, with the help of her favorite cousin. In one corner she had had her four-poster bed placed, with stretches of light pink Chantilly lace directly imported from France, hanging just so. Bored with taking directions, Madeleine had thrown herself onto the bed, immediately enveloped by a cloud-like sensation of ease and satisfaction. The holidays had been fantastic, her aunt and uncle spoiling her nearly as much as their own daughter. The plush bedding made with only the highest quality of the secret layer geese used to stay warm was almost womblike. She never wanted to let go of this feeling: to be swallowed by luxury, held by comfort.

"Get up! You need to move that chest of drawers so it separates the bedroom from the lounging area," Margot said authoritatively. Madeleine detested when Margot got into these moods. It rarely occurred but when it did, it stung the deepest part of her core. And this was the second time in one week Margot had been snappy and quite honestly condescending.

"Why don't you get Johnny to do it," she asked, not rising and placing her hands behind her head as if she was sunning herself by a swimming pool. Johnny was the handyman who lived on the property with his wife. The girls always liked watching him work. He was robust with broad shoulders and never spoke much. In the summer, when he worked the garden, the sweat would make his shirt stick to his skin so nothing was left to the imagination. He had been the subject of many fantasies where, in the shed, he'd lift up skirts to caress the inside of thighs. The poor man had not a clue.

"Why would I when you are right here," Margot replied, oblivious to the anger arising in her cousin. Madeleine bit her tongue and silently rose from the bed to the chest of drawers, using the brooding energy to displace the heavy piece. As she pushed against it, her anger grew.

She then marched to the gigantic round window in the middle of the room. It resembled a miniature version of the rose window in Notre Dame, minus the stained glass. Aunt Evelyn had had it custom made and it was extraordinary both from the outside as well as from the inside. Like a giant telescopic lens onto an imperturbable world of nature, a place of dominating stillness. There were only two openings, like doors onto the outside. So as to not damage the aesthetic appearance of the grand window, no external protective rail had been put in. Prior to Margot's decision to overtake the third floor, no one ever went up to that part of the house, only admiring the piece from outside. The attic had other windows which were normal and safe and Margot used those instead of the grand one. Madeleine opened one of the sides of the grand window. Margot gasped as they had been forbidden on multiple occasions to do so by her parents.

"Maddie, you shouldn't do that," she said nervously. "Close that one and open another if you want. Or don't actually, it's too cold out." Margot was again using the tone.

"Oh what, Margs, are you going to do everything your parents tell you to do? We're moving to Paris when we graduate, don't you think it's about time you do things for yourself," she fumed, looking down at the ground, three stories below.

"I'm not going to Paris anymore," Margot shot back. In the most authoritative voice she continued "I decided to go to college, to Vassar actually."

"What are you talking about? We're going to Paris."

"I don't want to anymore. Sheryl's sister was telling me about her time there and I want to try it out, " she lied.

"But . . . we didn't apply. And now it's too late anyway."

"Not for me! Papa has a friend and I received my acceptance letter on Friday. Aren't you happy for me?"

A rage washed over Madeleine. Her peripheral vision vanished. Her hands began to shake and her heart pounded deeply like a massive church bell being hit with a dense pillow. What was happening, she thought. How can she be doing this? Why? Surely she knew everything this decision meant. She would now be dumped back into her New Jersey town with nowhere to go, perhaps attend some nondescript local college the following year. Her parents might try to marry her off and have her leave the house before then. Or would they even care what she did? They hadn't in the past, why now. The life she had envisioned, all of the dreams spoken of about their future abroad came crashing down in complete and utter chaos. Did Margot not realize the implications of her actions? She knew the move was contingent on her coming. She had in one fell swoop ruined her life, purposely. It was obviously a means to reaffirm her power. Most of all, Madeleine detested having been taken for a fool.

Margot sensed the tension in the room and walked closer to her cousin.

"Maddie, come on. What? Why aren't you speaking? Oh goodness, you are acting like such a child."

Madeleine could barely even hear the words coming out of her cousin's mouth. There was so much confusion in her mind, so much swirling anger. She stood perfectly still but the spinning sensation continued. Her clenched fists turned both knuckles white in an instant while she drove her nails deep into the flesh of her palms.

"Maddie, we don't have to do *everything* together. You can come visit if you like and you will . . . I don't know, do whatever it is you want to do," Margot said, approaching. The very last thing Madeleine wanted to be was touched by this treacherous whore who had made it her life's purpose to humiliate her. As she came closer, a complete wave of clarity overcame Madeleine.

She opened her arms to embrace her cousin. Perhaps she could forgive her and indeed try and attend Vassar the following year. But what would she do for twelve months, with still no means of getting to Paris. Margot would soon regret this.

Like a wounded feline backed into a corner, Madeleine was ready. The second Margot embraced her, she spun around and violently pushed her out of the window. Margot fell backwards, her eyes in sheer shock and a scream which ended the moment her body met the cement walkway, shattering the life right out of her. She lay there, immobile as a warm, thick pool of burgundy liquid began to form; a halo of blood around her head.

Madeleine watched the body for a few seconds and stepped back, peering out onto the property. If Johnny was anywhere to be seen, had he heard the last sound to ever leave those betraying lips? She hurriedly grabbed her sweater and purse hanging on the back of the chair Margot had carefully chosen to match the desk she would have been studying on this summer. Before Vassar. On it she had placed the letterhead paper with her initials, the one Uncle Pierre had shipped from France. It was a decades-old tradition to have all of their family stationery embossed by a printer in Paris and when Uncle Pierre moved to the United States, he had continued to have them imported. Madeleine took a few sheets and put them in her purse, for she was now the only one in the family with the initials "MR."

She raced down the stairs, her feet quickly and diligently hitting every step until she finally reached the bottom floor. The cook would be back soon with the groceries to prepare the evening meal. The grandfather clock in the entranceway showed 3:37 PM and she suspected her aunt and uncle would be back around four. Aunt Evelyn liked to work on her embroidery in the afternoon while listening to the radio. This meant Madeleine had just enough time to leave. She wouldn't need an alibi because who in their right mind would ever believe she might do this? She'd gone home early, walking as she needed to clear her head. As Madeleine carefully closed the front door, she shot a last glance at Margot's once very alive body, splayed on the ground. Why had she gone and ruined everything? They should have been together in the city of lights and then, by her own doing, she had ended up in this situation, dead. Madeleine refused to be brought down in the same way and headed toward the garage.

Behind it was a small opening in the bushes that was a shortcut into another field and would only take her ten minutes to get home walking, slip into the house and wait for the news. As she was getting ready to pass the garage, she heard a motor. She froze, dead in her tracks, ears perked. Was that . . . ? The sound approached until it was just on the other side of the bushes. There was nowhere for her to go but inside the garage where they would be parking the car. As she stepped inside, she heard the grinding of the wheels on the gravel at the beginning of the driveway. Her eyes having difficulty adjusting to the light, she felt the way along the wooden wall. Her heart was nearly pounding out of her chest, there was no time. As the car was approaching and simultaneously while trying to find a place to hide, she rummaged through her mind for an explanation as to why she should be in the dark space, as she breathed in the stench of gasoline.

The doors opened suddenly. Madeleine only had time to slip behind a wooden box in the corner, barely large enough to cover her entire body. If anyone examined the corner carefully, she was visible. The car's headlights drowned the entire space. Madeleine retracted the foot which wouldn't quite fit behind the box. The car slowly pulled in, coming closer and closer. She stopped breathing, panicking between wanting to jump out and losing consciousness. But the car halted abruptly halfway as heavy footsteps approached the garage.

"Sir, sir! There's been an accident," she heard Johnny say, breathlessly.

"What do you mean," Uncle Pierre replied anxiously. Madeleine supposed Johnny's face revealed the gravity of the situation and she heard Aunt Evelyn frantically question the handyman as they followed him back to the house. Uncle Pierre had not turned off the engine. This was Madeleine's only chance. She delicately removed herself from the hiding place, squatting down along the side of the running car. She only had thirty feet to go to make it to the secret hole in the bushes. Closing her eyes and taking a deep breath, she promised herself to be fast and not turn back. She made a beeline for the bushes, and right before diving through the shrubbery, she turned to see three frantic adults around Margot's body. Aunt Evelyn had fallen to her knees and held her daughter's body close. A second before Johnny glanced in Madeleine's direction, she ran into the neighboring field, never stopping, every breath a liberation from what could have been.

She entered the Rivers house silently and slipped into her bedroom unnoticed, albeit soaked. She immediately changed her clothes, brushed her hair, and pulled out the collection of essays on Greek mythology she had been reading. Lying on the bed, Madeleine sighed before diving right back into Antigone's story, who refusing injustice, took matters into her own hands. Checking the clock, it was time to make her presence known for the news would arrive soon. She cracked open the door and shouted downstairs.

"Mother? Mother? Do we have anything to eat?"

"Madeleine? I didn't realize you were home."

"Yeah, I had some work to do and told Margot I'd come over later for dinner. But I want a little snack."

"Why don't you come down, you know I hate yelling."

Madeleine took her book and walked down to meet her mother in the kitchen who had already pulled out two slices of white bread and was spreading her homemade mayonnaise on it. She had a way of always getting the perfect amount to cover the entire piece evenly. Another nugget Madeleine had probably passed up.

She read at the yellow formica table, waiting for the sandwich and for the phone to ring with catastrophic news. Utterly calm, it was as if nothing had happened. Out of habit, she searched the underside of the kitchen table to find the hole she incessantly scratched away at. It had now gotten big enough to fit the tip of her index finger and sometimes she imagined being able to pick up the entire table with that one finger lodged in its perfectly shaped mold and throw it across the room so her parents might react.

The phone rang. Madeleine did not bat an eyelash and kept reading. She rarely answered the telephone anyway. Her mother put the turkey slice down onto the plate and walked over to pick up the receiver.

"Hello, Rivers residence."

Then silence.

"What are you . . ."

Then a deep gasp before the howling scream muffled in her hand. Madeleine turned to see her mother slide along the wall straight to the floor, letting the receiver slip onto the sunlight-colored linoleum floor. She ran over, taking the phone only to hear Uncle Pierre's heartbreaking cries.

"What? What is it?"

Unwillingly imitating her mother's reaction, she let herself fall, as if a very heavy load had been placed on her entire body. For the first time in years, she placed her head into her mother's lap, like she used to before her brother's fatal car accident. Her mother would stroke her hair and Madeleine loved it.

Here there was no stroking but it was enough. Mother's body couldn't stop shaking and all of the screaming had brought Father in. He knew from the wails that life had been cruel once again and his eyes closed at the sight of his wife and daughter, slayed by pain to the ground.

The investigation rapidly ruled an accident and not a doubt was cast on Madeleine's implication in it. Yet what she never found out was that Uncle Pierre *had* discovered the girls' idea of a transatlantic move after high school. Although he loved his native land, he wouldn't permit his daughter to live there. With every trip, a disgust lingered inside for the country who had knelt to the Germans. The horrific Nazi invasion and the treasonous Vichy government was nothing short of a source of humiliation and shame, which nearly two decades later, was still fresh in his mind. He was infuriated by the traitors; the ones who claimed to be in the "resistance" once the war was over but in fact had provided the Nazis with Jews, delicious praline chocolates, tender meats, and exquisite champagnes while people and country were murdered, starved, and tortured to death. Despite the years passed, Uncle Pierre could not forgive them. Until he buried the hatchet, no member of his family was moving to Paris. In his study, he'd sat Margot down to discuss her future, graduation being four months away, imposing college. That was how Vassar College had come into the mix. With a few friends on the board, Uncle Pierre had secured Margot a spot for the fall. She hadn't said a word, unsure how to break the news to Madeleine.

All of it was water under the bridge and today Madeleine was interested in maintaining the financial, rather than emotional support. She deserved the upscale life shown by her aunt and uncle, especially now that they were childless. What else were they going to do with all of that money? Hence, if Vassar sent her abroad, the chances of Uncle Pierre standing in the way of her dream were slim. And if he did, she was prepared to do anything to change her uncle's mind because for Madeleine, Paris was synonymous with reinvention. With a future. She saw none here. Farewell to Madeleine Rivers and hello to Madeleine Rousseau; the wealthy girl with no past, with no dead brother or cousin, with no disinterested parents. Leave and never look back. She was prepared to fully assume a carefully crafted identity and it certainly wasn't a wavering university professor in Poughkeepsie, New York who was going to keep her from it.

Vassar College,
September 12th, 1959

Dear Uncle Pierre and Aunt Evelyn,
    How time flies. The last few weeks have sped by, and I will soon be packing my suitcase. All has been swell here at school. Rose Suggs, my roommate for the year, needed some help with her work in order to join us so I created a timetable to divide the tasks, you would be proud Uncle Pierre! They are very excited about coming to New York. Phyllis has already penciled in a walk by the United Nations' offices. I cannot say I am entirely sure what she is hoping will happen by simply strolling in the vicinity! Perhaps someone will wander out of the building on a Saturday and offer her a job? To be honest, they probably should, she is one of the brightest minds I've come across and her future looks grand. Joanie, on the other hand, is a little nervous about coming into the city. She is also afraid of the big bad wolf! I told her we'd stay on the right part of town. Also, I did not mention to the others you'd bought her ticket. I figured there is no need to make her feel any more ill at ease than she may already be.
    On the other hand, our new friend Rose is head over heels at the idea of New York City! She is from Atlanta and has never been to the city. Can you imagine? She was hesitant and I strongly encouraged her to seize the opportunity. She loves jazz too so shall we go to Birdland on Saturday night, what do you say Uncle Pierre? You know, Margot would have

*loved these girls. I know we would have all been friends and
I am pleased they will be with us to celebrate her birthday as
if she were still amongst us. Some nights, I pretend I share my
room with Margot instead of Rose. I listen to her breathing
and imagine Margot and me being here at school together.
In that fantasy, we take the same classes, we share our meals,
and our study group. We stay up late like we did when we were
little girls, stifling our giggles into the pillows so you wouldn't
hear. On occasion she'd sneak into my bed, pretending to be
scared so we could sleep together. And when I come out of that
daydream, Margot still fills my heart; I keep her there with
me forever. Perhaps that's what makes the pain of her loss
bearable. She is with me, with us.*

*Oh my dear Uncle Pierre and Aunt Evelyn, how I long for it
to be next weekend already! We will celebrate Margot. Nothing
could make me happier in the present circumstance. We will
arrive on the five thirty-five train. Aunt Evelyn, thank you for
offering to send Alberto to pick us up. I will be happy to see
him again and get to you as quickly as possible. I'll catch you
up on my classes and everything else then.*

Love,
Madeleine

Madeleine admired the near perfect handwriting. That was one of
the few gifts from her mother. After her third grade teacher, Ms. Burns,
had given Madeleine a low grade in penmanship, she had forced Madeleine to practice for hours on end. It had carried on for so long that
a blister had formed on the side of her middle finger. But she did not
complain, hoping to win back her mother's affection. Finally when
her handwriting earned her the best grade in the class, she had run
home to show Mother, who had given her a forced smile and a dismissive pat on the head. Had she exaggerated too much in the letter? No,
she thought. Mourning parents needed to hear how still "alive" their

child is for others. Madeleine knew how to tap into that with the right amount of emotion. Satisfied, she neatly folded the letter into three and slipped it in an envelope. With a pair of the two-cent Frank Lloyd Wright stamps bought purposely because Uncle Pierre was a great admirer of the architect's work, the letter was ready to be mailed.

The presentation for Beardsmith was nearly complete thanks to the girls. Rose began packing for the trip and scheduled telephoning home on Wednesday in order not to have to ring her parents for another couple of weeks. Her mother was often overly excited, always intrusive, wanting to know about her life: was she cold, had she eaten enough, had she made nice friends, how was her roommate, etc. Rose answered, dissimulating the brewing enthusiasm about the upcoming trip to New York.

"Mother, I heard the school organizes a trip to New York City in the spring term, wouldn't that be nice for me to go? Since I've never been and all," she questioned, testing the waters.

"Oh sweet heavens, darling. I don't know who you are spending time with but I will sooner be tarred and feathered before letting you set foot into the city of sin," her mother's stern voice echoed in the receiver, dropping an octave. She was forever adamant about Rose never setting foot in New York, even accompanied, with the crime and the poverty rampant in the streets. At the end of the conversation, she concluded:

"Honey, please do not give me any more grief over this. You know I have a bad heart. You have gotten yourself into enough trouble for a lifetime. If your father EVER found out."

A familiar wave of annoyance swept over Rose. With a tight throat, she promised to call in a couple of weeks, hanging up quickly. Now more than ever was she ready to partake in the trip, against her mother's orders. She certainly hadn't needed the reminder about having nearly brought public humiliation to the entire Suggs name, yet her mother spoke of it "discreetly" as often as possible.

Rose had spent the first six months of 1959 at Aunt Vera's house in Savannah, Georgia. Her time was spent studying on the back porch, as the front one was off limits as prying eyes of the neighborhood might notice her growing belly. Despite the attempted instilling of shame and guilt by her mother and the priest to whom she had confessed, she loved feeling a life growing inside of her. No number of Hail Mary's could change what she had done. But she didn't care. Alone, every night in front of the standing mirror by the bath tub, she'd applied the honey-scented lotion to her stomach which was rounding, like her cheeks. Her breasts, swollen and tender but beautiful, preparing to nourish the baby inside; the child she would never know. Her mother had constantly repeated that she was but an oven, baking a cake for someone else to enjoy. That was God's way. Rose disliked the oven analogy though she did run hot all of the time. Wanting only cool beverages, Aunt Vera could barely keep up with Rose's ice cube consumption. As summer approached and the hot and humid Georgia climate settled in, Rose's belly had come to term. And by the fall she had arrived in Poughkeepsie with a flat stomach and a generous heart, grateful to have found a small niche of friends who had sacrificed their free time to help her come on the forbidden trip, ultimately changing the course of her life.

Chapter 11

Keeping busy rearranging the bookshelf by color, Madeleine regularly peered out of the window, scanning the visible part of the campus for Rose. She'd heard sniffling in the night. Why was she crying? She had called her parents the day before, the girls had done the work for her presentation, so everything was in motion for New York. Madeleine wasn't privy to Rose's intimate thoughts and worries yet. If she cancelled at the last minute, Madeleine would be absolutely enraged, obliged to go forth with the trip and leaving a potentially catastrophic encounter between Rose and the professor to occur without her surveillance. Deep in thought, she hadn't even heard her roommate walk in.

"Hello, Maddie!"

"Rose! I haven't seen you all day! Where have you been hiding? Is everything ok," Madeleine exclaimed, feigning more concern than necessary.

"Yes, everything is fine, I wanted to stroll the campus before the day started," she replied.

Madeleine came closer and fixed Rose's collar.

"Well, I'm here for you, you know. I don't want our weekend to cause you any anguish . . . ," she said, using the same soothing tone her aunt used when she'd needed her to stay perfectly still while she removed a splinter.

Rose smiled.

"I spoke to my parents yesterday and I had to lie to them. It's ridiculous. They can't trust me to be careful and safe."

Was Rose trying to back out? Or was she feeling a rebellious streak and wanted to go, full steam ahead. Maybe just one final push?

"I understand. You shouldn't have to lie. I don't want you to feel any pressure to come. Even if we did the work so you could, now it just means you have an entirely free weekend to rest or do as you please," Madeleine insisted.

At present, this was possibly the worst situation. A bored Rose, alone for the weekend on campus, with a stellar presentation to show the professor. This could easily backfire.

"I've made up my mind Maddie and I wouldn't miss this trip for the world. I can't thank you and the girls enough for making this possible."

Madeleine clasped her hands together in relief.

"Oh I'm so happy to hear it! We are going to remember this trip for the rest of our lives. New York City, here we come!"

Rose's face lit up like a child on Christmas morning. The sheer joy she expressed made pleasing her its own reward. An entire day could easily be spent observing Rose. Just watch her be, her expressions, her grace, her voice. All of it a marvelous delight.

"Let's think about what to pack," Madeleine said, opening up her closet and breaking free from the charm. "You can borrow anything of mine, and I even have more clothes in New York!"

"How fabulous! And what should we bring your aunt and uncle? I'd like to pick up a gift in town today. I was thinking a scarf for your aunt from the little store with the red awning next to the OK Cafe? What do you think?"

"That's very considerate. I'm sure she'd love it."

"But I will tell your aunt it is from all three of us. Joanie shared with me how you bought her ticket and I don't want her to have to spend money she doesn't have," Rose said.

Joanie had told Rose about the ticket. Interesting. Well, that was a surprise. Joanie was usually very discreet about her lack of funds, not wanting anyone to know. She must consider Rose a close friend. They had been spending a lot of time together and Joanie was quite impressionable, surely finding a sympathetic ear in Rose when confiding about her simple upbringing.

"What colors does your aunt like? I saw a few silk scarves the other day when I was browsing. There was a gorgeous blue one with flowers on it. Think she might like that? You know what would be best if you came with me! Can you spare some time this afternoon and we can find a gift and have a coffee," Rose eagerly suggested.

"What a splendid idea! I'll head over to the library to finish my outline and meet you back here at 2:30."

Madeleine didn't need to go to the library but was going to make an appointment with the professor before the trip. It was a good idea to satisfy him before being unavailable so no pent-up sexual energy might fester and attract potential competition.

The English department's secretary, Doris Hoxenbury kept the appointments in a large leather-bound diary she carefully wrote in with pencil, to allow for changes. Though she was rather odd, Madeleine had a pleasant rapport with her. She had only ever seen Ms. Hoxenbury wear a variation of three different jacket and skirt suits. Her long hair, always in a tight bun, sat at the nape of her neck. Not much older than Madeleine, she cultivated a conservative, borderline "old maid" style to inspire a sense of trust and credibility, off-setting her round, chubby-cheeked youthful face. Today, she was wearing the navy-blue ensemble. It was not exactly appropriate for the warm September day.

"Ms. Hoxenbury, how are you? How was your summer," she asked kindly, always entertaining polite chit-chat. Doris Hoxenbury loved to discuss the latest feline acrobatic performance of Dolly the cat and her mother with whom she spent part of the summers up in Vermont.

After a very abbreviated version of her Europe trip so as to not sound like she was bragging, Madeleine gave much attention and care listening to the description of Ms. Hoxenbury's train ride with Dolly, going into all of the details of the carrier she had used, the accident which had occurred, and the unpleasant man who had complained. As she reached in her bag to show a picture of Dolly, given by a photographer friend, Madeleine sneaked a peek at Beardsmith's schedule. She desperately wanted to see if there was a meeting with Rose scheduled in the books. Hoxenbury mistook attention for appreciation, and was going on about Dolly knocking keys off of the table, predictably like every other cat really, while Madeleine leaned over the desk laughing. The professor was scheduled to see Rose on Thursday at four.

"I'd love to see the professor on Thursday after my class. Is 4:45 all right? I know the office closes at five, but I only need to drop off my outline and have a few words."

The girls arrived at Penn Station with only two suitcases. Madeleine had suggested she and Rose pack together and for the girls to use one suitcase since they would be paired up in a room at the apartment. Madeleine inspected what Rose selected and though it wasn't her style, she approved of the classic and elegant outfits chosen. The good southern girls took proper care of their appearance. Madeleine pretended to hesitate about which one out of her Hermès scarf collection she should take, displaying them before Rose.

"These are incredible Madeleine! Each one resembles a sumptuous painting. I'm afraid it's impossible for me to pick," she replied, holding each one up, admiring the intricate details.

"If you think this is hard, you wouldn't stand a chance in the store. Aunt Evelyn and I went to the one on the corner of rue du Faubourg Saint-Honoré. There a saleswoman pulled out innumerable scarves from every color palette imaginable. You should have seen it Rose, from light beiges to bright reds, to turquoises of the Mediterranean Sea, to deep hunter greens, the silk fabric running through her fingers," she narrated. Madeleine picked one and held it up by two corners for Rose to admire. "Every year since I turned sixteen, my aunt buys me one for Christmas. It's not my only gift of course, but I love them. This year I chose this one."

The off-white silk square with red piping was a tribute to the French Foreign Legion, with soldiers from various countries, depicted in their traditional uniforms around a central piece. In the middle, on a green background, the backs of Foreign Legion soldiers along with their motto: honor and fidelity. Rose inspected it carefully.

"Well, this one doesn't resemble your other ones. It's quite beautiful but I like the horse-themed one better, I think. What is the 'Légion Etrangère," she asked.

"The French Foreign Legion. Have you never heard of it? It's an elite section of the military anyone can join. And when they say anyone, they mean a-n-y-o-n-e. You don't have to be French, no questions are asked about your past, and you don't even have to give your real name! Isn't that incredible? You join and become part of this world-renowned troop and leave everything behind," Madeleine described, lost in thought as she examined the scarf more intently. Transported by the story, Rose's eyes had lit up.

"That's fascinating. Makes you wonder who are the men that join, right? What part of their past are they running away from? Regardless, it is beautiful, and you should definitely bring it along, it goes splendidly with your coloring."

Snapping out of her daydream, Madeleine grabbed two more scarves.

"You may borrow them anytime you know," she said, wrapping one around Rose's neck. Rose beamed with delight and turned to face the mirror.

"How lucky you are Maddie! I could only dream of going to buy one in Paris!" Rose wrapped the scarf around her head, like Grace Kelly in to *To Catch a Thief* as she rode the hills of Provence in a convertible. She looked absolutely magnificent.

"You think I'll end up going one day," she asked her friend innocently. "Find myself a husband who will take me there to buy my own Hermès scarves . . ."

"Of course, you will! But for the moment, why don't we start with New York," Madeleine said as she slid the scarf off of Rose's blonde locks.

Chapter 12

When Madeleine reached for the suitcase as the train approached Penn Station, Rose immediately grabbed it from her. The girls refused to let her carry the baggage, as she was responsible for the whole trip. All four lined up in front of the doors of the carriage, prepared to exit, rearranging their skirts and hair before stepping out into the unknown. Friday afternoon meant the station was busy with travelers, too preoccupied to yell out a "Pardon me," as they bustled past.

"Pair up, it will be easier for us to get out of here unscathed," Madeleine warned, grabbing Joanie's hand as they walked down the platform.

There, by the locomotive, Madeleine recognized Alberto from afar. He stood in his impeccable black suit and driver's cap. When Madeleine and Margot were younger, they both had a not-so-secret crush on Alberto. Before Uncle Pierre hired him, he had been a young man in his early twenties working at his father's garage. The Renault Frégate, which Uncle Pierre had had shipped from France, couldn't be touched by anyone but Francesco, also known as Frankie, Alberto's father. Over the years, he had grown fond of Frankie's large Italian family and even more so when they'd lost one of their sons overseas, in the war. Frankie had avoided the draft with his club foot and Alberto had been too young. In a strange melange of emotion and culpability, Uncle Pierre had offered Alberto a job to partially absolve the guilt which ate away at him. He watched young men being sent across the world and getting killed to save his country, when he himself had not gone back to fight. In his mind, by ensuring Alberto's future he was paying his dues.

In their teenage years, Margot often feigned being too tired or too ill to walk so Alberto had to drive them around the city to their unimportant destinations. They giggled as they slid across the slippery leather of the back seat, catching Alberto's eyes in the rearview mirror. He would wink at them, making their laughter double. Those were some of the fondest memories Madeleine had, before the year when everything had changed. She'd felt carefree then. Not a concern about the past or the future. That was perhaps one of the sensations she longed for the most. To be rid of attachments stifling her, like a constant weight on her chest, to the point of suffocation at times. She imagined that same freedom awaited in Paris where she was going to ride the bus from the Eiffel Tower to Saint-Michel, and live a life without the baggage of her parents, friends, acquaintances, all who constantly busied and clouded her life.

As a young lady, she continued having flirtatious fun with Alberto. She enjoyed nursing the possibility he pleasured himself thinking of her from time to time. Only once had she secretly seduced him when she was seventeen and never again had the desire to repeat the experience. Madeleine gave Alberto a kiss on the cheek as he slid his hand around her waist. He'd be happy with the three new girls she'd brought for him to dazzle.

"Everyone in the station thinks I am the luckiest man alive to be taking four beautiful young ladies away! Come on *belle!*" Alberto always liked to punctuate his phrases with his native tongue to complement an already thick New York accent. Born in East Harlem, which was more Italian than Palermo, he wore his nationality like a badge of honor, proudly fighting anyone who dared question his loyalty. Uncle Pierre adored having the most rebellious driver in the city. And the most handsome.

Rose, Phyllis, and Joanie were initially quiet in Alberto's presence. Unfamiliar with the overtly seducing, sweet-talking, straightforward fellow, they had all lost their tongues. They seemed so provincial all of the sudden, not having been exposed to anyone beyond a narrow familial social circle. But within a few minutes, the awkwardness dissipated as they blushed and became giddy, intrigued by the new male specimen. Madeleine had purposely not mentioned Alberto, adding an extra element of surprise. He swiftly took the suitcases from Rose and Joanie and ran up to walk side by side with Madeleine.

As they all piled into the car, Rose had been taking in everything New York City was displaying before her. Madeleine reached over and squeezed Rose's hand.

"I am so pleased you came," she said.

"I am beyond thrilled to be here," Rose answered.

As Alberto pulled up to a towering stone building, the doorman approached to open the car doors. He was new and greeted Madeleine with a curt "Miss."

"I'm sure you were told about my arrival but so you can put a face to a name, I am Madeleine Rousseau," she barely smiled, not extending her hand. "My friends and I will be here over the weekend. And welcome, I'm sure you'll be happy here."

Although the new doorman was only ten years her senior, she wanted to impose her authority from the get-go, for him to know his place. He, on the other hand, was unimpressed, making no acknowledgment of Madeleine's attempted demonstration of power. This was not his first rodeo, he had been working in luxury apartment buildings all over the Upper East Side for the past thirteen years and had had his fair share of the children of the rich. He wasn't intimidated by them and knew how and who to please to keep his salary paid.

"It is a pleasure to meet you, Miss Madeleine. I know your family is most looking forward to your arrival," he said holding the door.

"I'll send your luggage up in just a minute. Go ahead, I'm sure they are impatient to see all of you," he said with a genuine smile.

Madeleine thanked him and led the way to the elevators. Before the doors opened, she turned back to the girls.

"No discussion is taboo with my aunt and uncle but so as to not be insensitive, my cousin Margot, whom we are celebrating, fell out of a window." It was fair to give them the only warning Uncle Pierre and Aunt Evelyn merited really. Besides a dead child, they were very refined, subtle people who would surely do their very best to put Madeleine's friends at ease.

As the elevator doors opened, Aunt Evelyn appeared in all of her beauty. Her flamboyant red hair was perfectly coiffed in a long bob, grazing her shoulders. She wore a beautiful navy-blue dress, exaggerating her waistline. She waved the girls in with enthusiasm and a perfectly manicured hand. Madeleine always noticed her own mother, though she cared for her physical appearance, didn't have the natural elegance Aunt Evelyn had. She had learnt from her aunt how to properly eat, talk, walk, and move. Neither of her parents had bothered to teach her the ways of the world. After the accident, they would not even have registered if she face-planted into her plate, let alone put an elbow on the table. At one point, she was lucky to have simply been fed. With Aunt Evelyn's teachings, Madeleine, alongside Margot, learnt how to wine and dine with the finest of guests. She was their very own in-house Emily Post and thanks to her the girls could be taken to local hamburger joints or invited to any black-tie dinner in the city, seamlessly. Madeleine thirstily absorbed the lessons, consciously striving to become the most elegant version of herself. With an innate capacity to adapt and benefit from a situation, she now blended in anywhere. Being a chameleon was the result of a cultured education she believed.

Aunt Evelyn had schooled Margot and Madeleine in the art of living by disguising lessons as games, their favorite being table manners. The two girls sat around the wide wooden dining room table, repressing fits of laughter as they held imported gold-rimmed Limoges plates with their elbows tight against either side of their torsos, learning to eat and drink, while taking up the least amount of space possible. A slight release of the tight, perfect posture and the expensive plates might shatter on the marble floor. They learnt to never speak with their mouths full, never make a sound when drinking, always place their cutlery appropriately and never ever have an elbow make an appearance on the table while eating.

Uncle Pierre couldn't bear bad manners, saying it not only reflected poorly on the person but on their entire family. Madeleine refused to be a source of embarrassment for her uncle and studied her aunt's teachings meticulously so as to never make a faux pas. When the lessons were over, Margot would run into the spacious playroom calling out for Little Mister, her white miniature poodle. She, in turn, would train and teach him tricks, much like Aunt Evelyn had trained them. Margot had loved that dog more than anything and he'd returned her affection. Though he didn't refuse Madeleine's caresses, he only ever obeyed his master. A permanent fixture in her bed, when Madeleine climbed in, he'd move to Margot's side, never between the two girls. Until he inexplicably disappeared. Madeleine desperately attempted to console her cousin but Margot couldn't stop crying for days. Finally, Madeleine moved into Margot's room and never left.

As the girls came into the penthouse apartment, their eyes widened and their jaws dropped. As they took in the grand entrance, Joanie's mouth was still agape. The floors were Italian marble with veins running across the large slabs of the shiny stone, crossing the Atlantic for months on ships to end up below their feet. The furniture was a mix of classic Louis XV style with beautiful lacquered light wood commodes and hand-carved crimson *fauteuils*, armchairs where Margot and Madeleine had dangled their little legs many afternoons. Phyllis had already engaged Aunt Evelyn in a conversation about charity work while Rose simply hung back. Madeleine knew the apartment would have its effect on the girls. It covered the entire floor of the building. Uncle Pierre kept the north part of it for his study and a meeting room if he didn't care to go into the office. In the living room, large bay windows gave onto Central Park and the entire city sprawled out before them, at the Rousseau's feet.

After everyone freshened up from the trip, Aunt Evelyn ushered the girls into the living room. Rose remained glued to the window, taking in all of New York City for the first time. Uncle Pierre finally joined after asking the kitchen staff to bring the chilled champagne. It arrived on a heavy silver tray with ornate handles, resembling twisted branches, in a silver bucket with six indigo Saint-Louis crystal glasses.

"Welcome to all of you lovely young ladies. Yesterday would have been our daughter Margot's twenty-first birthday. As you know she passed away a few years ago and not a day goes by without us thinking of her. We speak her name everyday and we are so grateful to our Madeleine for having brought you into our home to celebrate her. Margot surely would have been part of this great group of friends you have and I am sure she would have made an exceptional addition to it. Let us not be somber or sad, but rejoice in the gift we have of being together and honor her memory with laughter and amusement." And with that Uncle Pierre lifted his glass and put his arm around Madeleine.

They all raised their glasses to Margot. Madeleine eyed the girls. Joanie and Phyllis were visibly thankful, smiles having not left their faces. Rose still had a distant look in her eye. Madeleine walked over as she stared out onto the park.

"Is everything all right Rose," she mumbled discreetly, not wanting to draw attention.

"Yes, yes, Maddie. I . . . I'm blinded by all of this beauty. Down there, people are walking, going about their business, like millions of ants, while we stand here looking down," she replied, pensive.

Before Madeleine could inquire about the rather banal commentary, Aunt Evelyn invited everyone to step into the adjoining dining room straight away. She never appreciated the typically French *aperitif* moment. Uncle Pierre always teased her about it, saying she wanted to rush to the table.

"Come, come now. Let's have a seat and start. I am sure the girls are famished after their travels," Aunt Evelyn said as she pressed them along to the adjoining room. Uncle Pierre shook his head and smirked, winking at Madeleine.

"Their lengthy train ride is surely the reason we rush to the table," he kindly joked.

"Oh, darling, it's simply useless to fill up on bite-size amuse-bouches instead of sitting down to a proper meal. We aren't with the Rothschilds here, we can abbreviate that silly custom of your people tonight," she insisted.

"As you wish, my dear," he replied calmly to the perfect hostess.

Aunt Evelyn placed her guests with the purpose of ensuring interesting conversations, before indicating to the kitchen to begin serving. The menu had been constructed with Margot's favorites in mind, the rosemary lamb roast and the *gratin dauphinois* recipe from Uncle Pierre's childhood as the main course.

"I've never in my life tasted a dish like this. What in the world is in it? Mrs. Rousseau, it's delicious," Joanie exclaimed as she stuffed another bite of the thinly sliced potato baked in cream sauce and melted butter into her mouth.

"You're too kind Joanie, thank you," she answered, although it had been over twenty years since she'd set a foot in the kitchen other than to give instructions.

Rose had been seated next to Uncle Pierre and they were discussing music. Madeleine wanted to join in, opening her mouth to speak but never finding the right moment. Flustered, she touched her uncle's arm.

"I don't know if Rose has told you, Uncle Pierre, but she has a wonderful singing voice. It's absolutely splendid," she bragged about her friend, hoping to impress him.

"Really, *chérie*? You will have to sing for us," he encouraged Rose. "Madeleine and I love to listen to jazz, so I have arranged to take you all out tomorrow evening."

"That sounds wonderful, but Maddie is being too kind. I love singing but I'm not sure it is anything special," she said, modestly diminishing her talent the way well-raised girls are taught.

"I am a Frenchman, I will tell you the truth," he teased, laughing wholeheartedly. Madeleine was content, it had been a long time since she'd seen her uncle in such good spirits.

At the end of the sumptuous meal, a rolling table covered in a white linen tablecloth with embroidered initials emerged from the kitchen. Presented as if it were the *pièce de résistance* was the glistening three-layered chocolate fudge cake, traditionally served since Margot's fifth birthday. This year it had come out with twenty-one candles blazing. Phyllis and Joanie gasped at this culinary ode to the deceased. They knew no other mourning parents and strangely, once the initial shock had worn off, it was a beautiful way to keep the memory of their daughter alive. Every year since their eleventh birthday, on each of their respective birthdays, the cousins helped blow each other's candles out. So the ambulant fireball was placed in front of Madeleine. As she inhaled, prepared to blow out the candles, Rose stood. She began a rendition of "Happy Birthday" like no other. Her deep rich voice engulfed the room in a velvety curtain of music, caressing the notes, mesmerizing everyone at the table, including Uncle Pierre. How could she take such initiative during a delicate familial moment, Madeleine wanted to scream out. But she kept silent. As soon as she finished, Aunt Evelyn rushed over to give Rose a kiss, as did Uncle Pierre. Madeleine watched as her aunt and uncle encircled her roommate, a tightness wringing her insides. Stoically, she blew the candles out in one breath.

After such an emotional evening, everyone was ready to retreat for the night. Madeleine showed Phyllis and Joanie their room known as the pink one. It had soft rose-colored velour stretched on its walls. The bed had been placed in the center of the room, giving its guests the sensation of being a precious ring inside a luxurious gift box. Joanie fell onto the queen-size bed laughing, not believing her luck. Phyllis, disappointed to not be in the same bedroom as Madeleine, closed the door quickly. Madeleine was anxious to get back to Rose and pry about what strange mood had fallen over her since their arrival in New York and why on earth she'd sung "Happy Birthday" of her own accord.

But before the interrogation, she poked her head into what had once been Margot's room. After the terrible accident, it had been sealed off for months. Eventually, Aunt Evelyn had refurbished it into an office for herself, completely remodeling the space but saving a few pieces like the Tiffany's blown glass lamps with the fireflies. Margot loved fireflies and when she had seen those on display she had asked her mother to buy them for her bedroom. Aunt Evelyn had based the new decor on the red and yellow lamps, placing them on either side of the large 18th century carved wooden desk she had flown in from her favorite antique shop on rue Jacob. After her death, Madeleine inherited several of Margot's things like her record collection, a few items of clothing, and her stationery. Last spring, Aunt Evelyn had even given her *carte blanche* to redecorate the guest room entirely. They wanted Madeleine to feel at home here and come and go as she pleased. She had chosen each detail of the decor as a reminder of her cousin, down to the classic steel-blue-and-white *toile de Jouy* print, depicting nature scenes with fireflies drawn just above the river's bed. She had seen them and knew her aunt would too.

When Madeleine entered, Rose was sitting on the brightly colored silk bed throw, still fixated on the city's glimmering skyline. Madeleine knelt in front of her, taking both of her hands.

"Dear Rose, is everything all right? I hope you aren't disappointed in our trip and it is not what you expected," Madeleine lamented softly.

"Oh no, not at all! This is all so wonderful. I'm feeling overwhelmed at how beautiful your family is despite all of the sadness you share," Rose answered. Madeleine did not respond, careful to let her speak.

"It has nothing to do with you or this wonderful trip or your aunt and uncle," Rose's eyes dropped down to her lap. Madeleine was expected to pry.

"What do you mean Rose? You've been nothing but perfect. My aunt and uncle love you," Madeleine said, swallowing her irritation at this charade.

Rose was rapidly forthcoming with the real reason behind her mood swings since the arrival in New York City. During her sophomore year at Agnes Scott College, Rose had taken a class with Dr. Hartford Portman. He was a history professor and an attractive man whom she had also encountered at the Piedmont Driving Club and at various other social events around Atlanta over the years. Dr. Portman had a fiancé and was to be married the following summer at his family's mansion on West Paces Ferry. While taking his Renaissance class, she had fallen in love with him. Though she knew of the fiancé's existence, she considered it fair play and imagined herself, wife of the renowned Dr. Portman, whose family had the proper reputation to satisfy her demanding mother. This fantasy struck her as much more interesting than the promise of being married off to someone whom she'd "learn to love" as she had been groomed to be. Rose had hoped to lure Dr. Portman into leaving his fiancé and marrying her instead. A well-respected professor in his mid-thirties, he was an ideal candidate to save Rose from an uncertain future. And it is never very hard to seduce a man.

An affair had quickly begun. It was not the first time a student was a post-office hours appointment and repeatedly lingering after class to speak with him. When she had stepped into the classroom, she hadn't drawn particular attention to herself but when she spoke, she engulfed her listener entirely. As Aunt Vera liked to say, Rose could charm the dew off of a honeysuckle. Unsuspectingly, Dr. Portman had agreed to meet her, knowing their families ran in the upper echelons of Atlanta's social circle. And sure enough, the magic had operated as soon as they had found themselves alone and in conversation. With her extremely sensual hoarse voice and the light-heartedness of her being, it hadn't taken long for the meetings to become regular until they'd finally taken a more serious turn. Their story had lasted almost until the end of the semester before winter break. Rose had intended on seeing the professor at the Portman's annual Christmas party, one of the highlights of the season. But she had begun to feel ill early December. She was vomiting and exhausted. She had stayed in bed for a week and was concerned about missing final exams. The doctor had finally given his diagnosis. Rose was pregnant. Strangely enough, she had been excited at this idea as it would only precipitate the marriage with Dr. Portman.

But it hadn't been so when she announced it to the soon-to-be father. Dr. Portman reiterated he was going to marry his fiancé. The rest of that month had been a blur for Rose. She had revealed the secret to her mother who hyperventilated at the abominable thought of the tainted reputation before finding a solution.

Rose had stayed in school until late January and then sent to stay with Aunt Vera in Savannah. A fake case of tuberculosis would keep her away from school and a special exemption was granted for the final exams to be taken later. Once the baby was born and Rose back to an acceptable figure, she would return to Atlanta. But Mother was so disappointed in her daughter's behavior that she had decided on Vassar as a way to protect her from the man she thought she still loved.

Yet, Rose had recently received news in a letter from a childhood friend that Dr. Portman and his new wife had moved to New York to teach at NYU. So, she was now in the same city.

"I used to sing to him all of his favorite jazz tunes. He'd tell me we'd come live here, in New York, and he would teach while I became a famed singer like Ella Fitzgerald."

How anyone might want to leave this girl was beyond what Madeleine could fathom.

"But such is life right? Can you imagine if I had a baby to take care of now? Perhaps Hartford would have lost all of his hair and become a grouchy old man! Oh Madeleine, I'd been wanting to tell you but didn't want you to think . . . well, you know."

Rose cocked her head to one side and pulled her friend close, the scent of fragrant wild flowers drowning Madeleine during the embrace. She wanted to stay nestled in this comfort forever. How dare any man pain this beautiful angel? She took Rose's cheeks into her hands and looked straight into her eyes.

"How about this weekend we enjoy ourselves and forget about all of the rest? We'll go to the park, to see a picture. Uncle Pierre promised to take us to the very best jazz club! He knows a lot of people my uncle . . ." Madeleine pouted her lips and winked at her friend.

Rose laughed.

"Yes, Maddie, yes, that would be fantastic! Let's make it the most memorable weekend ever!"

As they slipped into the cool crisp white sheets of the freshly made bed, Madeleine kissed her on the forehead, assuring tomorrow's excitement required proper rest. Before long Rose was sleeping soundly. Turning off the lights, Madeleine wondered about Rose's behavior with Professor Beardsmith. Could she be attempting to recreate what hadn't worked the year prior? She was not so daft. Yet things could not go awry for the volatile desires of this incredible young woman. Once she was finished, Rose could have him. Staring into the darkness, listening to Rose's slow, rhythmic breathing, her mind raced.

Chapter 13

By the time the three guests arose and crossed to the other side of the residence for breakfast, Madeleine had already eaten with Uncle Pierre. He promised to make a couple of phone calls to finalize the evening excursion to one of the jazz clubs he frequented. Aunt Evelyn's table was laid out with freshly made croissants and brioche by the in-house pastry chef they had hired and brought over from France, an array of cold cuts of meats and cheeses, bagels and lox, sausages, bacon, pancakes, and fluffy omelettes made to order. A luxury hotel couldn't possibly have a better breakfast buffet thought Joanie. And she was right. The girls discreetly overate. A hearty meal was recommended for they would be busy until lunch. Madeleine had scheduled a visit to the Museum of Modern Art, a walk by the United Nations for Phyllis, a ride through Central Park, all before lunch. As everyone left the room, Joanie grabbed one last croissant and slipped it in her purse.

Alberto was waiting downstairs for his employer as the girls walked by, on their way to the park.

"You ladies are a sight for sore eyes," he called out to them, making Joanie laugh until she blushed. As the four walked arm in arm, their colored dresses contrasting against the grey sidewalk, they were prepared to take on the day. The sun shone brightly on this September morning and the city seemed to welcome them with open arms.

It wasn't until lunch at *Rue de Paris* that a proper break was taken. The four were seated in a corner table, leading onto the populated terrace.

"Madeleine, where are we headed after this? I might need a rest," Joanie asked, usually never one to complain, but her feet were hurting. She wasn't used to this much walking.

"You'll feel better after we eat. Why don't you have *steak-frites*,[4] it's wonderful here," Madeleine suggested with a perfect accent. "My uncle comes here every Wednesday to have it."

She had also chosen the restaurant for its proximity to the New York University campus. During the night, Madeleine decided Rose needed to be reminded of the pain she'd felt with Dr. Portman so as to disgust her from engaging with Professor Beardsmith. It was a harsh method, but in the night, it had sounded like an effective solution. Dr. Portman would probably not be working on the weekend, although there was a chance him and his new wife lived in the neighborhood. But Madeleine intended on passing by one of the university's building after lunch, to juggle Rose's emotions and hopefully provoke the desired effect.

"Maybe I'll have the onion soup," Joanie said, relieved to have snuck the extra croissant in her purse. She hadn't thought they would go out to a restaurant and reading over the menu, she realized she barely had enough money in her purse to pay for an appetizer although she was famished. Madeleine waved the waiter over to order as a group of chatty students walked in, laughing loudly and were placed a few tables away. As they continued to draw attention to themselves, Rose saw the "NYU" logo on a folder.

"Are you ready to order," the middle-aged waiter asked in a monotone voice, wishing he was anywhere else than taking orders from the young and wealthy.

Rose abruptly stood. "I'm not very hungry actually, I'll meet you back at the apartment," she whispered, leaving the table before Madeleine could respond.

"Wait, we can . . . ," she called out to her, but Rose was already out of the door and in the street where she energetically walked off. Her plan had worked.

The waiter sighed loudly, as Madeleine turned sternly back to him.

_____

4 Steak and fries

She ordered enough food for six, making Joanie's anguish peak. As soon as he walked away from the table Phyllis piped up.

"What in the world just happened? Maybe she felt sick from the lox this morning," curious whether she might too, having had more than her fill.

Madeleine reached out to Phyllis and Joanie.

"She probably needed some air. Either way, I'm sure she'll be fine," she said reassuringly.

"I don't know how anything could get in the way of us having a grand time," Phyllis innocently stated, sounding more naive than usual. Wearing a high ponytail with her thick bangs perfectly resting on her forehead, she appeared even younger than she already was. Phyllis had skipped a grade and was therefore Madeleine's junior by a few years; an inexperienced yet old soul.

Joanie's main concern throughout the meal was, now that Rose had left, would they split the bill in three instead of four? Trying to dissimulate her concern, a dwindling appetite only allowed her to nibble through lunch. When the disagreeable waiter came over with the check, her stomach ached.

"So that was a lot of food. How do you want to . . . ," she started. But before she finished her phrase, Madeleine picked up the check.

"It's on me. I'm only sorry we couldn't have enjoyed it all together," she lamented. Immediately, the regret of not having had more food overcame Joanie. She'd shamefully hidden in the restroom to eat the stolen croissant from the morning.

Having recuperated Rose at the apartment, they continued the discovery of the city. Unlike Joanie who was happy to still be alive and well in a place which promised a threat at every corner, Phyllis was intent on adding an additional stop to the well-planned schedule. Besides admiring the United Nation's offices, there was a very special place Madeleine's uncle had suggested, the Argosy Bookstore. On his advice, Phyllis was to ask for a certain Patrick. He was the most knowledgeable fellow and also the only one FDR had ever trusted to provide a selection of publications worthy of the former President's attention. The visible enthusiasm provided by the idea she might obtain insight on the President's personal taste in literature was so incredibly out of character that the three others happily obliged. As she entered the store, Phyllis's heart was pounding with excitement, like a child in a candy store. After only browsing for a few minutes on the other hand, Rose and Joanie were ready to leave. Phyllis could have spent the entire day perusing the works but was considerate of her friends and quickly decided to purchase every book recommended by the said Patrick. Madeleine had the books directly delivered to the house so the girls could continue onto some more traditional fun the city might provide.

Rose was wide-eyed as they passed the theaters, the restaurants, the bustling life of the Big Apple. Joanie was impressed with its grandeur. Half of the time, their delicate necks were cricked to admire the steel skyscrapers, the movie posters, and the advertisements splayed across the gigantic billboards in Times Square, all of them dazzled by the enormity of the Planter's Peanut man and the thirty-foot Pepsi Cola bottle. To them, New York was a city one spent looking up at. What was happening on the street level and below was much less obvious. It wasn't until later that night that they would change their minds.

In order to take a break from all of the walking, Madeleine suggested the five o'clock picture of *Some Like It Hot,* starring Tony Curtis, Marilyn Monroe, and Jack Lemmon. They cooed over Tony Curtis's charm and Rose doubled with enthusiasm about seeing Marilyn on the big screen. Madeleine bought the four tickets despite the discussion about everyone wanting to pay for themselves, even if Joanie did not put up much of a fight. When they entered the theater, Madeleine strategically placed herself in between Phyllis and Rose. The lights went down as they settled comfortably in their red velour seats. Phyllis was thrilled about catching the newsreel before the feature picture. As soon as it began, the theater went quiet and the three stars graced the screen. But it wasn't until Marilyn Monroe's performance of "I Wanna Be Loved By You" came on that Madeleine glanced over at Rose. Her eyes couldn't have been wider. It was as if she was trying to swallow Marilyn whole with them. Was she envisioning herself on a stage and being adored by everyone? Is that what she longed for, Madeleine wondered. She grabbed Rose's hand in the darkness and squeezed it. It felt small and frail. Rose squeezed back. Phyllis noticed the hand holding and became much more interested as to what was happening off screen than on.

At the end of the film, they gushed about the most remarkable scenes. Rose was still dreamy-eyed about the love story between Monroe and Curtis, questioning where her Tony Curtis was. Madeleine, though she didn't share with the others, found Jack Lemmon's character the one to be envied. He had ended up with a rich man who hadn't a care in the world despite the fact he had lied about who he was, which was a rare find. Unfortunately, people found the truth so important. And with that, Billy Wilder's last line of the movie, "Nobody's perfect!", became the quote of the weekend.

It was early evening by the time the foursome headed back to Fifth Avenue. Alberto had picked them up from the theater luckily, much to Joanie's delight. Her feet had swollen from all of the walking in new black Mary Janes. She had wanted to save them for the spring but the trip to New York absolutely qualified as an exception. No open blister could ruin this weekend. Madeleine had seen but remained discreet, not wanting to embarrass her. She would be sure to lay out some bandages in the bathroom for Joanie when they got home. As Alberto took the scenic route back for the pleasure of his passengers, Madeleine played with her pearl necklace, wondering if she had successfully disabused Rose from the idea of seducing Professor Beardsmith. A pearl had loosened between the two small knots of the silk thread of the necklace she wore and she continuously rolled it between her thumb and index finger, pondering a life elsewhere. Less than a year from now, looking out onto the Seine, she'd enjoy a *café crème* with five cubes of sugar, turning it into a sweet syrupy beverage to mask the bitter coffee taste she disliked. She had set her sights on the Latin quarter, near Odéon. It was close to the Sorbonne where she might attend the summer lectures. There, at the terraces with intellectuals, she'd be overhearing discussions of free will and the fallibility of objectivity and other such philosophical notions. She dreamt of partaking in the long and lively diners held in the Parisian apartments where Sancerre, cognacs, and Gauloise cigarettes fed engaged conversations into the late hours of the night. Madeleine was prepared to endure nearly anything to obtain the reward for which she had destined herself. Phyllis watched her silently, from the backseat, wondering where she traveled to in her mind when she got so pensive.

Reading in the library, Aunt Evelyn looked up from her book when Madeleine entered the room.

"How it is going dear? Did you manage to reassure your friends about the scary city," she mocked kindly, as Madeleine had confided Joanie's fears.

"Wonderful. We've had great fun. Rose was tired at lunch so she came home to rest but we picked her up before the cinema."

"I hope she didn't go hungry," she worried. "I was with the ladies playing bridge until three and then Olive and I went for tea." Aunt Evelyn was an avid bridge player, participating every year in the White-head Women's Pairs bridge championship with her partner Olive Frutiger. Having been widowed at a young age, she had turned into the kind of woman who would now be encumbered by a husband. Olive was known as a force of nature, matching her stocky build, but mainly due to her determination which knew no bounds. The two had been runners-up three consecutive years and Olive had her eyes set on the 1960 trophy of the spring tournament. Come hell or high water, she had promised Evelyn.

"I'm sure she asked the kitchen. Has Olive been a tyrant about your practice," Madeleine jokingly asked.

Aunt Evelyn laughed. "Absolutely. If we don't win this year Madeleine, I'm afraid of what she'll do to me!"

"And you're sure you don't want to come tonight?"

Aunt Evelyn was never quite keen of the jazz scene, or of jazz at all to be honest. The chaos and asymmetry of the music made her feel on edge, ill at ease.

"I am in quite good company for the evening with Mr. Stendhal, thank you," she said, pointing to the cover of *The Red and the Black*.

"Darling, I can't tell you how much the thought of you taking your uncle out pleases me. He'll love having company at the club for once and will certainly gloat about being with such lovely young women."

Madeleine gave her aunt a quick kiss on the cheek, eager for the night to begin. As she speedily returned to her room, each corner of this apartment held memories of her teenage years. The ox blood curtains, for example, separating the communal areas from the sleeping quarters, had a tiny hole on the bottom left-hand corner. Margot and Madeleine had hidden there to smoke a cigarette they had stolen from Uncle Pierre's study one night. They had snuck in and even used his precious carved jade table lighter, given to him by a Chinese intellectual, whom fleeing his country after Chiang's defeat, found not only refuge but also a dear friend in the United States. Her uncle always encountered fantastic people with the most incredible tales. As she passed the curtains, her hand grazing the soft fabric, she wondered about Pierre Rousseau's life before he had married into her family.

He had come to the United States, sole inheritor of his family's enormous fortune. He rarely spoke of his life during the 1930's when the nation was recovering from the crash, but Madeleine daydreamed of what it must have been like to be a wealthy young man in New York City at the time, the world at his feet. She longed for the same: the possibility of a new life, in a new country, where one could reinvent themself. Although, it hadn't been entirely true for Pierre Rousseau, whose family's reputation preceded him. They were of noble descent on his mother's side and his father's family, though not aristocratic, were what was referred to as *bourgeois* and one of the wealthiest families in France. Much like the way Getty had exponentially expanded his wealth, Uncle Pierre had grossly profited from buying up cheap oil stock. Then the money seemed to multiply itself uncontrollably, ensuring financial security to several generations after him. But after Margot's death, Pierre had no direct descendants. He had wished to have many children and now he had none, only his favorite niece Madeleine who had been like a sister to his own daughter. The already fine line was often blurred with what he gave Madeleine. He was overly generous, almost selfishly so, desperate to ease the constant gut-wrenching pain of losing his daughter. At times, he felt very Cartesian about her disappearance. So was the definition of life, death. It happened to everyone and time on this earth was temporary, he thought. But at other moments, the despair crept into his heart and seized it unexpectedly. An innocent smile from a toddler in a stroller and the wind would be knocked out of him, his mind flooding with images of Margot at that age, of her at fifteen, too old to be scared but still slipping her small hand in his for the reassurance he always guaranteed. He would have shielded Margot from any pain, from any hurt, with his own life if necessary. But no amount of money or will could protect against death. When *la mort* [5] came knocking, no excuses were valid, taking with her the souls of the young and the old, of the healthy and the sick, indiscriminately. As the scar in his heart still ripped open at times, unannounced, Pierre always felt better when Madeleine was around. He doted on her the same way he had on Margot, needing a living receptor of his bountiful fatherly love. His niece, always an oddly mature child, had quickly adapted to her own unfortunate situation and behaved irreproachably with her uncle and aunt, earning their respect in addition to their love. Evelyn and Madeleine's mother had been pregnant at the same time and though they hadn't been particularly close at first, the pregnancies had proved a bonding experience. Pierre often wondered if it had played a role in the particular relationship the two cousins had entertained; almost as if they were twins.

Looking dashing in a suit and tie, hat in hand, Uncle Pierre called out to his escorts of the evening,

---

5   death

"Ladies, *allons-y.*[6] We are not meeting the Queen of England. We must leave now." He despised being late and checked his watch once more as the girls hurriedly grabbed their coats from the maid's arms.

In the car, Madeleine sat up front between Alberto and her uncle. She didn't mind being a bit squeezed, quite the contrary, it made her feel powerful as they sped down 52nd street to the club. Uncle Pierre, his arm around his niece, was entertaining the back with lively conversation.

"So, anyone who knows anything about jazz in New York goes to Birdland, isn't that right Alberto," he began prepping the girls.

"Yes, sir. It's the best," the chauffeur answered, happy to give his two cents to the conversation. "The line wraps around the block every weekend."

Uncle Pierre had called the owner to make sure to get a good table for his guests. Phyllis and Joanie had nearly no appreciation of jazz but what they lacked in knowledge they made up for in enthusiasm.

"I hope you ladies aren't too dazzled by celebrities because there are often some," Uncle Pierre bragged.

"Like who," Rose questioned excitedly.

"I've personally seen Ava Gardner, Marlene Dietrich, and let's see, do you know a man by the name of Marlon Brando?"

The backseat gasped in unison.

"Really Marlon Brando might be there tonight," Joanie whispered, wishing she'd had a more remarkable dress to wear.

"I haven't seen him in a long time but he was quite the regular, especially when he was only a Broadway actor. After he made *A Streetcar Named Desire,* not so much. But the real stars are on the stage. You might not recognize them but they are some of the most talented musicians in the world!" Uncle Pierre animated his explanation with his hands, hoping to convey his admiration and fervor to the musically virginal crowd. "You might witness Thelonius Monk, Charlie Parker,

---

6 Let's go

and . . . ," he paused, disappointed as the names seemed to not be ringing any bells from the back.

"Miles Davis," Rose ventured, remembering Madeleine had mentioned the trumpet player.

"Yes Rose," he answered, elated she at least knew one name. "Yes, Miles Davis plays here often! Although last month a policeman beat him in front of the club, despite his name being right there on the marquee. So I'm not sure if he'll want to come back."

Alberto mumbled an Italian insult under his breath about cops, but not loud enough for his employer to hear. He had had a few run-ins with the police in his youth and despised their very existence, leaving no room for exceptions.

Joanie paled at the idea of the danger lurking in this part of town. This was exactly the type of thing she read about in the papers. When she scanned through her favorite section, the obituaries, she sought out the ones who had died too soon, by accidents, diseases or murders to feed her paranoia. But if she could bear to live through this moment, she'd surely impress any future date by having been to Birdland for an evening. That perspective filled her with courage.

As the car pulled up, the neon sign above the club read "Birdland, Jazz Corner of the World."

Uncle Pierre sighed with satisfaction, never taking for granted every time he came to witness magic being made until the wee hours of the early morning in the carpeted bullpen. Leading the way, he familiarly greeted the large man at the door and ushered the group to the room on the left. The cabaret room on the right was reserved for clients without the proper introductions.

Margot had loved jazz like her father and therefore Madeleine had decided to love it too. All of the jazz records Madeleine had in her dorm room in actuality had once belonged to Margot. At the funeral, Uncle Pierre had had Margot's favorite jazz piece played live. Everyone sat listening to "Monk's Mood," shifting uncomfortably in their seats after only a few minutes of the eight-minute piece. But Madeleine had closed her eyes, imagining Coltrane's saxophone coming to grace Monk's piano. The day of the funeral had been a bitterly cold but sunny winter day. The sky was blue and the air so sharp and crisp, it practically seized the lungs if a breath was drawn too quickly. As a child, Madeleine did not believe bad things could happen on sunny days. She thought accidents were relinquished to grey, rainy days, when overcast skies were an indication of looming disaster and the power of sun rays burnt the evil of the world like mother nature's cleansing solution. But if that were true, perhaps she would have melted a long time ago.

The five sat around a table close to the stage. The lights were already dim and the musicians on stage, joyously chatting. The instruments gleamed, catching the reflections of faces as they were being tuned. Rose was entirely overwhelmed with the experience. It seemed her eyes didn't have time to take in what was in front of her before they were darting off in another direction to inspect the bar, searching for the celebrities, heightening the night's already promising evening.

Madeleine ordered a gin and tonic and after glancing at one another, Joanie, Phyllis, and Rose followed suit.

"I'll have a martini, make it extra dry with two olives," said Uncle Pierre, emphasizing the number with his long fingers. Immediately Rose spoke up.

"Please change my order. I'll also have a martini."

"With one or two olives, miss," the waitress asked, hurriedly. The place was packed and she had other tables to wait on but the gentleman was a regular and always a generous tipper. An alarm had sounded in Madeleine's brain with the last-minute change of orders. Rose had been very keen to impress Uncle Pierre. Now that she thought about it, Rose had also been seated next to her uncle at the dinner table. It could have been purely by chance, but Madeleine rarely believed in chance. Especially when women were involved. She laughed at all of his jokes, which were not always deserving of such appreciation. Surely it was polite but was Rose trying to seduce him? She'd been desperate enough to entice and trap her Agnes Scott professor with a child. What was she trying to attain by acting this way with Uncle Pierre? No, no, no, Madeleine pushed the idea out of her mind, she was reading too much into details. Rose may like to have fun but her upbringing would surely have her embrace the role of the nice wife, like in her mother's favorite show "Father knows Best." With an apron around her waist and a homemade cherry pie for dessert, she'd lovingly await her husband, drink in one hand and slippers in the other.

"Do you ever watch *Father Knows Best*," asked Madeleine over the brouhaha of the growing crowd.

"Oh, I love it! It's a grand show," answered Rose with a wide grin. "Mr. Rousseau, do you think there'll be any movie stars tonight?"

"Call me Pierre, Rose. I wouldn't be surprised. They like to make an entrance before the musicians. I'll let you know if I spot anyone." He greeted different people with a wave or a nod of the head from across the room.

"You really *do* know everyone here," Rose uttered, dazzled.

Madeleine couldn't get the thought out of her head now. But Uncle Pierre won't be sensitive to Rose's charm. He wouldn't be a fool and fall for flattery, the easiest trick in the book. The lesson of La Fontaine's popular fable of the crow and the fox came to mind:

> *Learn that each flatterer*
> *Lives at the cost of those who heed.*

He had obliged Margot and Madeleine to memorize this one and several more, in French. As Phyllis distracted Madeleine with a question, out of the corner of her eye she swore she saw Rose putting her hand on Uncle Pierre's forearm, leaning in to speak to him. Yes, the noise level was rising as the tension in the room was building but their seats were close enough together that he should be able to hear just fine. Maybe Rose was trying to exclude her? That would be a gross miscalculation on her part. Madeleine was the reason Rose was here in New York in the first place, and now she was flirting with her uncle? Why hadn't Madeleine sensed Rose might be problematic in this way? She had played the naive girl so well, Madeleine had fallen for it.

As the lights were lowered, Madeleine glanced around the packed room one last time before the darkness swallowed everyone. A woman in a long beige overcoat and a scarf wrapped around her head caught her attention as she slid into a reserved booth. She could have been anyone but a gold lock of hair framed her very recognizable face, Madeleine gasped. The spectacular Marilyn Monroe had entered the club only but a few seconds before the lights were dimmed, barely drawing any attention to herself. Distracted for a moment from her own growing concerns, Madeleine stole another peek. It wasn't so much her acting or singing she admired, but her fortitude. Reduced to her shapely physique and soft voice as a stereotypical "blonde bombshell" and nothing more, when in fact, she had an extremely enviable career and financial independence. Marilyn Monroe played everyone at their own game to get what she wanted. Now that was true intelligence. Madeleine took a long sip of her gin and tonic, thinking about what to do next. The girls, and *especially* Rose would be over the moon to see Marilyn Monroe, crowning the weekend with such a vision. But Rose had frustrated Madeleine, so she turned to the stage and said nothing, wondering if the ingrate might even appreciate the glorious music filling the room. Madeleine checked Uncle Pierre's face. Was he honestly flattered by the attention of a cackling ingenue? A semblance of average, menial behavior on his part made her wince in disgust. She had the highest of expectations for her uncle whom she considered extraordinary. With his navy-blue suit, tailored perfectly to his broad shoulders with the cuff of his white shirt peering out from his sleeve, he was the most handsome man in the whole club. Usually, she was proud and admired him but tonight she was worried about the effect his demeanor was having on Rose. At that instant, Thelonius Monk sat down in front of the piano, his fingers dancing on the keys, and the rest of the world melted away.

The set was about to finish when Uncle Pierre indicated it was time to retire. He signaled to Madeleine, who quickly ushered her friends out at the end of the piece through a side exit. In fact, he was prepared to listen all night long as he'd tipped the bartender extra to make stronger drinks, but there was another stop to be made. The New York night air cooled the girls' cheeks, rosy from the alcohol, as they climbed the stairs back to the street level.

Rose had taken Uncle Pierre's arm while Madeleine was holding on to Joanie, who had enjoyed her gin and tonics a little more than everyone else. Her sensible heels were now small and challenging surfaces to balance on. Luckily Alberto pulled up with the car as soon as they stepped out. As Madeleine helped Joanie into the middle of the back seat, Rose slipped herself between Alberto and Uncle Pierre in the front.

As they rode into the city's dark streets, the chattering in the car was incessant. The girls' excitement for this nocturnal adventure was palpable. But none of them knew Uncle Pierre's next surprise, not even Madeleine. Alberto made a sharp right, avoiding the direction of the penthouse where they would eventually all go to lay their heads and instead headed down to the East Village. There by the corner of 2nd Avenue and 4th Street, he came to an abrupt stop in front of another dimly lit joint. Silence overcame the girls as "Club 82" lit up an arched doorway.

"What are we doing here," Madeleine whispered.

"I wanted to make a quick stop here before we head home," Uncle Pierre replied with a twinkle in his eye.

Before they understood exactly what was happening, the four girls were guided past heavy curtains, down a flight of stairs and into the most incredible club, packed with men dressed as women, women dressed as men, and a flurry of folk from all walks of life who came to watch extraordinary performances. Joanie grabbed Madeleine's hand, who was attempting to remain composed despite the desire to ogle and stare. He led them to a free table and spoke to a person whose physical appearance was beautifully ambiguous. Phyllis took in the scenery with an expressionless face. Rose on the other hand was in awe. Every cell in her body was at peak excitement. Uncle Pierre knew the risk taken by exposing these proper young ladies to this underground world. But he never saw a reason to dismiss art because of sexual preferences, race or what have you. He relished in the chaos of this club, the grit it brought, and the talent it exposed while pushing the norms of a conventional society he was bored with. It was doing the girls a favor but to show them real life he sincerely believed.

On stage, a quartet of gorgeous crossdressers was wrapping up its performance, greeted with applause and whistling.

"This is the so-called amateur night," Uncle Pierre explained. "I have yet to be disappointed by anyone I have had the pleasure to watch on this stage. Rose, Madeleine asked me for a favor. Your name is next on the list. Are you all right with that?"

All eyes turned to the southern belle. Madeleine had mentioned it in passing and was surprised Uncle Pierre had even remembered. He often forgot small details or what he considered frivolous demands. She had mainly asked so as to impress Rose but now bitterly regretted it. This would be all of too much for the poor Rose. But when Madeleine laid eyes on her friends, it was as if a light from the heavens had shone down upon her.

"I am absolutely honored and hope to make you proud," she responded.

Had Rose known all along? Had Uncle Pierre confided in her and not Madeleine? But before she could say anything, Rose stood, smoothing her dress out and headed toward the stage with determination and perfect posture. Somehow her unusual looks were an ideal fit for the place.

The moment she stepped onto the stage, it was impossible to look away. It was as if she belonged nowhere else but on that stage. The music began and as if touched by an unspoken grace, her low tone enveloped the room into a warm haze of musical magic as she began Edith Piaf's "La Vie en Rose." The accompanying piano elevated every note she held. If a moment of confidence could seduce, Rose had everyone in the audience at her feet.

A wave of admiration, heavy with envy, washed over Madeleine as she watched her friend caress every soul in the room with her voice. There on that altar, in the glow of the spotlight, Rose seemed even more irresistible than ever. Was there anything this girl could not do? How could such grace and talent come together in an unconventional and yet glorious physique. Uncle Pierre's eyes glistened, with a smile stretching across his face. Joanie had tears streaming down her cheeks and Phyllis sat perfectly still, drinking every note like a misted flower in the desert.

By the time they had returned to the penthouse on the Upper East Side, Madeleine was fuming. She ignored Alberto's wink and slammed the door of the car. When they reached the penthouse, Phyllis quickly led Joanie into their room as Madeleine impatiently waited in the entrance for Rose to finish her conversation with Uncle Pierre. She rested against on the rosewood desk Margot had gotten a black eye from while cutting the corner a little too quickly when they were nine years old. Madeleine had been afraid to get scolded because in fact she *had* been chasing Margot yet no blame was attributed to either of them. It was chalked up to being an accident luckily. But as this memory resurfaced, Madeleine made a startling realization. Watching Rose, she noted her blonde hair was the same shade as Margot's. Though she didn't have Margot's fine features by any means, that strange sensation she couldn't put her finger on, was terribly similar to her deceased cousin. Was that what Uncle Pierre was feeling? Did he find Rose a better substitute for Margot than his niece? Because of some physical resemblance or a presence? All sorts of thoughts sped through Madeleine's head, her pulse racing. The more she watched the two talking, the clearer Rose transformed into a threat. Her forehead began to tingle, the heat from the anger rising to her face, she had to put an end to it. Grabbing Rose's arm a little too forcefully, she got on her tippy toes to give Uncle Pierre a peck on the cheek as she had since she was a child.

"Good night, Uncle Pierre, I've really got to get to bed, I'm exhausted."

"*Bonne nuit, chérie,*[7] I had a splendid evening with you and your friends. A demain," he answered before turning back to Rose. "And you Mademoiselle, I hope you had fun despite having an old man for a chaperone!"

"I couldn't have wished for a better chaperone," she replied and with that, planted a kiss not on one but on both of his cheeks.

Madeleine's grip tightened on Rose's arm.

"Maddie dear, you're hurting me," Rose said to her friend. Madeleine's face had changed. Her brow was furrowed and her eyes had gone dark. Her face was flushed but she did not let go of Rose's arm and led her down the long marbled-floor corridor to their room.

Rose quietly slipped out of her sun-yellow dress and into a new nightgown and robe Madeleine had never seen. As she went into the bathroom to brush her teeth, Rose looked back at Madeleine. Their eyes met. If looks could kill, she'd be comfortably horizontal, six feet under. She tried smiling but Madeleine's face was fixed. Her eyes bore through Rose until she retreated into the bathroom. As Madeleine sat on the bed, pulling her nightgown back, revealing her legs. On her knees, lots of small scars were visible. And one more would be added as she bit down as hard as she could to release her rage. Her teeth broke the skin and blood came to the surface of the oval shaped dents, espousing the alignment of her jaws. Madeleine inhaled deeply. That was enough to feel better. Over the years, the nerve endings on both knees had been damaged enough, she no longer felt much pain. It had never been an intention for self-harm but rather a self-sufficient way to release the bouts of rage that reared their ugly heads on occasion.

---

7   Good night, darling

Madeleine did not particularly enjoy surprises and could not possibly be prepared for what she was about to discover. As she approached the reception area, she heard muffled voices. She pushed the door and immediately came face to face with her own parents. Her entire being, from head to toe, was submerged by a sensation of emptiness. Her mother turned to Madeleine,

"Hello, dear, how are you," she asked in a monotone voice that barely invited a response. They hadn't seen one another in months.

"Hello, Mother, hello, Father. How lovely to see you," she replied.

Why had her parents come for Sunday brunch? Why were they coming into her life when they hadn't been invited?

"Your parents were coming into the city so when you said you were coming for Margot's birthday, so I thought with one stone, two hits," Uncle Pierre grinned.

He often made literal translations of French expressions where the meaning would come across, but the saying was all wrong. How after so many years in the United States had he not gotten a proper grasp on expressions, obviously not bothering to learn proper terms as long as he was understood.

Madeleine stretched the muscles of her face into what could be perceived as a smile. Her father, in a light beige sports jacket, walked over to give her a pat on the back, the familiar light waft of whiskey trailing behind him.

"Why did you need to come to the city," Madeleine questioned.

"Well you know, I like to visit once in a while, do some window shopping, catch a picture, if we have time."

No, Madeleine didn't know. She didn't know anything about these people who stood before her. Not about them, their habits or likes and dislikes. She vaguely remembered them as parents before the accident. After that, they had become recognizable strangers.

Elizabeth Rivers was one of those people whose eye contact needed to be avoided at a dinner party in order not to get trapped in a long-winded monopolizing story. Except when it came to her daughter, then it was like pulling teeth. Joanie had introduced herself to Mrs. Rivers and had not been able to interject since.

Madeleine crossed the room toward Uncle Pierre and her father, drink in hand, while her mother continued with the narration of their travel from New Jersey to the city for Joanie and Aunt Evelyn.

In the last year, Andrew Rivers had decided to go by "Drew," perhaps a way of reinventing himself, Madeleine thought. She had hoped this meant her father was turning over a new leaf, but apart from the name, there wasn't much change. She found her father far more tolerable than her mother, as his behavior was not radically different with others than with his daughter. He was a consistently quiet, broken man with a routine so rigid it made Madeleine suffocate.

Watching her father and uncle side by side was quite the sight. They were diametrically opposed in every way, where one was somber, the other was loud. Her uncle was spontaneous and adventurous, her father went to the hardware store every Saturday before lunch, never earlier in the week, never later. He had the regularity of a Swiss watch. Madeleine wished she could melt into a puddle on the floor and not have to go through the motions of an entire meal of being gently ignored in front of her friends.

Rose came into the room looking radiant, wearing Margot's royal blue dress. With hair a little looser than her habitual coif, she appeared ethereal instead of disheveled. If Madeleine squinted, she could have easily been mistaken for her cousin. Did anyone else notice? Aunt Evelyn was in the corner, staring over Phyllis's shoulder, watching Rose cross to the other side. Indeed, Uncle Pierre headed right over to introduce Rose to Madeleine's parents. Instantly the admiration in Elizabeth Rivers's eyes was like a dagger into her daughter's heart. She couldn't remember the last time her mother had looked at her in that way. Luckily, she could depend on her father being imperturbable. He was numbed from any interest in people. Only fishing and painting miniature soldiers of the Civil War kept his attention. Madeleine liked to believe she had inherited meticulous planning from her father's capacity to concentrate on minute details. At least she could claim something from him since she'd since unofficially renounced his name. How Aunt Evelyn and her brother could be so different was a mystery. It was a true wonder the two of them had been raised in the same household.

Joanie was charmed by Madeleine's mother. Their migration to one another was predictable. For once, someone was impressed by her mother's "nuggets." Madeleine imagined Joanie going back to her dorm room and writing in detail in her brown leather notebook each and every one of the precious pieces of advice Elizabeth Rivers had slipped into the conversation to impress the young housewife to be.

Madeleine stood back and watched as everyone conversed with one another; all of this commotion. If only the ground opened up and swallowed her whole. Or if it swallowed everyone else and only left her standing, alone. Anyone else might treasure a situation like this one: family and friends, all gathered because of her. Well, in actuality, everyone had been gathered for Margot but Madeleine was the one who had made it happen. Surely Margot's birthday was the excuse but they were all there because she was the one still alive. And now this Rose was altering the equilibrium. Madeleine hated all of it, the entire situation. How much more would she have to endure? All of a sudden, Paris seemed so distant, so unattainable. It was only September and the summer classes at the Sorbonne began in June. The committee would vote in only a few weeks and when they announced her name, she would then be able to tell her aunt and uncle the *real* great surprise. No one was to know she would not return after the summer. Madeleine needed to get away from it all; from all this brouhaha which pained her ears.

Chapter 15

What felt like an interminable brunch for Madeleine was on the contrary a delight for Rose. Being gathered around a table, with multiple conversations happening all at once was a reminder of Sunday lunches at Grand-mama's house. All of the aunts, uncles, and cousins on her mother's side reunited every weekend, some would say religiously as no one wanted to miss the matriarch's famous roast. She willfully ignored the fact several of her descendants were not attending mass prior to the dominical gathering in the dining room. She prayed for them even more, while sitting in the front pew, listening to Pastor Stone give his sermon. Rose had loved Grand-mama dearly and therefore accompanied her to mass twice a month. Though Rose was not particularly religious or a believer, she did love to please. The pleasure it procured Grand-Mama to show off her granddaughter dressed to the nines was worth the effort. She would flaunt Rose to all of her friends, praising her grace and kindness, and, of course, her figure. Luckily, she had passed away before Rose's body had become a home to an unwanted baby. Rose suddenly felt very homesick watching Maddie's family: her parents, her aunt and uncle, her friends. It was a gift to be surrounded by such kind and caring people.

But catching Madeleine staring intently broke her out of the reverie. Her attitude had shifted since the night before. Rose had wanted to chalk it up to the remembrance of her deceased cousin, but there was something else. She had seen the way Maddie had gotten angry because of her entente with Uncle Pierre. But she hadn't even had time to explain that having spoken with her uncle had really opened up a world of possibilities about what to do after graduation and even more so, about her future entirely. Hearing him speak of France, Paris, the music scene, the life, everything sounded so grand and better than anything she could ever imagine. With his connections, he had made her believe it was all at her fingertips! Rare were the young women who could envision going abroad on their own. But now Uncle Pierre had opened her eyes, the world was her oyster! Next summer's exchange program Professor Beardsmith had mentioned at the Sorbonne had taken on a whole new meaning. He had not gone into the details as Rose had not seemed overly enthused. Only three girls from Vassar would be chosen and she might be one of them. Pierre had even said if she went to Paris, he promised to put her in touch with good people and that perhaps they'd even visit! When speaking with him she'd felt heard, taken seriously, as if what she said mattered. It had been a long time since that had happened with anyone, let alone with a man of his status. Sure, she had flirted with a few boys from Yale and even had a date with one of them, but Maddie's uncle was of another rank. Besides innocently flirting never killed anyone. It was done with no malicious intent, only just for a bit of fun. Pierre didn't seem insensitive to Rose's attention and charm. So, she had casually put her hand on his forearm while speaking with him at the club, pretending not to hear and leaned in, so he could easily see down the front of her dress her cleavage encased in the prettiest black brassiere. She hadn't *really* wanted to seduce Maddie's uncle, only wanting to see if she could. It was one of her bad habits. She had burnt herself with Hartford, pushing for love. But the sensation of power when men paid attention to her was so very enjoyable. She wasn't supposed to like it, but she did. Her mother always said to let a man play the role of a man, never forgetting to ask him to do things that will make him feel superior, dominating, and strong. The truth was when Rose played innocent and helpless, they did love coming to her rescue. It had become second nature and once again this weekend, it had had its effect on a middle-aged man in, what appeared to be, a happy marriage.

The discovery of the potential cat-and-mouse game between Rose and Uncle Pierre had ruined the lovely Sunday lunch. Madeleine was suffocating at the table, and her parents' presence only heightened her anxiety, making it unbearable. She was ready for the weekend to be over. In fact, at this very moment, she could no longer bear anyone's presence. Their very breathing, all of them, was excruciating.

"Pardon me, I'm not feeling very well," Madeleine mumbled discreetly before rising. It was best for her to excuse herself before she flung Aunt Evelyn's pink forest-scene Wedgwood plate at Rose's face or flipped the entire table over, trapping her mother and everyone else on the opposite side with it.

"Are you all right? Do you need me to come with you," Joanie asked politely, hoping to stay seated in front of her plate embarrassingly filled with food, as she reached for her hand.

All of the color had drained from Madeleine's face, the white rage inside was tensing every muscle in her body. Joanie's touch felt like an abrasion against raw skin. She drew her hand away quickly without answering and left the dining room avoiding any eye contact.

With each step, the anger rose and before it burst, Madeleine locked herself in the nearest powder room. The glossed ebony-panelled room resembled the interior of a luxurious sailboat, a safe cocoon. Hands on either side of the sink, she stared at her reflection. As a child, she genuinely believed there were two Madeleine's living inside who never agreed. A good one and a naughty one. That was why her eyes were different colors, one wanted green and the other one wanted amber, so they each took one. Had someone told her that story or had her vivid imagination invented a reason for the differentiating trait everyone saw? Staring back at her was the reflection of a young, beautiful girl of twenty, in a sumptuous apartment in New York's finest neighborhood.

Footsteps came rushing down the hall.

"Maddie? Maddie? Are you unwell," Rose said as she knocked.

Madeleine brought one leg up on the smooth yellow marble counter of the sink. Preparing to bite down on her knee, the traces from the night before were there, barely healing.

"Do you need a doctor? Shall I ask your uncle to call someone?"

Any excuse to bring him in, of course, Madeleine thought. Her breathing became more rapid and the need to alleviate the burst of anger about to implode became urgent. Grabbing a hand towel, she stuffed it into her mouth and as she flushed the toilet, bit down harder than she ever had on anything in her life, letting out a scream that would have shaken the city had it not been muffled.

Once the ringing ears and blazing fire in her stomach had subsided, Madeleine was in no state to examine the situation objectively. Something had to change in this equation. What piece on the chess board needed to be taken out to get closer to a checkmate? Rose, with her gentle southern drawl, continued speaking from the hallway.

Taking a deep breath, Madeleine leaned the left side of her face against the cool wood door, listening to Rose's increasingly panicked voice.

"Rose, speak to me. Just keep talking to me, I'll be fine."

"What do you mean? You just want me to talk? Oh Maddie, I do hope you are feeling better. What a wondrous time we've spent together. I could never have envisioned this in a thousand years. You took me in and introduced me to your friends, your family . . ."

Madeleine abruptly opened the door and Rose stumbled in. Madeleine caught her arm before she fell to the ground. Her emotions muted, as if buried under layers and layers of soft cotton, she was in control again.

"Thank you. You know, your voice has a wonderful calming effect on me," Madeleine said holding her close. And just like that, the two girls walked back into the dining room as if nothing had happened. Joanie looked around and took cue from the rest of Madeleine's family. They had not paid any mind to the situation. Perhaps this was not a rare occurrence.

Alberto had been as flirtatious as ever while driving the girls back to the station. Madeleine had paid him no mind but the others certainly were fond of the overly confidant, handsome Italian trying to teach them phrases in his native tongue as they swooned in delight. Madeleine was in her own thoughts, playing out scenarios in her head.

As the train pulled out of the station, Madeleine watched the city disappear into a blur. After a short while, Rose began singing softly. She did have the most wonderful voice, worthy of soloist of a southern Georgia Baptist church choir. It nonetheless irked Madeleine that she had, once again, boldly taken it upon herself to distract them and everyone else within earshot as she would have preferred to sit in silence. Joanie, on the other hand, was mesmerized, not losing a single note coming out of Rose's mouth. Phyllis, who'd purposely sat next to Madeleine, leaned on her friend's shoulder, shutting her eyes and escaping into a secret fantasy. Talent was a simple matter of indiscriminate luck, thought Madeleine. Therefore, she only had admiration and respect for those who dedicated hours to hard work, like Phyllis. Yet despite herself, she was enjoying Rose's melancholic song as the New York countryside flew by. The whizzing row of bushes closest to the train gave the sensation of dizzying speed as her eyes darted back and forth trying to gather images as rapidly as possible. But when she looked out to the farthest point on the horizon, it seemed like the train was barely inching forward. It was truly all about perspective.

By the time the taxi had dropped them off at school, dusk had settled. Joanie checked her watch.

"Anyone interested in grabbing a bite of dinner," she offered. Joanie hated skipping meals, finding reassurance in these fixtures of life.

"I've got some reading to do and am not particularly hungry," Phyllis replied, resuming her studious role.

"I'll come along Joanie, I'm famished," Rose said, grabbing her arm. "Maddie?"

Madeleine had wanted to slip into bed and let the weekend's adventures percolate through her brain. Yet she did not want to miss a beat if Rose was also trying to manipulate Joanie and form an allegiance. So, with a heavy sigh, she took her coat and ran to catch up with the girls, taking Joanie's arm as they headed to the dining hall.

"Rose you must try out for a solo in the choral group. Or maybe you could sing somewhere in town? Madeleine, do people do that," Joanie questioned the one who always had an answer.

"Oh absolutely! We'll find a way to get you out there, Rose. Start here at school and then we'll get your name in the papers," she agreed, silently congratulating herself for coming. Had she not, Rose could have easily brainwashed Joanie and stolen her away.

On her plate, Madeleine found a few leaves of salad and a half-sized portion of lasagna was plenty. The idea of more food made her stomach churn. The lasagna was messy enough it could be made to look like it had been eaten, without ingesting much. As Madeleine took her tray, she purposely waited to strategically place herself next to Joanie.

While Madeleine was rummaging the lukewarm layers of pasta around her plate, occasionally putting her fork in her mouth, Joanie was eating with her usual healthy appetite. She couldn't remember one occasion where Joanie had skipped a meal since they'd met. Even when she'd gotten the flu last year, she'd eaten all of the chicken noodle soup Madeleine had brought from the OK Cafe. Joanie should remember that instead of being charmed by Rose and her voice. The novelty of a new toy.

"Maddie, you really do have such a wonderful family. Your parents, your aunt and uncle are all so kind and entertaining. You know, your uncle even said he thought I could go and sing jazz in Paris! Can you imagine? It's impossible, I know, but I love just thinking about it. He told me in his delightful accent 'Rose, you must dream big!," Rose imitated Uncle's Pierre accent perfectly.

"He's absolutely right Rose, you should dream big. It never killed anyone," Madeleine replied with the kindest of smiles as her jaw tightened. Was she saying this on purpose? Did she also want to steal her uncle AND Paris away from her?

Rose had sensed Madeleine's quiet return from the city had to do with her. Especially her and Uncle Pierre. It wasn't her fault he had been so charming and genuinely interested. She'd be furious if she only knew their knees had accidentally touched under the small table at the jazz club and Rose had not moved away. And neither had he. And she'd caught his eyes drop down to her cleavage. She considered it a small victory. He was attracted to her! At least a little bit.

Rose always craved a sign to know she was special. For those with whom a story was almost impossible, Rose only needed a tiny signal; like knees touching. Dr. Portman had been a different story and she hadn't stopped herself from throwing all caution to the wind hoping to win over a man promised to another. But succeeding in her seduction had not resulted in the ultimate goal of marriage, like her mother had asked.

Besides, she hadn't been the only one to be flirting with lines of decency. When bidding the girls goodnight, with *la bise*, the familiar greeting in France of a kiss on each cheek, the corners of their mouths had met. Before she could draw in a breath of surprise, Uncle Pierre had moved on to her other cheek. This time she had parted her lips ever so slightly and again their lips brushed against each other for an instant. Though quick, Rose's heart had skipped a beat before Madeleine had yanked her away. Had she seen anything? As she was being pulled down the hall, Rose had tried to catch her breath. What just happened had to remain a secret but all Rose had wanted to do was dance around the room. Why had such a small and meaningless and perhaps accidental gesture meant so much? Rose felt chosen. That was as big as Rose could dream.

"They'd be lucky to have you in Paris, Rose," Joanie exclaimed, the adoration pouring out of every cell in her body. It was obnoxious and unbecoming, thought Madeleine. What was happening to her dear friend? Why was she in such awe?

"Rose, isn't your presentation for Beardsmith's class tomorrow?"

Madeleine attempted to steer the conversation away from Paris. And yet as if Joanie knew what buttons to press to enrage Madeleine, she threw her hands down on the table.

"ROSE! Beardsmith sits on the committee that selects students for summer school in Paris! At La Sorbonne! Maybe if you tell him you are interested and impress him with your presentation, he could put in a good word on your behalf!"

Madeleine's face flushed hot. Was everyone turning against her? Why would Joanie suggest this to Rose? Madeleine hadn't confided in Joanie that sleeping with the professor was her method of securing her spot but still. She closed her eyes and clasped her two hands tightly to keep herself from elbowing Joanie in the face, breaking the bridge of her nose so thick dark blood would run down her face. At least that would keep her from talking.

"Madeleine, are you all right?" Rose asked, noticing her closed eyes and red face.

"Yes, I must have eaten something that isn't sitting right. Girls you'll have to excuse me." Madeleine shot up and ran out, down the stone steps of the dining hall. Night had settled on campus and she wanted to be engulfed in it. She took a deep breath, drawing the cold air all the way down to the very dark corners of her lungs, cleaning them out. This was the image in her mind. Perhaps it might take away all of the anger that crept out of the depths of her being. So, Madeleine breathed in deeply, slowly before calmly walking back to the dorm.

By the time Rose got back to the room, Madeleine had turned in. She had wanted to isolate herself from the world and fall asleep before Rose came back. The last thing she needed was another discussion with anyone, let alone her roommate.

Later, Rose settled down on her bed, opening some letters she had picked up on the way back from dinner. One was from her mother. Four pages of an update of the Atlanta's social scene: the Dubois-Brooks wedding, the charity dinner for the playground for the local public school (the not-so-fortunate as her mother liked to call them), Ms. Love's nephew from California, and so on. Rose always enjoyed reading her mother's letters as they made for a great distraction and a good laugh. She always thought that when the person who wrote the social column in the *Atlanta Journal and Constitution* retired, her mother may be an ideal replacement. She had the upbringing and the wit to humorously comment without ever seeming rude. This was the gift of properly raised southern women really, and her mother was its best shining example. Rose was so absorbed by her mother's description and comments she forgot where she was and laughed aloud whole-heartedly. Immediately, Madeleine propped herself onto her elbow. A darkness in her eyes instantly stopped Rose from laughing. Her stare tore right through Rose who'd frozen completely. The exchange lasted but a few seconds but felt like forever. Only when Madeleine turned away, back to face the wall, did Rose release the breath she had unknowingly been holding. It's as if Madeleine had grabbed her chest with a giant hand and squeezed it tight and upon release, had her flop to the ground like a limp Raggedy Anne doll.

"Sorry," Rose whispered as she tucked the letter away. She grabbed her toiletries bag and headed to the bathroom. Hopefully by the time she returned, Madeleine would have fallen into Morpheus's arms.

Before seven, Joanie rushed into the room, newspaper in hand, to find Madeleine still in bed. She silently hushed Joanie who had opened the door without knocking and waved her over, throwing back her sheet so Joanie could slip in. Madeleine handed her the obitu-ary section and the two went about reading in silence, forgetting the existence of the other being in the bed across the room. Joanie loved this ritual. It soothed the craving she'd had as a little girl who dreamt of crawling into the safety of her parents' bed. Alas, her parents were very strict and even when Joanie had an accident in bed, she'd have to wait, cold and wet, until morning to get her mother. Only when the sun came up was she allowed to knock on their door.

Rose's presentation was today, so Madeleine would swing by Beardsmith's office right after. She wanted to mention her participa-tion if he was impressed with the work. She didn't want the professor to discredit Rose, but rather simply to be aware Madeleine had had her part to play in the success of the presentation.

Rose stirred at the noise of the crumpling pages of the newspaper.

"Morning girls! How are you feeling, Maddie," Rose asked kindly. Why did she have to be so chirpy and considerate before even setting foot on the ground, Madeleine wondered.

"Much, much better, thank you. I'm sorry I had fallen asleep before you got back," Madeleine replied.

"Oh don't worry. I'm sorry I woke you with my laughing. I got so distracted by Mother's letter," Rose said with a sheepish smile, widening her big eyes as an additional demand for forgiveness Madeleine supposed.

"Don't worry, you didn't wake me. I fell asleep as soon as my head hit the pillow. I didn't even hear you come in," Madeleine said.

Confused, Rose continued. "But you looked straight at me. You stared at me, and well, I cannot say it was the kindest look I have ever gotten."

"How could I have looked at you, Rose, I was fast asleep I told you! Or perhaps you were dreaming," Madeleine shrugged.

"Maybe you were sleepwalking. But without the walking. You could have been sleep staring," Joanie ventured like a child whose parents' fighting she had learnt to manage. She wanted the conversation to move forward and reconcilement to be found.

That look was not from someone who was sleeping. Or was it? Either way it had paralyzed Rose. The same eerie chill the stare had procured ran through Rose's body again.

Chapter 16

Madeleine slipped on a pair of black capri pants and matching flats, an Audrey Hepburn inspired ensemble from "Funny Face." Rose had not yet returned from class so she had the entire space to get ready. Brushing her dark hair into a low ponytail, she tied it with a tortoise shell barrette which had once belonged to Margot. It was as if her cousin was always with her, a part of her. To complete her ensemble, a fitted black sweater would work perfectly. Madeleine did not have Hepburn's small chest and therefore appeared far more seductive. Now she looked the part to go live in Paris, she thought. With a very light tint of red on her inviting lips, as if they had just been bitten and a touch of Guerlain's *L'Heure Bleue*, the romantic scent inspired by the magical hour of dusk, Madeleine was prepared for her encounter with Beardsmith, fully ready to seal her future.

Madeleine waited until the end of the afternoon to visit Beardsmith's office. His hours would soon be finished and with any luck, he might invite her for dinner. She had slept over at his place only twice, claiming to the previous R.A. she'd spent the night at the hotel with her parents who were in town. Perhaps there would be a third time. Beardsmith's office hours ended in twenty minutes and she needed to catch him before he left. Hopefully the queue of girls lining up to meet with him would be short. They all wanted to flirt and seduce him but as long as she got what she wanted, Madeleine couldn't care less about what Beardsmith did with his time or with the other girls. She was leagues ahead of these women.

Madeleine got to the English Chair department office and saw Beardsmith's office door was closed. Madeleine frowned, walking over to Ms. Hoxenbury who always seemed to actively be doing nothing.

"What a lovely green jumper, Ms. Hoxenbury. Really suits you. I'd like to see Professor Beardsmith quickly before he leaves. I need to get some notes from him for my paper this week." Madeleine made sure she smiled from ear to ear, showing all of her teeth.

Doris Hoxenbury peered from over her glasses and up from her busy work to meet Madeleine's sterile but smiling face. Interesting how words coming out of her mouth were never in correspondence with what her body language was communicating, she thought. She had rarely witnessed such discrepancy between the two. Unbeknownst to anyone in the department, Doris was studying to enter the FBI next year as a researcher. She was deep into Raymond Birdwhistell's recent publication on non-verbal communication and analyzed everyone she saw, practicing reading people before they had opened their mouth to speak. Madeleine was no exception. Before her was a polite and thoughtful young woman, but her body revealed impatience and disdain. To the untrained eye, Madeleine was another sweet student, but to Doris Hoxenbury she was an expert manipulator.

"Thank you, Miss Rousseau. Unfortunately for you, Professor Beardsmith completely skipped his office hours today. He called and cancelled them right after his last class," Doris replied.

Madeleine frowned, her thoughts racing a million miles an hour. His last class had been the one Rose was presenting in, which was exactly why she had wanted to see him afterward. Why had he canceled? Where did he go? Could he have invited Rose to discuss her presentation?

"Do you want to make an appointment for Thursday," Doris interrupted in a kind, maternal voice. She was trying out one of the exercises she had read about to comfort the person with whom you were in conversation.

Madeleine struggled to answer. There was no need for alarm, maybe nothing happened. He could have taken ill. A missed appointment. A friend dropping by from out of town.

"Thursday is absolutely perfect. Thank you. There's no real rush, I was only hoping to catch him." Madeleine said as she walked out. "No need to worry."

There were girls who regularly lined up to meet with Professor Beardsmith in his office, hormonal and desperate for attention. But Madeleine was different and Professor Beardsmith seemed to think so too. Doris strongly suspected there was something going on between the two of them. It wasn't any of her business, but she had heard some muffled noises once when coming back for a forgotten notebook after hours. The light had been on in his office and as she had walked past, she had also smelt the very distinctive aroma of the perfume Madeleine Rousseau always wore. But Doris had remained discreet. By the end of the school year, she would be passing the exam she was sure to ace and leave this place where no one thought much of her anyway.

Madeleine briskly crossed the quad in her elegant black outfit, desperately trying to reassure herself. Rose was maybe back in the room, studying at her desk or listening to a record. She would ask in her throaty voice how Madeleine's day had been and probably comment on her outfit because she had been raised to value politeness before anything.

Madeleine ran up the steps worn down by thousands of women's feet. She only used the sides that held their original shape, never wanting to step in the sloped middle, where everyone else did. Breathing heavily, she pushed the door open to an empty room.

Madeleine hadn't considered anyone could upset her perfectly laid out route to Paris, but Rose had. From her desk, she grabbed a couple of books and a notebook to write in. Checking her wallet was in her purse, she placed it on her forearm, ready to step off campus. She had to know if Beardsmith had brought Rose back to his house. Glancing at herself in the mirror, she reapplied lipstick and dabbed some on her cheeks and the tiniest smudge on her eyelids. This way, she looked flushed and healthy and it made men think of sex. Or so she had heard.

While rushing down the corridor, Madeleine ignored everyone. As she passed by other girls walking, she was already rehearsing what she would say to the professor when she got to his house. Last semester she had come uninvited and it had been very well received. They had had a long afternoon of pleasure and reading and eating and more pleasure. Certainly the professor had been surprised but Madeleine saw no interest in beating around the bush when they both wanted the same thing, and she needed to coax him a little while longer.

As she sped down the hall, Joanie was just opening her door.

"Madeleine! Madeleine," she called out to her friend, but not loud enough to grab her attention. Where was Madeleine running off to at this time? Joanie knew Madeleine's schedule by heart and she had no classes necessitating scurrying across campus like that. Joanie checked her watch and was pleased to see she would be early to the library where she was meeting Rose. They had a study date, hoping the two guys from Yale they had spotted the week before while working on Rose's presentation were there again. Stuart, the one Joanie liked with the auburn hair, had dropped a note asking if they'd wanted to go have a milkshake off campus. Rose had written back they weren't available because of the trip to New York but perhaps the following weekend. Rose reassured Joanie that nothing would be lost by not going when the guys asked, the fact they were unavailable made them stand out, which was a good thing. Joanie listened like a good student for she did not have the romantic maturity Rose did. She was not particularly interested in acquiring it to be honest. Joanie wished she could skip over meeting, flirting, dating and everything one had to do before getting married. She wanted to marry as soon as possible. But in order to do so, she had apparently had to go through the motions and hearing Rose speak about it, she was obviously an expert.

Meanwhile, Madeleine was rushing to get to Professor Beardsmith's home. His house was located off campus, between Vassar and Poughkeepsie. It was a simple yet strikingly well decorated home Madeleine had always thought. He did not seem to have a penchant for such aesthetics so the refined and elegant style was surprising; a decor usually attributed to the touch of a woman. She had never asked about it, only bothering to gather the maximum amount of information about the professor in order to better cater to his needs and desires. That is how one became essential and got exactly what one wanted. Every time. But Rose seemed to have flung a wrench in that arrangement, so she'd had to improvise, which she was not keen on at all.

As Madeleine knocked on the blue front door, her face transformed completely from sharply focused to kind, genuine concern. There was movement coming from upstairs in the bedroom. After a few moments, she finally heard the sound of steps coming down the staircase. From what she could tell, there was only one set of them. Unless someone had stayed in the bedroom. There was also the possibility that Rose had been here, they had frolicked, and she had left.

If only Madeleine could inspect the rooms and see if she could find traces of her roommate or another woman. Another woman was not bothersome. Just Rose. She bit her lips to make the blood rush to them and pinched her cheeks in case the lipstick had rubbed off. The door opened and the professor was standing in his bathrobe and wet hair. Madeleine's heart raced. So, he had been with another woman! Was it the cafe girl, another student, or Rose? Now that she was thinking about it, hadn't Rose become a little too interested in everything Madeleine did? Already she had wanted to call her Maddie, a very personal nickname despite the fact they had barely met. Then ever since the weekend, there were a number of things that she had asked about Uncle Pierre and Aunt Evelyn. She had also borrowed her face cream because she had apparently run out of hers. Madeleine was also convinced that Rose had taken her razor without asking. She had once told Rose to feel free to borrow a silk scarf and ever since, Rose had worn it at least three times. She was inching her way into Madeleine's life with great ease.

"Miss Rousseau. What are you doing here," asked Professor Beardsmith. With a dark brown towel in his hand, he was rubbing the back of his head.

"I ran into town for an errand and thought I'd swing by on my way back. I then remembered you'd be at your office but I was already at the door and thought I heard you, so I knocked anyway!"

She was kicking herself for having given too much unnecessary information revealing herself to be the liar she was, ruining any chance of discovering his secrets.

"Well, I'm not properly dressed but if you want to come in, I can fix you a drink," Beardsmith offered.

And just like that, the game was back on. Madeleine walked in, regaining her confidence and grazing his bare chest with her fingers as she passed, heading into the living room.

"Let me put some clothes on. Give me a minute and then I'm all yours," he said before running swiftly back up to the second floor.

He hadn't mentioned why he had missed his office hours. His bathing at the end of the afternoon could point to sexual activity. While he was upstairs, Madeleine began looking around to see if there were any clues left behind. She didn't smell any perfume in the air but perhaps it had disappeared or was in the bedroom. It seemed difficult to get a glimpse of any clues upstairs. Madeleine stuck her hands between the couch cushions, knelt down to look underneath it to see if a barrette, a notebook, a slip of paper, anything would reveal Rose's presence. There was nothing on the couch or underneath it. Hardly any dust under the couch could be explained by a cleaning lady but no jacket on the back of a chair or even papers on the table was surprising for an unannounced visitor.

The sound of the bathroom door closing echoed in the house as she heard Beardsmith's steps above on the hardwood floor. He would be down in no time. Running into the kitchen adjacent to the living room, she found what she was looking for. Two glasses in the sink, with the melted remnants of ice cubes, the condensation still present. One had lipstick on the rim. Did Rose wear lipstick? She did. A light-colored one making her full lips appear like a blush pillow you'd softly land upon and would plump right back up. Madeleine had no way of determining if the lips which had stained the glass were Rose's. Andrew Beardsmith had been quicker down the steps than she had expected so opening a cupboard, she pretended to look for a glass.

"Couldn't wait for me to make you that drink," he joked, grabbing her by the waist. With that he leaned into her and like a magnet, his mouth instantly met hers. She enjoyed kissing and had longed honed her skills by practicing every chance she got, be it with distant cousins over the summer holidays or with boys she met in secret. She'd pin the boys down and slowed their suffocating adolescent mouths and tease them with gentle, soft to progressively firmer, wetter accolades.

She hadn't needed to do so with the professor though. He was no amateur. Thoroughly enjoying herself, Madeleine couldn't help but wonder if only a few hours ago, Rose had been right here experiencing the very same thing.

"Seems you didn't need for me to come to have one," she said raising an eyebrow, head tilted toward the glasses in the sink.

"Am I not allowed to have friends over?"

"What you choose to do with your life doesn't concern me," she stated bluntly as she ran her hand down the front of his pants. It was best to take pleasure when it presented itself.

As his tongue found hers, she closed her mouth around it. All of the sudden, she wanted to eat him whole. Her body reacted immediately and her chest swelled, pressing against his. Breathing heavily, his pelvis pushed between her legs. Hard against her inner thigh, she maneuvered so when he was properly placed, and the instinctual rocking motion took over. By now the professor had taken her left breast out of her décolletage. His warm tongue slowly but firmly pressed against her skin, as if he were licking an ice cream from top to bottom to keep it from melting. At the top, he took her nipple between his lips, suckling hard while stroking with his tongue. Looking down to this grown man at her breast, a sense of domination and power came over her as much as the throbbing sensation at the top of her thighs. Professor Beardsmith would pick Madeleine to go to France, she would make damn sure of it by giving herself entirely to him. Now was the right time as it would surely erase the memory of any woman before her.

Chapter 17

Slouched over her desk, Phyllis was taking notes from a textbook while Madeleine scribbled away, sitting on Joanie's bed as she walked in.

"Where were you two? I came back after the meeting to see if you wanted to have dinner and then I went on with Mary Anne and that crowd," Joanie explained. "Are you ok?"

Phyllis looked up at Madeleine, who in return winked at her. Joanie was not aware of the affair with the professor. The less people knew, the better.

"We met and had a walk in town, then at the library and then came back here. I guess we just lost track of time," Madeleine explained.

"Wait, you went to town together," Joanie asked looking over at Phyllis. "You could have asked me to come. I didn't have anything to do there but the walk would have been nice."

"How was the meeting? Are they installing showers everywhere or not," Phyllis asked, feigning concern. It was best to launch Joanie in another discussion since Phyllis hated lying. They hadn't gone into town. Madeleine had done her senseless business with the dull professor all afternoon long and had only met her at the library toward the end of the day and they had returned to her room not long ago.

Phyllis had covered for her on numerous occasions and though she would *never* get herself involved in that kind of situation, she owed it to Madeleine. Also, she liked sharing a secret no one else knew. How many girls would love to find out this piece of gossip? Wouldn't Mary Anne be disappointed if she knew all of her loud bursts of laughter in class and her incessant leg crossing in the front row to impress the professor were in vain? That her own best friend was the one whom he had decided to risk getting caught red-handed for. Phyllis understood him. Madeleine was beautiful and mysterious and worldly. She had long fascinated Phyllis during freshman year. They had been in *Introduction to Macroeconomics* together. Madeleine had walked in ten minutes late and the professor had already begun the lecture. In this situation, most people would have chosen the closest seat to the door or in the back to be as discreet as possible. Not Madeleine. She had walked to the very front and sat right next to Phyllis, giving a small head nod to the professor as a means of communicating an apology.

After the lecture, Madeleine had asked her if she had missed anything of importance. While speaking, she had touched Phyllis's arm. A warm wave had traveled through her body from where Madeleine's hand had made contact with her skin. What an unfamiliar feeling, she remembered thinking. As Phyllis had turned to look at her more carefully, she had been mesmerized by the different color of each of Madeleine's eyes. Phyllis had never seen anything like it. Offering a glimpse of her notebook, when she had leaned over to read, Phyllis had smelt the delicious scent of her hair. She'd been torn between wanting the interaction to end quickly all the while hoping it never would. Everything happening was uncomfortable. Phyllis's armpits had begun to tingle, tiny beads of sweat forming on her upper lip. She'd grabbed her notebook, ripping the first several pages and shoved them into Madeleine's hand as she had run out of class.

Madeleine had called after her but Phyllis hadn't stopped until she had crossed the entire campus and locked herself in the third-floor bathroom of the main building. Breathing heavily, she wanted to wipe clean the memory of these feelings as rapidly as they had arisen, flush the emotions down the toilet. Nothing like this had ever happened to Phyllis. Why couldn't she reason with herself? A blur of sensations spun and clouded her mind. Surely, if she thought long and hard enough about it, she might make sense of the strange physical reaction she'd had to this new girl. It was uncontrollable and she hated it.

That afternoon, the registrar refused her plea to drop the class for it was too late, the deadline had been the Friday before.

From that day forward, it seemed everywhere Phyllis turned, Madeleine appeared. When they saw each other in the halls or crossing the quad, she'd smile and wave. Phyllis had made casual responses only to then look away, hurrying to reach her destination, often finding refuge from these encounters in the library. On the second floor, behind the mathematics section, a pair of tucked away tables behind the stairs to the third floor were safely out of sight. It was where she could do her best studying with the least distractions. On this particular Wednesday, Phyllis had gathered all of the reference books for her European Diplomacy class. She was preparing the outline for the end of term paper. Surely, she was ahead of schedule by a few months but she had done so much studying to avoid Madeleine over the last couple of weeks, she'd already completed the reading and most of work for the rest of her classes. As Phyllis was deep into Kissinger's *Nuclear Weapons and Foreign Policy,* she vaguely heard the librarian shushing someone. A few minutes later, a loud sound of a chair being dragged drew her annoyed attention to the other side of the aisle. There, perfectly in view, was Madeleine in all of her splendor. More beautiful than ever, she had tilted her head when seeing Phyllis. Phyllis's heart skipped a beat and she had immediately looked away. Should she gather her things and leave? No that was ridiculous, she'd thought. All she had to do was go back to concentrating on her paper. But her mind was not in agreement and all sorts of images of them walking around the lake together, arm in arm, laughing carelessly, having lunch, helping each other study with Phyllis's impeccable notes. For the first time ever, she had found fantasies to be more interesting than work, spending nearly an hour mentally constructing pleasant situations and placing Madeleine in them. She was discovering the dangerous emotional neighborhood of her mind she had long neglected. And before she knew it, the vision of Madeleine walking over holding a loose sheet of paper dragged her back into reality. She dove into her book.

"The notes you gave me a few weeks back got crumpled when you ran out, so I copied them on a new sheet of paper for you. I hope you don't mind," Madeleine whispered as she leaned in to see what Phyllis was reading. Before Phyllis had answered, Madeleine continued "Is that for your paper? I'm doing research for mine as well. What do you say we study together? I feel like all of the other girls in there aren't even interested in what Professor Mallory has to say."

Phyllis couldn't agree more. She had an urge to throw her arms around Madeleine who'd finally said out loud what she thought silently all too often. Now this strange creature who understood had stepped into her life. Of course, she wanted to study with Madeleine, she couldn't think of anything she'd ever wanted more. Plus, she'd be a great partner because in reality, Phyllis was simply brilliant. She had what her father liked to call the "winning combination." Not only was she extremely intelligent, and had skipped the third grade, she was also an extremely diligent worker. Using her time wisely, she fed her mind constantly, never stopping, continuously reading, analyzing, discussing, all the time consuming more facts. As the information was absorbed, she felt her brain expand and become capable of storing additional knowledge. Sure her social life had suffered because of this but Phyllis had no interest in it anyway; she was made solely for intellectual stimulation. Yet, here and now, for the very first time, someone took interest in her *and* her studying. Is this what people referred to when they spoke about best friends? She couldn't be sure. Joanie, her roommate was sweet but this was different. There were all sorts of confusing and unfamiliar happenings in her body. One of them was this butterfly sensation in her belly. What was that? Was she going to be sick? No it didn't feel like the time she had a stomach bug in high school and had to run out of class, barely making it to the toilet. Her heart had beat faster when Madeleine's hair had slightly brushed her face and that distinct scent hung in the air again. Phyllis had never had to filter what came out of her mouth so before she could even think to refrain, she had blurted out:

"Is it you who smells so nice?"

Madeleine had thrown her head back laughing, letting another waft engulf Phyllis. It had been her.

"I hope so! Thank you for noticing. It's a perfume my aunt gave me and I wasn't sure if I should keep it," Madeleine had said while smelling her wrists. She had then put it right under Phyllis's nose "Is it this what you smell?"

Phyllis had approached with precaution feeling the heat emanating from the inside of Madeleine's bare wrist. No one had ever asked her to smell them. And as she had drawn a breath to take in the perfume, her lip had ever so gently grazed Madeleine's skin. She had pulled back instantly, as if burned, drawing her own hand to her mouth.

She had excused herself and Madeleine laughed, dismissing the touch and taking a seat at the table with Phyllis. Madeleine hadn't been bothered at all by what had happened. Later, when no one was around, Phyllis would take out the page of notes Madeleine had given her and admired the penmanship. She would run her fingers over the ink, the stains that made letters to then form words. Bringing the sheet of paper to her face hoping to again find Madeleine's scent, she wanted to stuff the paper in her mouth to feel a little closer to her.

That had been the beginning. Now Phyllis was happy to be on the same floor of Strong House as Madeleine, although if they shared a room that would be best. Yet the one she shared with Joanie was adjacent to the stairs and she liked it that way. In case of an emergency, all Phyllis had to do was turn right out of the door and run down three flights of stairs before getting out. Madeleine had just walked out and left the door ajar. Phyllis got up from her desk to shut it when she heard the blood curling scream coming from the opposite end of the hallway. Phyllis stepped into the hallway, while several of the other girls poked their heads out of their door questioningly yet not moving. The scream stopped and began again and this time she felt her heart drop. She recognized Madeleine's voice and ran in the direction of the scream.

When she reached her friend, the excruciating howl coming from her body had not stopped. And it was only when Phyllis looked inside the room did she understand why.

Chapter 18

Rose's body hung limply from the pipe running against the wall. Blonde hair covered her face and her shoulders slouched forward. Phyllis pushed past Madeleine, grabbing a pair of scissors from the desk, jumping on the bed to reach the pipe and cut Rose's body loose. The knot made with the silk material was difficult to cut with the dull scissors and Madeleine finally ran over, wrapping her arms around Rose's waist to help Phyllis release the body.

As Phyllis managed to cut through the taut material, Rose fell into Madeleine's arms like a small child, nestling in her mother's bosom. But there was no breath against her skin. When they laid their friend down on the ground, they saw her eyes were bulging. There was no color in her face or on her lips. Phyllis leaned in close to her face to feel for any warmth or airflow. Nothing. She put her ear to Rose's chest, desperate for a heartbeat. Madeleine had taken Rose's wrist, searching for a pulse too. No blood was being pumped through the veins, no air was filling those lungs. The casing of what was once Rose, lay on the burgundy carpet she had put down to keep her feet warm.

It wasn't long before the entire floor was gathered, screaming, crying; each girl drawing more attention to herself than the next.

"Grace, run down and phone the police and the dean right away, the rest of you go immediately back into your rooms and stay there, do not leave the building," ordered Janet as she shut the door to the hallway.

Inside, she swiftly moved to Rose's bed and removed the luxurious white cotton sheet her mother had carefully packed for her daughter, and let the billowed cloud gently espouse the shape of the body. Phyllis and Madeleine watched their friend disappear, dumbfounded.

As they waited for the police, Madeleine quickly went over the timeline of the afternoon.

"Phyllis, we must say we were together for the entire afternoon. If not, the professor will get fired and I will be suspended. So we were in town, then the library, then here. Just like we told Joanie ok?"

Phyllis listened, acquiescing. No words escaped her lips while her eyes darted over to the long white shape lying at the foot of the bed. Part of her was waiting for Rose to stand up and scream to scare them both, laughing heartily. But nothing happened. It was as if time has been suspended, a palpable stillness. She replayed the scene over and over in her head. For once in her life, she had acted on instinct, trying to save Rose. But it had been useless and now Phyllis was at a loss. There was nothing to do, only sit and digest, which seemed utterly impossible.

Madeleine stared straight ahead. She could hear her own scream still ringing in her ears; a sense of numbness and emptiness from all of the exertion. As she sat next to Phyllis, she felt nothing. She wanted to leave the room but had been instructed by Janet, like all of the other girls, to wait for the police. Madeleine reached out for Phyllis's hand, searching for some grounding while the world moved on.

When the police finally arrived, Phyllis and Madeleine had not budged or even exchanged more words. They were still holding hands when Detective Arthur Willoughby walked in. Immediately he took in the scene, standing at the frame of the door and scanning from left to right, up and down. He did this with every single crime scene since he had become a detective. Against the wall on the left was a messy desk, papers spread around, notebooks and schoolbooks piled on either side. A delicate looking pencil holder with large white magnolias painted on it and a gold rim with an array of writing apparatus inside. At the foot of the bed was the body whose lifelessness he had been called in to investigate. It lay extended and surpassing the foot rug of a dark blood color, matching the bed cover next to it. The bed was unmade and footprints were on it where he guessed the person who had released the body had stepped. In the middle of the two beds was a large window looking out onto the quad. He could see two colleagues in uniform talking to the students, most of them curious to hear about the incident. Willoughby knew the guys would have a field day in a women's college. By the time he looked at the other bed in the room, both Phyllis and Madeleine were staring at him. He had been in the room for a few minutes and had not addressed them.

The coroner walked in, nodding to Detective Willoughby, while two policemen began inspecting the pipe from which Rose's body had hung. A young officer approached and knelt down in front of the girls.

"Your names please," he asked hesitantly, his lips tightening into an uncomfortable smile.

Willoughby looked over at the other desk before proceeding to the two women on the bed, holding hands. Madeleine's work space was impeccable. A single white rose in a thin and elegant dark blue glass vase. It looked expensive and perfectly placed on the top left corner. Underneath, a small doily had been placed, protecting the cheap wood of the desk. The schoolbooks were aligned on the shelf by color and height, something Willoughby had never seen. As he wrapped up his visual tour of the room he turned back to the girls who had finished giving their details to the rookie on shift. Phyllis immediately looked down while Madeleine kept her eyes fixated on the detective. He waited to speak. This usually made people uncomfortable and found very revelatory what they chose to say in order to fill the silence. Phyllis couldn't bear the tension and spoke first.

"Are you the detective on the case? So, what are you going to do? Do you want me to tell you what happened?"

Somehow, Phyllis hoped that is she could answer all of the questions the detective asked and gave him the right clues, he would bring Rose back. Phyllis's logical mind understood that Roses's body still lay there in the room but wrapping her head as to where her friend had gone was impossible. She was angry at herself for being so irrational.

Without detaching her eyes from Willoughby, Madeleine slipped her hand out of Phyllis's and wrapped it around her own knee.

"I am," he replied in a deep, monotone voice.

Those were the only two words to come out of the detective's mouth. He wasn't there to make conversation, he was busy noting and examining details which might seem uninteresting or useless to the untrained eye. But he was far from untrained. He'd even noted how the dark-haired girl had pulled her hand away from the other girl. Something had made her shift.

Madeleine was curious as to how long this little game was going to go on. She wanted to be alone and lay down in her bed, yet that possibility seemed like a distant dream. So many things had to take place before she would be able to pull the blanket over herself and forget about the day. Phyllis's hand had become so sweaty she needed to let it go. It was disgusting; a clammy and cold, limp hand. She had wanted to feel grounded in the moment, held down in reality and all she had latched onto was this lifeless, weak gathering of fingers. Rose was there, lying on the floor, covered in a white sheet. Madeleine stared at the material outlining her nose, watching if there was the slightest movement due to her breath. But there wasn't. She was dead. All that remained was the human form whose soul had been removed. How long would they leave her there, Madeleine wondered. Her parents, her parents must be informed of this. Janet surely had already thought of that. She was one of those people who relished being in the midst of drama and the bearer of bad news. It allowed her to offer help and be essential in a situation, a true contrast to her otherwise dull existence.

Detective Willoughby asked for the girls to be separated. He needed to speak to each one individually, as a seemingly insignificant detail could come about. Phyllis returned to her room and paced there until the detective knocked. Phyllis had never been afraid of the police or of the law. Why would she be, she had always been an abiding, respectful citizen. She avoided each and every situation in her life which could have led her to any sort of sticky circumstance. When she was only fourteen years old, her parents had gone to their former neighbor's place for dinner. Having served herself a tall glass of cold milk, she'd settled down in the floral armchair with a book when she'd heard a knock at the front door. Her neighbor Harriet, with a flushed face and a big smile, stood before her.

"Hi Phyllis! I'm headed down to the river, wanna come," she asked, barely taking a breath.

"No thanks Harriet, I've got to finish my book, it's due back tomorrow," Phyllis had replied.

"Oh please? Come on," she had insisted, "Blake is going to be there, and I just need to see him for a little bit."

Harriet was in love, or so she claimed, with Blake, one of her older brother's friends. Blake was a senior and part of the popular group. He played football and had a wide smile that stretched across his face and made Harriet blush all the way down to her toes. Blake was a good guy and always kind to his friend's little sister, but never gave it any more thought. Harriet was determined to change his mind and had concocted a plan for this very evening. She wanted to drag Phyllis out of the safety of her home to run down to the picnic area by the river where all of the high school kids met up in secret to drink beers and neck in the woods.

"I really shouldn't. I didn't ask my parents if I could even leave the house," Phyllis had said, never wanting to disobey. She was such a good daughter, her parents had a hard time understanding how so many other families struggled with their children. They found parenthood easy and genuinely believed raising a child was only as difficult as you were willing to make it.

"You don't have to ask if they aren't home. Besides, we'll be back in no time," she'd convincingly lied. But Phyllis wouldn't budge, although if she thought about it, she *could* step out of the house. In all fairness, her parents had never said not to leave the house. Before Phyllis could express a tiny bit of hesitance, Harriet blurted out the truth out of sheer desperation.

"Listen, my mom won't let me go alone. So if you don't come with me, I can't go at all."

Phyllis was stunned at Harriet's bluntness. She hadn't been interested in her, only so she could have someone to walk with down to the river. It made sense though, the girls were neighbors but had hardly ever played together since elementary school. Harriet had taken advantage of Phyllis's hesitance and grabbed her hand, leading her out of the front door. But Phyllis had resisted before running back up the stairs to her bedroom. She grabbed her yellow cardigan for she knew spring nights by the river could get cool. A surge of excitement had taken over as Harriet led the way through the trees, following a trail to an open picnic area. She'd stopped in her tracks and placed her fingers on her lips so Phyllis knew to keep quiet. Her brother and his friends were standing around drinking beers and laughing. Harriet signaled that she was going first and for Phyllis to come after, as if they were meeting there as well. Harriet walked off and Phyllis heard some rustling. She saw police officers, crawling through the woods, ready to spring on the teens. Phyllis quickly evaluated her options: call out to Harriet and risk getting caught by the officers or run home, alone.

After that night, Harriet never again spoke to her. Though she had lost her only social interaction, Phyllis was rewarded by listening to her parents' praises about how proud they were of her grades, what a good girl she was. Meanwhile, the neighbors across the street had to worry about their children being disrespectful, drinking, and being liars. She found it easier never to make friends again. Throughout her lonely high school years, when she'd laid in her bed at night, staring up at the ceiling, Phyllis occasionally had allowed herself to feel. Her eyes would swell with hot tears. And there, with no one to witness, she regretted having abandoned Harriet and missed her wholeheartedly.

"Can you recount your afternoon for me please and then once you discovered the body?" Willoughby glared, unfazed by Phyllis's shaken demeanor. She answered, being as precise about time as her lie permitted.

"And then I finished my International Conflict Resolution class with Professor Perry at three, and met Madeleine right after for a walk around town. Then we went to the library from around four onwards. We got back to my room around six-thirty I would say maybe a little later. And then Madeleine went back to her room and found Rose . . . ," Phyllis said.

How did that lie escape her lips so easily? There had been no walk in town, and from three to four-thirty, Phyllis had been alone. And after that Madeleine had come in and out of the library but it was only when they'd gotten back to the dorm that they'd stayed together. Madeleine immediately had known there would be questions about Rose's suicide. She always knew everything. If Phyllis told the truth, Beardsmith and Madeleine would be kicked out of the school. After years of having no friends, Phyllis had let Madeleine in and she couldn't bear the idea of betraying her; she had vowed not to repeat the Harriet incident. Even if that meant lying to the police.

Detective Willoughby couldn't help but notice the thickness of Phyllis's bangs as she spoke. They were like a heavy curtain of brown hair drawn across her forehead. With his hair thinning, he now couldn't help but examine other people's capillary endowments. His father had been bald and it was a trait he didn't wish to inherit. Especially not at thirty-seven. The Phyllis girl had answered all of the questions with no hesitation, which made him curious. People in the face of tragedy are often hesitant, trying to both answer a question while still reeling from the traumatic event forever altering their existence. In his sixteen years on the force, he had found this to be true more often than not.

These two girls, the ones who claimed to have found the body had stayed together. There was a chance that they had had time to discuss what they would say to the police, should it be a variation of the truth. Willoughby kept that in mind with this case. As the girl spoke, he placed his hand in his grey overcoat. His fingers came into contact with a chestnut. It was smooth and soft, except for the slightly more rugged grey part. Since childhood, he always picked up a chestnut when it came to be fall. His father had told him it was what kept arthritis away. Yet the poor man had not even lived long enough to know what arthritis felt like. He had been killed while off duty by an Irish gang run by the Malone family back in New York City. Everyone knew who was responsible, but no one wanted to go after the clan whose influence reached higher circles. So Arthur had stepped in as the man of the family with his fifteen years of age. He was not the eldest, but the first boy. His father's death had propelled him into becoming the dutiful and emotionally detached man he was today; an ideal police detective. Despite his mother's pleas to not join the force, he had; unsuspecting of the paternal ghost preceding his every move. When the haunting, along with the drinking necessary to keep living with it, got to be too much, Willoughby had packed up his life, his wife, and left New York. He had been assigned to Poughkeepsie, hoping for a more tranquil life, which he had found. But the detective hadn't guessed it would be too tranquil for his bride.

After hearing Phyllis's statement, Willoughby was ready to move on to the other girl, a certain Madeleine Rousseau. With a name like that, there were chances she was an immigrant, maybe with an accent. Back in the city, he had come across so many different kinds of people and accents: Italians, Irish, Puerto Ricans. He had a good ear and paid very close attention to detail. He prided himself on being able to pinpoint where people were from, despite not having explored the world at all. But living in New York was an easy way to travel without going anywhere. Despite growing up there, he'd still made discoveries of entirely new populations. Like the murder in the Hassidic community right before he left. Willoughby had never even heard of them, though they had migrated to the city a little more than a decade prior. The crime had never been resolved, not due to language barrier he initially blamed, but because of the insularity of the people. They were a special group, they wanted to keep everyone out, even the law.

Willoughby's ear were perked, prepared to analyze, but when the girl opened her mouth, she had no accent. Just as American-sounding as he was. Unlike her friend though, she was unusually calm. Willoughby had about seen it all when it came to reactions to trauma. He found the Latinos, Italians, and Blacks to be expressive in their pain and shock. They wailed, screamed, and howled, asking God why he would inflict such pain upon them. The real question was why God would even care about each individual's sorrow, Willoughby thought. The whites, the Irish, and the rich on the other hand, were much less vocal about it all. Tears streamed down their faces, their bodies shaking with spasms they were so desperately trying to retain. Occasionally an embarrassed sob slipped out, only because had it not, it would have suffocated them to death. He had also seen a few like Madeleine, where the emotion had vanished completely and all that was left was a blank face and empty eyes.

Madeleine watched as the detective paced the room. He kept his left hand in the pocket of his coat and was moving it around. He was of normal build, dark, fine hair, and extra thick eyebrows. He had probably shaved that morning but the shadow of his beard was already beginning to show. Aunt Evelyn always said you could tell a lot about a man by looking at his shoes. Detective Willoughby's shoes were heavy durable leather, so not too refined, but made to last and most importantly, they were polished. Madeleine concluded he was therefore careful with money and his looks. Maybe his wife took care of it, she hadn't noticed if he was married, his left hand still tucked away.

"After Miss . . . ," he hesitated.

"Miss Phyllis Burrows," Madeleine replied.

"Thank you, yes after Miss Burrows came into the room, then the two of you released the body. You hadn't tried to get her down before she came in?"

"No. I was paralyzed until Phyllis came in. It was only when I saw her grab the scissors that I felt I could finally move," she recounted.

"Had you seen Miss Suggs earlier today or yesterday? Was she sad, did she appear troubled to you?"

"Not particularly, no. She seemed fine this morning."

"Nothing notable, a change in behavior, a letter, a phone call, anything you can think of?"

"I . . . I don't know how to say this. Nor would I want this to get out but there was something . . . ," Madeleine hesitantly offered.

"I'm all ears young lady," Detective Willoughby said, trying to remain detached in front of this rich twenty-something-year-old sent off to school to be educated before integrating another affluent family. For the moment he had asked one of his subordinates to look into the families of the victim and of the girls who were her close friends and social circle, to paint a proper picture of the world he was stepping into, though he already had a clue. Most cases in the upper intellectual stratum of Poughkeepsie were kept under wraps. When he'd moved six years ago, there had been questions about his arrival from the city to this smaller town but he had not given into them nor the gossip. Integrity did not ensure professional survival and he had learnt it the hard way. Back in the city, he'd denounced compromised behavior from colleagues, thinking his late father would be proud, only to find out that the trail went much higher than his pay grade. It was recommended he leave New York to remain a detective on the force. Additionally, the captain had hinted he was the first in his family to be a rat. Apparently, his father had known and kept silent; why wasn't he more like his old man? This had destroyed Willoughby and certainly made leaving the city and the ghost of his father easier. That and his overbearing mother. All was sealed in a file never to be opened again, forgotten in a basement of the NYPD.

"Rose had been acting strange," Madeleine said quietly, looking at her hands. "I had invited the girls to New York for the weekend."

Willoughby's ears perked up. He always suspected there was something strange with girls living together and being so close, sleeping in the same beds at times. He had heard of them bathing together and knew there was more to it than meets the eye. He listened intently, trying to subdue any vivid images forming in his mind.

Madeleine was picking at her nails, not making eye contact, waiting for him to ask. And he quickly obliged.

"Go on, Miss Rousseau, what happened," he pushed.

"Rose revealed she had had an illegitimate child with one of her professors from Agnes Scott. I don't want to gossip but I thought it was important for you to know. She was completely distraught when she spoke of it to me," Madeleine uttered in a quavering voice and hesitantly put a hand on her left breast, as if holding her heart all the while raising her eyes to the detective. While planting a false seed of suspicion as to the motive of Rose's suicide, she carried on, letting her eyes fill with tears:

"Oh, detective, I don't think anyone here at school knew but when she confided in me, I saw how painful the memory was. From then on, she did act distant and very strange. Do you think that could have anything to did with it . . . ," Madeleine whimpered, breaking down.

Willoughby couldn't help but rapidly glance at her full bosom. Her chest was inviting and she continuously drew attention to it somehow. It had been a while since he had touched his wife's small breasts. Automatically he had calculated his own hand could not hold one of Miss Rousseau's breasts entirely. But that was not the issue. She was suggesting the victim had had a reason to kill herself. That was interesting.

"Do you happen to know the name of the child's father?"

Madeleine nodded.

"Hartford Portman. I also know he lives in New York. And it is possible she went to see him when we were there. She ran off for a few hours on her own."

Detective Willoughby headed toward the window and peered out onto the quad at all of the women populating the campus. He wondered how being in such intimate proximity with one another, day in and day out, wouldn't eventually lead to experimentation. He wasn't born yesterday and knew the rumors about women's colleges. A dorm room was a veritable free for all for any girl who was "different." He wondered if Lacey had ever done anything like that before they met.

She certainly hadn't gone to college, let alone an all-women's one. She had started working with her parents in their grocery shop when she was old enough to count and stock shelves. They'd practically known each other their entire lives since Willoughby's mother would send him down to buy potatoes or whatever else she had forgotten for dinner. Through the years, Lacey had become essential at the store, especially after her two brothers had been drafted. There had even been talk of her taking it over one day. But her brothers were some of the lucky ones who'd come back from the war and despite being best suited to run it, Lacey had been kindly pushed aside upon the heroes' return. This way, they could drown the horrors of the human race they had witnessed with a mundane, normal life. No one ever imagining the contrast too grand.

"Is there anything else worth noting? Any other detail you might have seen or can recall," Willoughby insisted, reentering his thoughts. The fantasy was troubling his concentration.

"Well, it's probably not important at all but since you asked, the scarf Rose used to . . . you know . . . around her neck, it was mine."

It was the one Aunt Evelyn and Uncle Pierre had given Madeleine for her seventeenth birthday. Margot's had been dark green to bring out her eyes where as Madeleine's was deep purple and black, with gold thread used to highlight the metal details of the equestrian saddles of its design. The girls had loved wearing them at the same time. Madeleine had brought back it back from the weekend in New York and today it had ended up wrapped around Rose's neck, squeezing the life out of her like Isadora Duncan.

"I see. Had you given it to her? Or lent it to her by chance? Had she been wearing it today?"

"I had not, no. It was a gift from my family and though I had offered for Rose to borrow certain items, but this specific scarf was off limits . . . ," she trailed.

"Interesting," he noted, writing in his notepad.

"Detective, may I be excused? I feel I cannot breathe in here and would love to step out of this room for a moment," Madeleine asked. She gave him her best doe eyes.

In fact, she didn't particularly want to move at all. She wanted to lie down on her bed and pull the yellow mohair blanket over herself. Disappear for a moment, let all of the chaos around tend to itself, let the dust settle as it should. As he prepared to answer, the coroner walked over and whispered something in the detective's ear. Madeleine wasn't able to read his lips.

He was done inspecting the body and two hefty men in dark clothes lifted it onto the gurney, wheeling it right out of the room. A few officers were still jotting down information, their police hats looking much larger than Madeleine ever realized. They appeared quite ridiculous really. Was the size of the hat supposed to intimidate or induce a respect of authority? How strange. The two men were intensely but very quietly discussing seemingly important information. Madeleine strained to hear but could not catch a word.

Luckily, she had convinced Phyllis to say they had been together all afternoon. Now she needed to warn the professor before the police got to him and let him know she had an alibi which didn't endanger his career or her reputation.

"I will absolutely come by tomorrow," Detective Willoughby answered. He checked if Madeleine had reacted. Like a lost child seeking comfort, she had not batted an eyelash while awaiting his permission to move. The detective called off his men and told them to wrap up before turning to Madeleine.

"The coroner will hand in the report tomorrow, so you are free to go. If I have any further questions, will I find you here? Are you going to stay at school? Not in this room, I can imagine . . . ," he rambled.

"I may go to my aunt and uncle's in New York, but . . . this was the last place I saw Rose. And, her parents may have questions for me. I can only imagine how distraught they might be. Perhaps I can help them pack or begin to do it for them. I may be more useful here," said

Madeleine as she got up from her bed and reaching out to Willoughby. "And to you if I stay close by, of course."

"I'm sure they can find another arrangement for you to sleep on campus," he replied.

"You're too kind to worry about me, detective," Madeleine said as her hand slipped gently off of his overcoat purchased with Lacey when they had moved to Poughkeepsie. He had been proud of investing more than he normally did in a piece that was both classic in style and durable. He never would have worn it in New York. He could just hear the guys on the squad mocking him, thinking he was better than them, trying to buy his way up the social ladder. They were always too pleased to remind him of his roots and would probably say his father would roll around in his grave if he saw him in it. In all honesty, the latter part might have been true as his father had worked hard to get on the force, it had been a major achievement in the family. Though he'd never reached the ranks of detective, his reputation had at least been impeccable at the precinct.

The women in Strong House were lingering in the hallways, the last of them having their statements taken down by the officers. The detective waved to Stevens, the only officer with whom he had had a couple of beers with on occasion. Stevens gave him a head nod in return and went back to half-heartedly scribbling what the girl in front of him was spewing with shock and excitement. Once outside in the cooler air, Willoughby turned back toward the building. Strong House was not quite high enough to ensure death by defenestration, he pondered. Unless she had climbed onto the roof but it was still only about three-story fall and she could have survived considering the bushes. As his eyes followed the lit windows across the building he saw a service ladder running from the roof all the way down the south side of the brick building. Deep in thought, a movement caught his eye in the victim's room. Standing in the frame of the window staring straight down at the detective was Madeleine Rousseau. Tilting his hat to bid her farewell,

Willoughby wasn't sure she'd see him in the obscurity. She placed her hand against the windowpane. Despite the darkness, she had.

With the detective gone, Madeleine immediately ran down the hall and barged into Phyllis's room. She found her staring down to the floor, lost in a gaze. Joanie ran up to Madeleine and threw her arms around her, sobbing.

"Oh Madeleine, this can't be real! How could she? She loved us, we were having such a grand time, the four of us. Why didn't she tell us what was happening? Was she so sad? What are we going to do," Joanie asked in hysterics.

Madeleine fought off the desire to push Joanie away and slap her back to her senses.

"Joanie, we don't know what darling Rose was feeling or thinking. I'm very upset too. Can you go get me a cup of warm water with lemon in it," Madeleine asked, pointing to the door.

Joanie obeyed, satisfied to be finally active in a situation she couldn't quite grasp. Madeleine sat next to Phyllis and took her hand. Her fingers opened slightly so they interlaced. Phyllis breathed a sigh of relief and put her head on Madeleine's shoulder while big, warm tears fell straight onto her friend's pants, missing her cheeks because of the angle. Madeleine watched as the dark fabric absorbed the salty drops.

"I feel horrible that we lied. Maybe I should tell the detective the truth, Madeleine. Maybe he wouldn't have to tell the school you and Professor Beardsmith were together so only HE would know and . . . ," Phyllis suggested.

Madeleine held Phyllis's wet cheeks. She was hot from all of the emotions as the tears continued to flow, dripping on either side of her nose. She stared into her friend's eyes, coming close enough to feel Phyllis's breath on her lips.

"They will fire the professor and most importantly, they will ask me to leave school. I will not be able to return. We will not finish school together. I'll lose everything and most importantly, I'll lose you," she said. And with that, she ever so gently placed her lips on Phyllis's, who kept her eyes open, wanting to take in every second of what was happening to mentally replay it later. She inhaled Madeleine's skin, afraid the slightest movement might break the magic spell that had befallen her.

Chapter 19

Enjoying a bath before heading into work, Professor Andrew Beard-smith was reading Sagan's *Bonjour Tristesse.* Why couldn't he have published a great book early on? To be honest, it was good but fairly simple, a kind of writing he could easily imitate. Though her lack of social confines made the novel attractive, it was the descriptions which aroused him. Already he found being naked, submerged in warm water, extremely sensual. As he lay in the tub, a glass of whiskey nearby despite the morning hour, he closed his eyes, preparing for pleasure. Living so close to campus had its advantages. On occasion, he'd been known to run home between classes to indulge in these long baths as a means to relieve himself and also shielding from the conformity of the dull ordinary life of a college professor. He craved reminders that he wasn't like the others on the Vassar staff, the Greens and the Hastings of academia. Those two rested on their laurels and prided themselves on the praises of the incestuous literary community with whom he chose to not socialize. He had been the youngest professor at Vassar, which had come with its load of jealousy and attention, not always negative of course. When he'd first arrived, he'd been very careful about his reputation especially when it had come to students. But after six years, he knew how to walk the very fine line in order to indulge without endangering himself or his reputation. At least until Madeleine Rousseau. He was willing to go far beyond what he had initially imagined, raising the stakes and therefore the excitement. Yet he was always careful to never leave traceable evidence of their encounters, like he did for all of the others. Because, if their secret was to be discovered, it would be her word against his, and there was a risk the reputable college professor's word would not be decisive.

Thoughts of his seductive former student and the next great novel he would never write were interrupted by loud knocking at the front door. His watch, laying on the side of the sink, indicated nine-thirty. He was not expecting anyone. It was the second time in two days he had been interrupted during his favorite ritual. With the doorbell no longer chiming its annoying tune, pounding on the door was the only way to let him know he was wanted. Normally, had anyone knocked during a moment when he wasn't meant to be home, much less in a bath, he wouldn't have answered but this one had been insistent and had already ruined the sensation he was after.

Annoyed, Beardsmith grabbed his dark brown terry cloth robe, gifted by his mother two Christmases ago along with a pair of sheepskin slippers. Careful not to slide on the wooden stairs as he had in the past, he came down drying his wet hair with a hand towel, tossing it on the back of a chair in the living room before opening the front door, where his uninvited guest impatiently awaited.

"Detective Arthur Willoughby, Poughkeepsie Police Department," he said, presenting a badge.

The coroner had given Willoughby a preliminary hint before anyone else about the cause of Rose Suggs's death. The detective had skimmed over the statements made during the interviews and had noted a certain Professor Beardsmith come up on multiple occasions concerning the victim and her last known whereabouts. He needed a clear picture of who this Rose girl was in order to understand how and why this life ended in suicide or if and when there may have been any sort of foul play, as the coroner had suggested. On the doorstep stood a man, approximately of the same age.

"Hello, detective. What may I do for you," Beardsmith asked, expressing genuine surprise.

Willoughby looked down to note the time. Perhaps the professor was not working today? Strange. It was mid-week and he had apparently just finished bathing.

"I'm sorry, I seemed to have come at a bad time and dragged you out of the shower."

"Not at all, I had finished. Please, would you like to come in?"

Willoughby already did not like the visceral instinct he was getting from this professor. But then again, he was always suspicious of everyone during a case. For the moment, this was still technically a suicide, but the coroner had shared with Willoughby an important piece of information about the marking on Rose's neck. Though he was waiting for confirmation from him. Regardless, even with a suicide, he wanted to do a thorough and complete job, as he did for all of his cases, at times to a fault. Pushing an investigation too far had obliged him to leave New York. Still, until proven otherwise, everyone was a suspect.

"If you need a few minutes to slip into a more . . . comfortable attire, I don't mind waiting," Willoughby offered.

"Uhm . . . yes, that might be better I suppose. Pardon me, what did you say this was regarding again," Beardsmith asked, annoyed at the detective's directive to get dressed.

"It's concerning one of your students. But please, go ahead," as he indicated the stairs, "I'm in no rush."

Beardsmith nodded and let the detective in, climbing the stairs two by two. Had Madeleine said something? She had come over yesterday and perhaps someone had seen her? He knew he should be more careful, but the thrill had gotten the best of him! She could have come by for a paper or a book. Why the police? Nothing they were doing was illegal. He would get out of this. It was going to be fine. All he needed was a little time to settle down and remember he had done nothing wrong. Well, nearly nothing.

Detective Willoughby scanned the house to see what kind of man this Andrew Beardsmith was. The living room which he had indicated before rushing up the stairs was decorated in soft tones. The plush light blue couch with button detailing looked like a cloud in the middle of the room. A few pastel pillows only accented its dreamlike quality. In the corner was a leather armchair with a reading light placed on a rosewood round table which didn't quite suit the style. The bookshelves were filled to the brim and in the back of the room was a small alcove where a desk was hidden under a pile of papers and more books. Arthur pushed aside the almond green curtains and glanced out of the window to the backyard where a white iron table and matching chairs sat in an overgrown lawn.

Willoughby picked up a few papers off of the desk. Flipping through them quickly, he came across one with Rose Suggs's name. On it, written in red was the comment "Fantastic research! Very well-rounded argument and presentation. A delight to read. Please come see me after class." Willoughby heard the bustling upstairs and wanted to finish his indiscreet eyeing before the professor returned, hopefully fully dressed this time.

In the kitchen, a few crumbs lay on the counter and in the sink some dirty dishes. Amongst those were four crystal whiskey glasses. One of them had a smudge on the rim. Willoughby wasn't sure but he quickly grabbed the glass with his handkerchief and smelt it. On the rim he recognized the smell of lipstick, like the one Lacey used to wear when they went out. Inside the glass was an unfamiliar smokey odor. He was not a huge amateur of hard liquor but knew enough to make a few cocktails and enjoy a glass of brandy once in a while. It was definitely a sort of malt, whiskey or bourbon but the smoked component did not give him a clue. The professor had begun coming down the stairs so Willoughby gently placed the glass back in the sink and went around the back of the stairs, the way he had come into the kitchen. The professor found his guest leaning against the wall, staring out into the back of the garden.

"Oh yes, I really do need to tend to the backyard. It's a mess. I simply don't have the time," he explained without a prompt.

"Yes of course. Understandable," he replied, though he made time for morning baths, Willoughby thought. "I hope I am not keeping you from getting to work on time."

"Not at all. My classes don't start until early afternoon today," he explained.

The life of intellectuals; must be nice, Willoughby thought. Working only half days, teaching rooms full of young women.

"What can I do for you, detective," Beardsmith said indicating the cloud-like couch as he sat in the adjacent chair. Willoughby remained standing.

"A young lady by the name of Rose Suggs was found dead in her room yesterday. Currently it has been classified as a suicide but that remains to be confirmed. She was a student of yours, correct," Willoughby glared at the professor hoping to catch the slightest inflection of his voice or the tiniest twitch of a muscle.

Beardsmith was startled. His eyes widened in shock, his pupils dilating almost instantly. Rose had made a wonderful presentation. It had been so great he had asked to speak with her to see if she'd be interested in doing research for his next book. She had been so diligent in her preparation that it would save tremendous amounts of time if she accepted to do the brunt of the work. It was also the part he detested, having to pore over piles and piles of books only to extract a few key ideas. She had demonstrated an extraordinary capacity to do so. In all of his years of teaching, it was one of the most thorough and well-constructed presentations he'd witnessed. When she had been hesitant about the workload the project might entail, he had asked her to come and discuss the idea at his home. She had seemed fine, her normal self. There was no indication of a depressed girl, quite the contrary. He had even offered the opportunity to secure the junior spot for the Paris exchange if she accepted. And that had tipped the scale. She had been over the moon about the idea and well, then they had kissed. But no one needed to know that, especially now that she was dead.

"She is, I mean, was. Yes, she was in fact, quite a promising student really. She had given such an impressive presentation. I can't imagine this had anything to do with her killing herself. I don't understand. When we last spoke, she was thrilled because I was going to nominate her for a summer program we have in France. And she was absolutely delighted. Couldn't have been further from sad to be honest."

"Interesting. What is this summer abroad in Paris? Something she wanted or might it have caused an enormous amount of nervousness, to the best of your knowledge, of course?"

Willoughby was detecting genuine reactions, with a little hint of anguish. Was the professor thinking ahead, worrying about hiding something?

"Not at all, quite the contrary. She was overly excited and had wanted to rush back to tell her parents," he answered, his hands beginning to sweat.

"When was this," Willoughby probed, verifying the timeline.

"Yesterday actually." The professor took his face in his hands. "I just can't believe it. She was so . . . so . . . it sounds ridiculous now, but so alive. I never imagined she might do such a thing. Perhaps her parents refused the Paris idea . . . that could be."

The detective observed attentively and remained perplexed by the man. The professor was peculiar with the femininely decorated house and original bathing hours. He acted like a housewife with no husband. But the Paris suggestion was interesting. If Rose had some sort of fragility, a blow from an authority figure like a father could break a person. But Willoughby wanted to see if the professor did any dabbling with his students.

"Are you married, sir," the detective said, looking around the room.

"No, no I'm not," acknowledging the discrepancy between the home and his masculinity. "My sister is desperate about it actually and decorated the house in hopes of making it more inviting for a permanent female presence," he chuckled awkwardly. His sister had never set foot in this house. It was he who had chosen everything in his home and he loved every last piece. But it was a perpetual source of questioning how he might be able to have such taste. So now he lied every time.

The detective did not respond, continuing with the interrogation.

"And your relationship with Miss Suggs was strictly a student-professor one? Pardon my asking but I am obligated," he apologized, though he needn't to. But it made people trust him, made them more apt to confide.

"Umm . . . yes, yes of course it was," the professor babbled. Rose wasn't going to rise up from the dead to blurt out they had kissed and his hands had wandered.

"So there would never be a reason for her to have come to this house," pursued Willoughby.

"Well," he answered slowly, "she might have passed by to hand in a paper or something. Oh yes once, she did, she dropped off an assignment and took a book back to her roommate for me, Miss Rousseau."

"So you know Miss Rousseau and Miss Suggs were roommates? Are you aware of the sleeping arrangements of all of your students, Professor Beardsmith," Willoughby pressed, silently congratulating himself for his instinct. It is difficult for the untrained to lie seamlessly under pressure. The professor had slipped and revealed a possible intimate relationship with not only one but two of his students, and one of which had turned up dead. Willoughby kept the burgeoning excitement under wraps but if he had been alone and was sure to be unheard, he would have hurled his fist up in the air and given a yelp of joy. This is why he loved his job.

The professor's cheeks had flushed. He took a deep breath in. There was no need to say anything about Rose but should he reveal his affair with Madeleine? The university would fire him undoubtedly for gross misconduct. She would get dismissed as well but her family had money; now it sounded like it was his career on the line really. Why hadn't she come to tell him anything? What a selfish girl. They should have gotten their stories straight for God's sake. Now he felt that everything he was saying was being written in stone while the detective watched, suspiciously.

The telephone rang. The professor let it ring twice, examining the detective's response. Willoughby was still standing, purposely exerting physical dominance over the Beardsmith. Willoughby nodded to the phone and the professor quickly got up and stumbled, catching his shoe on the corner of the carpet.

"You should have your sister fix that," Willoughby said before Beardsmith picked up the receiver.

"Hello, Professor Beardsmith," he heard on the other end of the line. It was Madeleine's voice. His instinct was to hang up immediately, claim a wrong number. But the detective was scrutinizing his every move. Had he heard Madeleine saying his name? Did he know it was her? What was this overwhelming feeling of guilt, paralyzing his normal behavior? Now he must be coming off as strange because of his racing thoughts. He calmed himself by remembering he was a well-respected college professor whose intelligence had been recognized. He didn't need to feel intimidated by this grotesque questioning.

Willoughby watched as the agitated man's forehead grew moist in a matter of seconds. He wasn't sure what involvement the professor may have had, if any, in the death of Rose Suggs but there was sufficient shame and guilt to make him a person of interest. Willoughby was prepared to jot any little clue to establish the complete picture of the student from Georgia whose body lay in the morgue.

Chapter 20

If only Madeleine hadn't invited Rose to New York, there would be no need to inform her aunt and uncle of the current situation. But Aunt Evelyn and Uncle Pierre had really taken a liking to all three girls, and especially to Rose. In that respect, she was no longer a threat to her uncle's love for his niece. Surely there was no comparison in his heart between the two but the weekend in the city had been a pivotal moment for the idealistic manner in which Madeleine viewed and respected her uncle. And even today, despite the tragedy, she still harbored anger toward Rose for having exposed that reality. Yes, he was only a man, one who could falter, but the very idea of it disgusted her.

Madeleine chose to write a letter, in the heat of the moment. A phone call may be more appropriate but wasn't prepared to handle their reaction; a reminder of Margot's death only a few years earlier. Madeleine pulled out a couple sheets of the thick paper with Margot's original letterhead to announce another girl's death. Her fingers reached into the drawer to find a pen. It reminded her that ever since she had lied about having lost the gold one, the janitor repeatedly asked her about it every chance he got. It grew tiresome and annoying really. Had he nothing better to do than to hound her about a lost pen?

"Poughkeepsie, New York
September 22, 1959

"Dear Uncle Pierre and Aunt Evelyn,
    How I hope this letter finds you well. I wish things here were
all right but unfortunately they are not. I am sorry to inform
you that my friend, Rose, whom you met last weekend, has

passed. She was unsuspectedly a very sad girl. To be honest, and I can only say this to the two of you without feeling as if I am betraying her, I had noticed a few things that now make more sense. Rose did a very good job at being a beautiful, radiant, and the light being we believed her to be. But there was a darkness, a force inside of her that was too much for her to bear. It breaks my heart to inflict more sad news onto you and I know your minds have jumped to think of our dear Margot. Know not a day passes where I don't reach out for my cousin, turn my head to speak with her, seek her out in the crowd. I feel she will never leave me. My only hope is that Margot has welcomed Rose up above with the love and kindness which defined her. It is a sad day, my dear aunt and uncle, but I find repose in the thought of them together, watching all of us from above and guarding us until we can all meet again, in His kingdom."

Perhaps "His kingdom" was a bit much. Uncle Pierre was what one would call *culturally* Catholic. He didn't believe in much, but he played along; knowing all of the prayers and the words to the hymns by heart. Aunt Evelyn had converted from being a Methodist to a Catholic when they married. As long as Jesus was the son of God, she was happy and made do with the rest of the variants. At the Catholic school Madeleine attended with Margot, they had been obliged to do their first communion and later, their confirmation; publicly asserting their religious beliefs. Madeleine always struggled with the idea anyone stood between herself and God. He knew who she was, there was no need for a layman to translate anything. So when it came time for confession, she would invent credible sins which required minimal penance; never beyond one Our Father and four Hail Marys. A little white lie told to not hurt someone's feelings, borrowing a pencil and purposely forgetting to return it, she had a pool of harmless sins to pick from. The real dark secrets of her soul, she carefully stowed away;

even God didn't want to see those. As she grew older and socially attended religious ceremonies, be they baptisms or weddings, she systematically went to receive the host given by the priest, only meant for the Catholics who had recently confessed. Filled with withheld sins, she stood solemnly before every holy man announcing "the body of Christ" while holding up the consecrated wafer as it was placed into her cupped hands. Responding with the customary "Amen" before putting it in on her tongue, Madeleine thought they'd taste better dusted with cinnamon, in which case, she would have grabbed a handful.

It was time to warn Professor Beardsmith as the police might decide to speak with him. The detective on the case seemed like a thorough man. He visibly cared for his appearance and Madeleine was sure he did the same in his work. It was probable he would contact all of Rose's teachers but he was the only one who had been busy frolicking with a student on the afternoon Rose died. She wanted to tell him to say they had not seen one another. With Phyllis's alibi, she was safe. It certainly wasn't worth risking telling the truth about being together. If the professor told the truth, it would be his word against hers and she was very convincing. Besides, why would he contradict her? He had much more to lose than she did. She needed him to feel safe in their secret and continue to trust her.

The first floor of the Strong House had three telephone cabins to the left of the entranceway. Girls often left the accordion doors wide open, wanting their conversations with boys or general gossip to be overheard. Madeleine shut the door to the cabin as tight as possible, glancing through the small window into the entrance. Women were coming and going, greeting one another with the news of the southern girl who had killed herself. Like watching a silent film, the same scene repeated itself over and over again, with the same dropping of the jaws, hands covering their mouths, their eyes wide in disbelief. Madeleine turned abruptly back to her mission, dialing the professor's number. As soon as he picked up the line, the tone in his voice immediately revealed he was perhaps not alone.

"Hello, Professor Beardsmith? Yes professor, I'm so sorry to disturb you. I just called to inform you of Rose Suggs's passing. I wasn't sure you'd heard . . ." she said in a high-pitched, innocent yet heartbroken voice.

"Yes, I'm just here with Detective Willoughby who has just given me the awfully sad news. Thank you for your call. I'll be in touch. Thanks again," he'd replied and hung up abruptly.

The professor had purposely omitted her name. Though she hadn't been able to inform him of her alibi, she had communicated with him. He would reach out when possible. As Madeleine stepped out of the booth and turned to the staircase, a small hand intertwined its fingers with hers. Taken aback by unexpected physical contact, Madeleine pulled away swiftly to see the culprit of this unpleasant and unwarranted experience. It was Joanie, whose eyes were red from crying.

"Oh, Madeleine. I simply cannot believe this to be true. How could she? Why? We were all so happy . . ." she repeated the same words as the night before, not paying any mind to Madeleine's stricken expression. She had to act fast, bringing Joanie close for a hug, her purple cardigan made of itchy wool again began to irritate the inside of Madeleine's arm, like someone was tickling her skin with a feather. Rubbing Joanie's back to alleviate the sensation, she comforted her wails of sadness. All of the sudden, it was also unimaginable for Madeleine to muster yet another comment about "poor Rose." The other girls were walking by, looking over sympathetically, with their eyes full of pity, their lips pulled tight. Joanie caught sight of them and quickly took Madeleine's less resistant hand and guided her toward the stairs, away from the crowded lobby.

As the two were climbing the stairs, Janet, in yet another one of her unflattering outfits, stopped them.

"Madeleine, I wanted to let you know that I have organized for you to sleep in my room tonight and I've made other arrangements. I don't want you to have to go back in your room. We'll soon find another solution."

How to make people understand that she was fine to sleep in her room where they had seen Rose's dead body hanging off the ground and then carried away on a gurney? The fact of the matter was that there weren't any blood stains anywhere, so it wasn't unsanitary or such. Last night was one thing since it had only been a few hours since they had found Rose, but tonight, she wanted to be alone. Madeleine was exhausted at the idea of having to find an explanation as to why she was fine to sleep in her room. In fact, she was more than fine, it was the only thing she wanted. She looked at Janet and gave her best compassionate smile. The one which said, "Thank you for your kindness and catering to my feelings," and reached out to squeeze her arm. This was the most heart Madeleine had ever shown her and for some inexplicable reason, she was moved. She had managed to please a girl like Madeleine Rousseau, the kind of student who always made her feel ill at ease.

Madeleine gently pushed Joanie's fingers away and walked up the last flight of stairs. With her eyes forward, walking with intent, not turning to peep into Phyllis's room, her footsteps echoed in the hall. The few stragglers watched as Madeleine headed to the room in which Rose had been found dead. Each pair of eyes were following her every move. When Madeleine reached the door, she looked back down the hall for a second and saw all of the girls, eagerly awaiting some sort of expression in her face, in her eyes. A pin drop could be heard. There was nothing, the world had come to a standstill it seemed. No one dared to move or even breathe, expecting anything. Madeleine opened the door and closed it right back behind her, giving them nothing at all.

Chapter 21

"Detective Willoughby. How goes it? I figured you'd be coming by," said George Habersham, dressed in his coroner's attire. He was a strange bird. In fact, he resembled one. He had fine features, visibly high cheekbones, which caught the paper-thin skin of his face, giving it an angular shape. His wispy brown hair was nothing remarkable either but his deep-set eyes gave him a particular owl-like appearance, making small children either stare or hide behind their mother's skirts in fear. Willoughby figured he was the type of man who had always looked old, waiting for his age to finally catch up with his physique. They got along well, a kind of mutual respect strictly within the professional realm.

The coroner had invited him out once for a drink and Willoughby lied saying he had to get home to his wife. Lacey had been long gone but there was no reason to keep anyone on the force in the know about his marital distress. He was afraid that after a couple of beers, he might falter and talk about his failed marriage and perhaps even shed a tear. He needed the reputation of being weak like he needed a hole in the foot. Because of that, he was always put on his toughest demeanor around the coroner, giving him firm slaps on the back to thank the man who in fact, had sensed a fragility and had reached out when Willoughby had most needed a friend.

"Dr. Habersham, you know me all too well. When you said there may be more to this case, you had to know I'd be here right away. What has the body told you," Willoughby repeated the same phrase the coroner liked to use.

"Well, I'm not sure you are going to like what I have to say, detective, but I have a feeling you already knew that," Habersham said, pulling back the sheet to reveal the dead girl's chest. Willoughby kept his eyes on the coroner, wanting only to follow the doctor's finger which pointed to two distinct dark marks around the neck. But before he knew it, he stole a glance at her breasts. He wasn't even interested but curiosity got the best of him and only now could he really focus on what was being said instead of desperately trying not to drop his eyes. It was done, he had seen them. They were rather small for her size but nicely shaped, he noted.

"So as you can see there are two markings on the neck, this angled one and this lower one, straight across," the doctor said, indicating the dark bluish lines which ran across Rose's neck.

"Indeed. And what does that tell us, Doc," Willoughby urged.

"The body tells us it was not a suicide, detective. You see, straight across the neck here, indicates that someone strangled her from behind. Only then did they attach her to the pipe to make it look like she had hung herself. If she had hung herself, there would only be one marking on her neck and it would be at an angle. I'm afraid you've got yourself a homicide."

This had been the case to take on. Willoughby wanted all of the distractions available and this was ideal. Work long hours, avoid the loneliness, the questions, and most of all his mother who had arrived a couple of weeks ago. This was a case that needed solving and could earn him the respect he deserved after nearly six years in Poughkeepsie. Lacey hadn't lasted but four years here before traveling back and forth to New York only to ultimately run off with another man. At first, Willoughby had said she was staying with her ill mother in Staten Island for an indeterminate amount of time when people asked. He had gone as far as to fake conversations on the phone at his desk so others would hear.

"Yes honey, of course I understand, darling. I know you only have one mother, tell me about it! Yes, I have everything I need, don't worry about me."

After a while, his mother-in-law's terminal illness hadn't terminated her life. He couldn't bring himself to lie about her dying so the situation maintained his suffering and humiliation as it dragged on. Finally, the guys at the precinct stopped asking about Lacey and her sick mother. A few had even offered for Willoughby to come have dinner, alone, in their homes while she was away. He always kindly refused and now his own mother had come to care for her only son despite his reluctance.

"So, she was strangled? You are sure of it," Willoughby asked, writing in his notepad.

Dr. Habersham looked up at him with his wide owl-like eyes, not answering the question.

"Of course, you are. All right, well, I'd better go and file some paperwork for the homicide and let the guys know we've got a different situation on our hands," he stated, replacing the notepad back in his coat pocket.

"Do you have any idea who could have done this to her, detective? Anyone you already have suspicions about?" Dr. Habersham enjoyed asking detectives; curious if their instincts worked as well as they bragged about in the break room.

"Doctor, I'm suspicious about everyone and everything. So yes, I've already got an idea who I might need to speak to about this young girl's death," Willoughby replied.

And with that, for some unknown reason, he took the white sheet and drew it back over Rose's rigid body, accidentally grazing her left breast as he did it. Immediately flustered, he moved away from the table, awkwardly patting Dr. Habersham too hard on the back and walking out of the room before his visible embarrassment showed.

"I'll read your report in the morning, doctor. Thank you, again," he yelled as he ran up the stairs, feeling the rising heat in his cheeks.

Rose's side of the room had been left intact. Her things were sprawled out, no indication she wasn't going to be returning from a date with a boy shortly or walking in with her arms full of books from the library. As she scanned the room, Madeleine wondered if Rose's parents intended to collect her things. They might send for them, not wanting to see where their daughter had died, forever ingraining the vision in their minds. Along the wall ran the pipe which had held the knotted scarf around her neck. Madeleine ran her hand over the part that was only a few feet off of the ground. It went all the way to her side of the room, and she had used it to prop a few frames on it. She had a beautiful black and white photograph in Central Park which Uncle Pierre had taken. There were pigeons flying around and Aunt Evelyn was protecting young Margot and Madeleine with a shawl. It had originally belonged to her cousin and she had asked Aunt Evelyn to take it to school, saying it would always make her smile. But tonight it did not make her smile. She stared at her dead cousin's face, familiar feelings of utter void and emptiness.

Sitting at Rose's desk, she opened the center drawer, ruffling a few loose-leaf sheets of paper, her fingers exploring where her eyes couldn't reach. At the very back and under a handkerchief was a small rectangular velvet box. She pulled it out, curious to discover what was inside. A beautiful gold ballpoint pen laid on a bed of velour. Tucked into the top of the box was a folded piece of paper.

> *"Dearest Maddie,*
>
>   *Thank you for having been such a wonderful friend. I know how sad you were to have misplaced your gold pen. This one won't replace the sentimental value of the other, but I hope you may accept it as a token of our friendship and my gratitude for your trust and generosity.*
>
>   *With all my affection,*
>   *Rose"*

Rose had mentioned to Madeleine she had a surprise for her. Such a thoughtful gesture and surely a thank-you gift for the trip to New York. She must have gone there when she'd left the girls at lunch. And here Madeleine had been convinced she'd been upset about her former lover, when in fact she'd gone to buy her a gift. The true coincidence was she had purchased the pen from the very same store Uncle Pierre bought all of his writing apparatus in the city. Uncanny really. It was the exact match to the one she had dropped in the lake; how could she have known? Unless Uncle Pierre had taken Rose there of course. She quickly pushed the enraging thought out of her mind.

Needing some fresh air, she changed her shoes for black patent leather flats so as to be more discreet in her movements as it was nearing curfew. Rose had complimented her on those very shoes, saying she had long been looking for the same style. Madeleine had lied, about having bought them in Paris, hoping she wouldn't go looking for the exact same pair. Before heading out, Madeleine caught sight of herself in the mirror. Reflecting back was smooth skin without even an ounce of fatigue. With the light at this angle, the color difference between her eyes was flagrant. She covered half of her face with her right hand and then did the same with her left. Mother had been concerned her heterochromia would make an already particular daughter stand out even more, but that was not the source of Madeleine's unruly behavior. The year before little Mary's broken arm incident, Madeleine had spat in a boy's face and sprained his finger. The same finger he had used to point and mock her different eyes. She had shown no remorse for it whatsoever, explaining logically to her mother it was her right to defend herself, even physically. Eventually, Mother believed Madeleine had matured, but in fact, she had simply become smarter and more discrete in her revenge plots; creating, and executing them without a trace.

She checked the time as any comings and goings would duly be noted by at least one of the girls from the floor. They were probably keeping watch, wondering how she could be in the same room where her roommate was found hanging. Madeleine walked silently down the hall of the dormitory and heard shuffling behind her.

As she neared the end of the hall and approaching the stairs, Janet appeared again out of nowhere.

"Everything all right Madeleine? Have you changed your mind? I'm more than happy to let you sleep in my room," she spurted out, uncomfortably.

"Thank you but I am just going to see Phyllis and Joanie if you don't mind. I know it's past curfew but I just . . . ," she said quietly, veering toward their door, side-stepping her desire to be alone, outside in the darkness.

"Given the circumstances, please do."

Madeleine gently knocked on Phyllis and Joanie's door and walked right in. The two of them were on their respective beds, reading in silence. They had exhausted all conversation and found comfort in each other's muted presence.

"Madeleine. Are you okay? Do you want to come and stay with us," Joanie immediately asked, longing to ease their mourning together.

Madeleine smiled as best she could. Janet wouldn't stay in the hall forever.

"I just wanted to see the two of you for a bit. I'll go back in a minute," she explained.

Phyllis hadn't said a word. She opened up the blanket as an invitation for Madeleine to come and crawl inside. And she did just that, removing her flats and sliding into the warmth, searching for Phyllis's feet with her own. The contact between their two bodies made Phyllis's heart palpitate, but she kept reading her book. Madeleine turned toward Joanie and they were speaking quietly about Rose and the remains of the day. Madeleine's feet kept rubbing Phyllis's, trying to remove the cold.

After about twenty minutes, Madeleine turned to Phyllis. "Thank you," she said and opened up the blanket to extract herself from the safe cocoon. Phyllis wanted to reach out and keep her from leaving. She fantasized about the most physical contact possible while they were in bed together; a head nestled into a shoulder, a thigh laying across her waist. But Madeleine had already stood up. She leaned over, tucking Phyllis back in and kissed her softly on the cheek, leaving behind her usual arousing perfume. Intoxicated by Madeleine's fleeting presence, Phyllis hoped only that the sweet scent might have lingered on the pillow. She rolled her face right into it as Madeleine closed the door and inhaled deeply. It had.

Janet meticulously continued roaming the halls like a shepherd guarding her flock, forcing Madeleine to retreat back to her room. Discouraged she couldn't step outside, she opened the window between the two beds and took a deep breath letting the cool night air rinse away her thoughts. Across the quad, in one of the other dormitories, she watched as the lights turned off in the windows, one by one, preparing the campus for darkness. A gust of wind blew, sending miscellaneous papers on Rose's desk flying. Madeleine watched them land on the ground, wondering what words had last been written by her dead roommate. Her pondering was interrupted by a loud knock at the door. She was stricken as she heard men's voices outside. There was another insistent knock as she shut the window, tore off her sweater, and stood in her brassiere. The door opened and Detective Willoughby stood before her, followed by a few officers in uniform.

Madeleine gasped and crossed her arms over her nearly bare chest. Detective Willoughby, embarrassed, immediately turned around as did the rest of the men.

"Uh . . . Miss Rousseau . . . pardon the interruption . . . ," he rambled awkwardly.

"What are you doing here, detective," asked Madeleine, seeming offended he hadn't awaited a response to barge in.

"I am going to need you to leave the room as is. This is now a crime scene," he answered with confidence this time. He did not like her tone.

"Excuse me? What do you mean a crime scene? You want me to walk out right now, out of this room in front of you and your men in this attire? What in God's name . . . ," Madeleine managed to say all in one breath.

"Miss Rousseau, do not touch anything, as you leave this room.

Your roommate was murdered and we now have a homicide investi-gation on our hands," Willoughby stated without any emotion.

"What? Murdered?" she cried out in disbelief.

"I cannot discuss this with you at the moment, we need to examine the room with a fine-tooth comb. Please leave," he asked her again, his back still turned to her.

Madeleine leaned toward her bed to grab the sweater she had just thrown off.

"Arrest me if you need officer but I am putting my sweater back on before you and your men get any more inappropriate enjoyment out of springing into young women's rooms without being asked to enter. Shame on you," she ranted.

Sheepish, Detective Willoughby was surprised at his own reaction. It was his absolute legal right to demand she exit the room immedi-ately. He quickly glanced over as she pulled the sweater over her head. Her brassiere was black with fine lace; quite unexpected for a girl her age. He'd once bought Lacey an expensive set as a surprise, to try and rekindle the flame a few years back, but it had been to no avail. The flame had withered and been blown out for much too long, and today she was probably wearing the lingerie with her new beau, prancing around New York City with nearly half a month's salary under her clothes. If Miss Rousseau's family had money to spend on such under-garments, he was curious about who they were.

"Miss Rousseau, I'd like to ask you a few questions in the morning. Where will you be staying," he said, attempting a nicer tone.

"It seems I can't very well stay in my own room so I will go and find other accommodations for the night. This is honestly very abrupt and very shocking; after everything I have already been put through . . . ," and as her voice shook, her eyes welled with tears. She grabbed her purse from the desk, her new gold pen inside, and her navy coat from the hanger, turning to the detective.

"Do you mind if I take these or do you need them for your investigation as well," without awaiting an answer, she stormed out of the room, leaving the detective and his men speechless.

Madeleine's exit had been a spectacle only to end up knocking on Phyllis and Joanie's door. Where else would she go at this hour, head into town and get a hotel room? The safest and easiest solution was this one for the time being.

When Phyllis opened the door, Madeleine fell into her arms, her eyes still wet. Phyllis held her tight, more than happy to console her.

"Madeleine, where are you going with your coat? Are you leaving?" panic setting into Phyllis's voice.

"No, no, well . . . yes, I mean, may I sleep here again," she asked, wiping away tears.

"Of course, you can. I told you it was too much to be in that horrible room. Here, give me your coat," she said as she hung it up in the closet.

As Madeleine pulled back with a half smile, she had to give them the news.

"Girls, the reason I can't sleep in my own room is because the police returned."

"What? What are they doing here at this hour," Joanie had shot up from her bed to have a peek down the hall. "Oh, you're right, they are there!"

"This is atrocious. I cannot believe it is true. They must be mistaken," Madeleine said, shaking her head from side to side. "They believe Rose was murdered," she whispered. Joanie gasped loudly, clasping her hands over her mouth. Phyllis just stared at Madeleine.

"What? But we saw her . . . hanging," Phyllis said as she sat down on the bed, her face drained of color.

"Do they know who did it? Should we be scared? I'm putting a chair against the door. Maybe someone is going to come back here and kill us! Oh my, what's going to happen," Joanie was spiraling, her breath shallow and rapid. Grabbing Joanie by the collar, Madeleine slapped her hard. Joanie's cheek reddened as did her entire face. She stood there, stunned.

"You are going into hysterics. There is nothing for us to do right now but try and get some rest. We'll surely have questions to answer again in a few hours. Being in a panic is not bringing back our friend, so breathe, calm down, and get to bed. I cannot talk anymore about this or my head will explode. Please," Madeleine spoke firmly to Joanie who obeyed immediately like a scolded child. Immense fatigue swept over her as she turned to Phyllis, who'd watched the entire scene in dismay.

Phyllis wanted to say something in Joanie's defense. Surely the behavior she'd witnessed was due to the extraordinary circumstances and really only wanted to console Madeleine again. So instead, respecting the demand for silence, she handed her friend a nightgown. It would surely be too large for her petite figure but at least it was more comfortable. While Madeleine changed over by the desk, Phyllis peered at her friend. Despite knowing each other for the past several years, she had rarely seen Madeleine's body. It wasn't that either of them was particularly prude but there simply hadn't been many occasions as they did not share a room. On their trip to New York, she had gotten stuck with Joanie again. With burning curiosity, she discreetly peered over, pretending to tidy up her side. As Madeleine pulled off her sweater, wearing nothing underneath, not even an undershirt, only the outline of black lace stood out against the pale skin of her back. When she unsnapped the bra and turned briefly to place it on the chair, Phyllis caught a glimpse of the side of her left breast. It certainly was not the lack of light in the room which made her pupils dilate and hold her breath. Pushing Rose out of her mind, she jumped into bed and turned to face the wall, shutting her eyes tight as can be to burn the beautiful image into her brain, saving it for later, when alone, she could imagine touching it.

Madeleine, in the oversized nightgown, got into the bed gently, pulling the blanket high over her shoulder. Coming close to espousing the shape of Phyllis's body with her own, she reached over and took her hand. Phyllis couldn't help but smile. Here was this strong girl, always in control and organized it seemed, knowing what to say and do, but at times, like now, she was like a child needing to be comforted and cared for. Phyllis knew she wouldn't sleep a wink but didn't care. Despite the news of the murder, with Madeleine close by, she felt safe.

Chapter 22

Willoughby returned home late purposely to avoid his mother. He wasn't so keen on the company but couldn't complain about the homemade meals. It beat the bologna and mustard sandwiches he had perfected by adding slices of kosher pickles and a touch of honey. His mother's cooking was one of the few things he did love about her. It was long past midnight when Willoughby finished turning the dorm room inside out. He didn't care that he'd annoyed the forensic photographer by asking him to return in the morning for the exterior of Strong House, specifically with the metal steps attached to the side of the building he had spotted on the first day. He was thorough like no one else.

On the formica table was a note to heat up the lasagna but Willoughby was too lazy to wait the twenty-five minutes as instructed. He wasn't even particularly hungry but when opening the oven door, a warm and delicious smell tickled his salivary glands instantly. His mother had kept the oven on low and stayed up as late as she could, knowing her son wouldn't take the time to heat the meal. Arthur took the pink Pyrex dish out and, not bothering with a plate, he dug in with a spoon. Lacey used to make her famous peach cobbler in the very same dish. He thought he had done everything right to make her happy, but it wasn't enough. As the tasty ground meat melting into the sheet of pasta entered his mouth, he made a mental observation: remember to be grateful his mother was here when in the morning her pestering questions began along with his irritation. He anticipated the conversation: why did he come home so late, how was he ever to meet someone new, were they officially divorced, if she ever comes across Lacey in the neighborhood, she was going to give her something to cry about, and so on and so forth. The phone calls to the station also had to stop. It had gotten beyond embarrassing. The Poughkeepsie station was small and everyone could hear when his new secretary, Frances, read out his messages. Glances were exchanged, but nothing was said. His mother had even asked whether Frances was potentially an interesting prospect for him. Far from it, Frances was older and exactly what he needed to keep him straight at work. She was diligent, minded her own business, and did the odd bit of digging if he asked. He was careful to only use those favors when absolutely necessary. But Frances was in no way physically interesting to him. Strangely enough, he couldn't get the Madeleine Rousseau girl out of his mind and wondered about the potential involvement in the death of her roommate. Why had she gotten so aggressive when he'd asked her to leave? Had she wanted more time in the room to hide evidence? She had said that the scarf the victim used was hers, but that didn't mean she used it herself. Or did it? She had a frustrating way of wiggling herself into his imagination. Was it her righteousness, which annoyed him immensely? The tone she had used with him now felt both dismissive and condescending as he replayed the conversation. He hated when people believed they were better than him. While rummaging through the dorm room, touching her luxurious knits and lingerie had nearly given him an erection. He had slipped his hand over one particular light yellow Angora sweater and imagined her full breasts underneath it. They would be firm from their youth and yet still have the softness of well-rounded bosoms. Before it became obvious to the other officers on the scene, he had had to shake off the fantasy. As always, he'd thought of baseball to clear his mind. Would the Los Angeles Dodgers beat the Milwaukee Braves in the tie-breaker games for the National League he'd wondered, moving away from the girl's personal effects.

Arthur Willoughby was eager to get the files of potential suspects and important witnesses which would be ready in the morning, including one on the Rousseau girl. Apparently, she and her friends, including the victim, had gone to New York the weekend prior and stayed with Rousseau's family. Perhaps they might have noticed something during the trip. This was the ideal occasion to return to the city while questioning the Rousseaus about their impression of the victim. He had not gone since Lacey left and for the first time, his excitement grew at the thought of seeing New York again. The idea made him feel more alive than he had in a very long time. The tide was turning and he was ready for this change in his life. Solving the case, divorcing Lacey, all of it would set him free and that's what he believed he wanted now: freedom. But for tonight, he'd settle for finishing up the lasagna, lying down, and closing his eyes.

Chapter 23

Borrowing a robe from Phyllis, Madeleine tip-toed out of the room and headed to the bathroom before either girl awakened. In the hall-way stood an officer, guarding the door to her bedroom at this early hour. Since they were now part of a crime scene, all of her things were inaccessible until the police were done combing them for any types of clues. How long would she have to wear the same clothes? Phyllis was half her height and double her weight and Madeleine wouldn't be caught dead in Joanie's clothes. She was going to have to try and sway the man into letting her take a couple of things before Detective Willoughby returned.

More easily than she expected her mission to be, Madeleine walked across campus in the black dress she'd procured using her charm, see-ing the other girls whisper as soon as she passed by. She didn't give them a second thought, marching confidently to the English Depart-ment with *Season in Hell*, and other of Rimbaud's works stacked in her arms. It was best to not risk going to Professor Beardsmith's house for the time being as the campus was still crawling with police offi-cers asking questions about Rose. They did not need to uncover the extracurricular activities in which she was partaking. Dressed in the traditional mourning color, she entered the office with her head down. When Doris Hoxenbury saw her, she removed her reading glasses and swiftly circumvented the desk to hug Madeleine, her eyes filling with compassion. Madeleine had had barely enough time to create a bar-rier between their two bodies with the books, limiting the intimacy the secretary seemed so desperate for.

"Madeleine, dear. You have my deepest condolences. Truly. I can-not imagine how you must be feeling at the moment," she said observing her keenly. "Miss Suggs was in here a few days ago. I cannot believe she is no longer with us."

"Thank you. I must speak with Professor Beardsmith," she began, "It's about Rose actually." She wriggled herself away and toward the professor's office.

"Oh, of course, go right in. I'll hold off any calls or visitors," Doris offered as she stood there, crossing her arms. She had satisfyingly proved her hypothesis concerning the Rousseau girl's aversion for unwarranted physical touch.

Beardsmith had risen from his chair to greet Madeleine as soon as she walked in. Any more touching might make her ill, so she quickly went to sit across from him, safely on the other side of the desk. Taking the hint, he placed both of his hands on the armrests and gently eased himself back down, sighing loudly.

"Can you believe it? That poor girl," he lamented. He barely made eye contact before glancing down at his desk again. His predictability now annoyed Madeleine. Couldn't he find anything more original to say? From a cultured man to stoop to the levels of basic disbelief removed any remaining attraction she had for him. Waiting for her cue to discuss details of their whereabouts the afternoon Rose was killed, the professor played with his pen gently shaking his head.

Careful not to reveal her brewing annoyance, Madeleine took a deep breath and sighed heavily too, allowing tears to well up on command.

"I can't. I simply can't believe she's gone." And here she needed him to feel manly and protective of her. "Oh Andrew, I can't help but imagine that if I had been there, not with you, then perhaps I could have saved her."

Beardsmith rose from his chair and knelt before Madeleine.

"Oh, darling, you mustn't think that. Thank goodness you were with me. She was murdered, you could have gotten yourself killed as well. You are perhaps still alive because we were together."

As the words came out of his mouth, Madeleine watched the wheels turning. She interrupted, bringing them to grinding halt: "Should we say we were together? I've already said I was with Phyllis and she agreed to lie since she too was alone. Do you have an alibi . . . ? I know it would mean your removal from the school and my dismissal . . . Oh Andrew, what do we do," Madeleine continued, breathless. She had a natural knack for dramatization, easily inspired by Joanie's recent performances. Beardsmith was weighing the possibility of having a strong alibi but with the assurance of being fired and ruining his career.

"For the moment we must say nothing. I did not mention your visit. I said I was home alone and there is no reason they would tie me to her death; I had no reason to kill her. Anyhow, they said she was murdered between two and seven p.m. and though I don't remember what time you left precisely, it was still daylight. So that still means that there are a few hours I truly was alone . . . ," he said, silently reflecting on his last phrase.

On his desk was a file with *Summer Exchange: La Sorbonne, Paris, France* written across it.

"And here she was, so excited about Paris this summer," she said.

The professor got up, glancing out of the window for a few moments. In all fairness, he had used the program as a motivator to exchange more with Rose than notes on her presentation. He hadn't thought she confided in Madeleine.

"I saw how much it meant to her," he said, pensive. "And with your family connections, I know getting to Paris is not a problem. This was her only chance of experiencing it with her parents perhaps agreeing to it."

The explanation angered Madeleine. Unbeknownst to the professor, this *was* her only ticket and he had tried to hand it off to someone else after she'd put in so much time and effort securing it. Madeleine stood up rapidly and he followed suit, taking her in his arms, nuzzling in her neck. She stood, rigid, forcing herself to relax and wrapping an arm around his back.

"Besides, I was hoping you would do some summer classes here instead," as he began to gently kiss her face, searching for her mouth. Every additional second spent in contact with the professor was proving extremely irritating for Madeleine.

"You know Professor Steinberg fought tooth and nail for Elizabeth Kraus to go, so maybe I should let her have the junior spot anyway."

A rush came over Madeleine, she felt her blood surge to the surface and her grip tighten on his back. She wanted to rip his skin right off or better yet, sink her teeth into his soft flesh. Disgust made her clench and Beardsmith mistook her firm grip for arousal, pressing against her even more. Afraid to not be able to stop herself and knee him in the groin, Madeleine leaned into his ear and whispered:

"Let's make a promise not to say anything to anyone. About where we were, about Rose, about Paris, all of it is our little secret," and with that she bit his ear, hard enough to make him pull back. Satisfied with having pained him, she smiled coyly and turned to leave the room. All of the sudden he slammed his hand on the door, keeping Madeleine from opening it.

"Don't tease and then leave. It's very unbecoming. And you know how much I despise it," he said, clasping her wrist tightly and forcing her to face him.

"I have an appointment with Detective Willoughby," Madeleine swiftly responded. "And seeing as you have no alibi for when Rose was murdered, I don't think I should keep him waiting."

Beardsmith's fervent desire cooled quickly. Madeleine often surprised herself with the lack of hesitance with which untruths came flying out of her mouth. The professor released his grip at the mention of the man who had come into his home and probed with persistent questioning. Madeleine stared into his eyes with an anger he'd never seen. He took a step back. She said nothing more and left. Doris Hoxenbury, not visible from behind the filing cabinet, saw the disheveled student wipe her eyes, fix the scarf around her neck, and smooth her dark hair before walking out of the department office.

Chapter 24

Upon Detective Willoughby's request, all of the evidence had been placed in a small unused room of the station, solely dedicated to solving the Rose Suggs murder. Frances had arranged along the wall the photos returned from the crime scene. Most of the victim's personal items were displayed on the long table against the window, including the silk murder weapon. It was an unusual request to devote an entire room to a case, but then again, it was unusual to have such a case in Poughkeepsie. The town was calm and quiet, so the local police was rarely overwhelmed with homicides, let alone murders. But Willoughby knew to seize an opportunity when it struck. This was the one he needed to solve to get his life back on track. Already, a journalist from the local paper had gotten hold of the story, obliging the detective to work even faster.

Frances came in with a steaming cup of coffee as Willoughby pored over each and every element belonging to the victim. Each paper from Rose's desk, her clothing, her jewelry, everything was now in this room. The detective wanted to immerse himself completely in her life so he might find a clue as to who had wrapped a scarf so tightly around her neck and taken her last breath away. It was only when he began rummaging through the clothing and accessories that his patience and precision proved fruitful.

From a cardboard box, he removed a dark green purse with a large flap and a golden metal clasp. It was small and square shaped, almost like an oversized wallet rather than a handbag. Inside were a few folded papers, a pencil. But in the lining he felt something. In a secret fold of the material, Willoughby found an opening. With difficulty, he got one finger in the tight pocket, pushing the zipper open. He felt a small notebook and after a few seconds, managed to get it close enough to pull it out. It was a very thin black leather notebook with the initials "RS" embossed in gold lettering on the cover. He ran his fingers over them before turning to the first page.

"Atlanta, November 9, 1958

The dearest Rose of my heart,
May this be the resting place for all of your secret thoughts
when we are apart, even the ones which make your cheeks
redden. Write them here for safekeeping, for them to be sacred,
for them to only be ours. I long for you to lay in my arms again.
With more love than this ink can hold,
H . . ."

Willoughby couldn't quite make out the signature. The inscription had been written nearly a year ago. As he continued through the notebook, stopping to read a couple excerpts only to discover this was the same man who had gotten her pregnant. From confiding her innermost thoughts about their future life together to the birth of newborn she parted with, the penmanship had taken a turn as well. Rose's handwriting at the start of the notebook was perfectly cursive, smooth, with the right curves and inclines. As the entries progressed, the writing became tighter and heavier, not as tidy and airy as before. Willoughby had trouble reading the later entries, deciphering a few words. It had softened again, coinciding with the period of her arrival at Vassar College. Rose was enjoying herself again, writing about a new life and new friends far from the boring gossip, the history, and the weight of expectation of her life in Atlanta. It seemed the young woman had made up her mind and had no intention of ever returning to the south, noting the quickest way would be with a man. She mentioned Professor Beardsmith a couple of times but it was the entry after the return from New York which was revelatory. Willoughby could practically feel the excitement in Rose's handwriting.

> *"I suppose when a rich, handsome, intelligent, kind man says you have talent, it's worth believing. Pierre (he asked me to call him that instead of Uncle Pierre, which makes sense since he is NOT my uncle!) He truly believes I should try singing professionally, he even offered to reach out to a few people at the clubs."*

So, Pierre Rousseau had offered to help a young college girl, friend of his niece. Willoughby had asked Frances to make some calls, only to find out he was one of the wealthiest men in New York City. This made it difficult to imagine a person of his status interested in such a girl, nevertheless he'd add the French man, along with father of Rose's child, to the list of people to speak to directly. He would leave no stone left unturned.

When the call from the Poughkeepsie Police Department was patched through to Dr. Portman's office at New York University, his secretary hurriedly ran to cut short the professor's class, sensing the urgency of the call. Dr. Portman was wrapping up his lecture and often lagged behind at the end of class. He fared well with his Paul Newman-like eyes and southern drawl, captivating certain students more than others. Faculty rumors about his flirtatious attitude eventually made their way back to Portman's ears, who had addressed them head on, laughing them off and explaining they were mistaking his agreeable personality and upbringing for inappropriate behavior, of which he was incapable, seeing as he was happily married and a soon-to-be father. Disarmed by the manner in which he had handled the situation, and with the excitement and the publicity his next publication was going to bring to the university, all was easily forgiven and forgotten and the newly arrived Dr. Portman could continue blurring the lines of decency undisturbed.

"This is Dr. Hartford Portman," he said as he picked up the receiver in his office. He needn't insist on the "Dr." part of his name, Willoughby thought. To which he replied:

"Detective Arthur Willoughby here. How do you do?"

A pregnant Mrs. Portman walked in silently, showing her watch. They had a lunch appointment in twenty minutes with another couple whose social circle she was trying to integrate. She hated being late. Dr. Portman, not wanting to hear about it for the next few days, wrapped his arm around his wife and kissed her hard, buying himself a few minutes. Flushed, she took a step back and smiled at her charmer of a husband.

"What can I do for you, detective?"

"Do you know a young woman by the name of Rose Suggs?"

Dr. Portman's appearance remained calm but his mind raced. What had she done? Was this about the child? Was she about to ruin his life? He had not told his wife about the incident last year before the wedding.

"I do," he answered, wanting to reveal as little a possible, but the slight inflection in his voice made Mrs. Portman turn to him.

"She was murdered in her dormitory at Vassar College . . ."

Portman had stopped listening. He was sorry such a beautiful creature had passed but it also meant there was no risk of a knock at the door in the future, with Rose and a child on her hip, prepared to reveal his darkest secret. He'd thought of multiple nightmarish scenarios where this occurred, one more catastrophic than the next. Her family would have never allowed it but Rose was fearless and capable of anything. That's also what had attracted him.

"I am heartbroken to hear that. She could have had a wonderful future. I know her family, what a tragedy."

His wife looked at him wide-eyed and he gave her a saddened, tight-lipped nod, as if to say, "We have to accept the injustices of life."

Willoughby heard the insincerity with which the words were coming out of the man's mouth.

"You had fathered a child with Rose Suggs, is that correct, doctor?" Willoughby asked, purposely pressing Portman.

"Uhm, I suppose you could say so."

The detective wanted the professor to know he knew about the baby. But it served no true purpose. Unfortunately, Portman had an indisputable alibi as he had been teaching classes all afternoon, therefore over fifty eyewitnesses to vouch for his whereabouts. There wasn't enough time between his last class to travel to Poughkeepsie and back. Willoughby didn't want to pin a murder on an innocent man but the arrogance which had seeped through the phone was enough to provoke a call to the Portman residence later in the week and hopefully speak to Mrs. Portman, perhaps even casually dropping in the conversation the existence of an illegitimate child.

Willoughby pulled out his small notepad and crossed "Portman" off of the list. Above it was written "Pierre Rousseau." Frances popped her head into the office, paper in hand.

"I spoke to Pierre Rousseau and he said him and his wife are en route for Poughkeepsie and are happy to meet and answer any questions at your convenience."

And above Pierre Rousseau's name, was Madeleine Rousseau.

Chapter 25

The school announced a moment of silence to be held for Rose on Saturday at two in the afternoon. Phyllis had taken refuge in the library; a place where everyone followed the rules. The silence was like a comfortable blanket she wrapped herself in for hours. Spreading books and papers across the entire table, little room was left for anyone to join. Phyllis had not come to Vassar to make friends. Joanie and Madeleine were merely incidental. She hadn't expected for them, especially Madeleine, to become important in her life. This morning, a letter had come from her father announcing he had finally obtained the interview at the State Department. If next summer's internship could be secured, she would be well on the way to paving her road to success.

Despite trying to concentrate on the future, she was constantly distracted by the lie told to the police. She was proud to be a law-abiding citizen. Always. The way Madeleine initially had suggested it, it had sounded like an innocent lie. She was her friend and didn't want her to get into any sort of trouble because of a ridiculous escapade with a professor. Besides she was bound to get bored with him sooner or later. Phyllis wasn't able to comprehend what it was that made so many of Professor Beardsmith's students swoon. She found him utterly classic in both his views and his looks. He had never surprised her with an original point of view she hadn't already thought of or read in a literary magazine. But now that Rose's suicide had turned into a murder, she was obstructing justice by lying. This could go on her record, her police record which was as virginal as she was. She had to speak to Madeleine. Surely, she would know what to do.

As if she had willed her into existence, Madeleine opened the heavy wooden front door of the library and headed for the stairs, hoping to find Phyllis at their usual spot. In her presence Phyllis's soul was soothed and this time was no exception. They were in this together. Despite the chaos of the situation, Madeleine was still impeccable. Her hair was pulled back into a low ponytail with perfect dark brown curls on the ends. Her pink and black silk scarf was wrapped just right around her pale neck, tied with a small bow tucked to the side. She sat down and took Phyllis's hand in hers, making her feel warm all over.

"Oh honey, I think it's best we not change our story. What do you say," Madeleine asked. Phyllis had never seen her friend's eyes look as different as they did today.

"I suppose. Or we tell the detective the truth? I don't want you to get in trouble though . . . but Madeleine, Rose was murdered! The man who did this may still be roaming around here and I think telling the police the whole truth might be the safest way for us," Phyllis blurted in a shaky voice. The sensations of warmth and anxiety spreading with every pulsation in her temples.

"The campus is crawling with policemen Phyllis. No one is going to hurt us. I too was thinking of telling Detective Willoughby the truth but then I thought of you . . . Of course I would be dismissed and the Beardsmith fired for gross misconduct but you, well, you've already lied and most importantly, what alibi do you have all afternoon? What if they pin the murder on you," Madeleine responded in a hushed voice.

Phyllis gasped. She was not prone to dramatic reactions but had never considered being a potential suspect. "But I was here and then in my room studying . . . ," she said, thinking out loud. Madeleine watched as it dawned on her friend.

"Exactly, you were close to the murder scene, with no one to account for your whereabouts for hours and Joanie was at the meeting. Therefore, if we change our story, you become a potential murderer. Oh, Phyllis, as soon as I realized this, I wanted to warn you. I can't have anything happen to you." Madeleine hugged her close, purposely letting her lips graze her neck.

"We will get through this," she mumbled, brushing a piece of hair out of Phyllis's face. "May I sleep with you again tonight? They've arranged another room for me, but I'd like it better if I could be close to you. If you don't mind . . . until my aunt and uncle arrive. Then I'll go to the hotel."

Phyllis wanted to snuggle in the small twin bed with her as long as possible. Even if it meant she laid awake all night, watching Madeleine's thin delicate fingers and perfectly filed nails resting on her forearm.

"Of course you can. I . . . Do you really think they'll consider me a suspect? That's ridiculous, why in God's name would I do that to Rose. I have no motive, we were friends. As if I could ever kill anyone . . ." Phyllis felt her cheeks go hot and her eyes get wet. All she wanted was to go back to studying, bury herself in facts, analysis, and research. Things she could control.

Chapter 26

The Warnock House was Poughkeepsie's most charming inn. A welcoming front porch lined with red wooden rocking chairs, to be put away for the winter, and a lovely autumn wreath on the front door giving it a quaint, provincial style. Madeleine walked up the front steps, preparing to meet her aunt and uncle. They had been called by the police and informed about the homicide. The decision was to rush and be with their niece to answer the local police directly. Madeleine's parents had phoned but she was in no haste to return their call. She had brushed it off as usual. They were useless to her. Out of sight, out of mind, she thought and ran up to the suite Aunt Evelyn and Uncle Pierre had reserved and knocked on the door.

It swung open and Aunt Evelyn stood with open arms, welcoming Madeleine who eagerly accepted the invitation.

"Oh my sweet, sweet Madeleine," she said firmly holding her shoulders. "How on earth . . . let me see your beautiful face. How are you my sweet girl? Here I made some tea, sit down and tell us everything."

Madeleine slowly peeled herself from her aunt as she heard Uncle Pierre's shoes clicking in the hallway walking towards them. She inhaled deeply and slid her hand into her aunt's, seeking an anchor to get through this. Uncle Pierre without hesitation came over and embraced Madeleine.

"Oh, Rose," Uncle Pierre lamented. Madeleine's entire body stiffened.

"Why are you calling me Rose?"

"Oh, *chérie*, I was not calling you Rose, only saying her name. I'm so, so sorry, Madeleine," he continued while wrapping her shoulders. Normally, Madeleine might embrace her uncle's fit torso but this time she held Aunt Evelyn's hand tight. Had he been crying? Madeleine stared into her uncle's eyes; they were red.

Aunt Evelyn led her to the living room part of the suite where she had disposed three delicate china bone teacups and the matching teapot along with a plate of assorted cookies. She scrunched her face at the sight of those with the unidentifiable piece of red candied fruit on top. Her inexplicable despise for those particular biscuits had originated in the forgotten memory of her brother forcing them into her mouth as a toddler. Examining the rest of the table, she wondered how in the world her aunt found a way to make every place she was in her own. Madeleine sat next to her while Uncle Pierre took a seat in the flower-patterned sofa on the other side.

"I cannot thank you enough for coming. It's been a horrible twenty-four hours of my life. I haven't even wrapped my head around the fact I will never see her again and . . . there was a murderer in my room," Madeleine whimpered and held her breath as well as their undivided attention for a few extra seconds before saying what she knew would break their hearts and make them want to protect her for the rest of their days. "It could have been me."

And with that phrase, Aunt Evelyn inhaled a gasp, launching her into a coughing fit. Madeleine quickly grabbed a cup of tea and gave it to her aunt. Uncle Pierre had not even moved.

"You can no longer stay there, Madeleine. Let's answer the police's question and the three of us will go back to New York. You can transfer to NYU or Columbia and come live at home. No need for you to be here any longer," Uncle Pierre said sternly.

Madeleine looked down at her hands and then straight into Aunt Evelyn's eyes. "I just don't know what to do, I might want to get away from it all for a while. You know, maybe go to Paris for a year. All of this has been overwhelming, and I feel like I may want a fresh start. Everyone in New York will know and . . ."

"Madeleine, that's out of the question. We can't have you so far. And you don't know Paris, it's not suitable for you. The collaborators are there still prancing around Paris as if nothing had happened, going to restaurants . . . ," Uncle Pierre stated.

"Oh Pierre, it's nearly been fifteen years . . . ," Aunt Evelyn said getting sidetracked by her husband's habitual argument.

"Uncle Pierre, that barely happens anymore. Things are changing," Madeleine carried on.

"No, you need to stay here. Your parents will want you close and so do we," Uncle Pierre's voice had risen and left no hesitation on his stance. Aunt Evelyn took Madeleine's face in her hands.

"This is all talk for later. Right now, I want you to finish your tea and slip into the bed over there in the second bedroom, I turned the covers down for you. Come on now, no need for decisions to be made," she said, scooping Madeleine up by the arm and leading her away. Madeleine shot one last look at her uncle whom she once so blindly adored.

In the soft sheets of the hotel bed, Madeleine had pulled the covers over her head to drown out the world. She slept for a solid three hours since the night before, in Phyllis's twin bed, she had mainly tossed and turned. Right before waking from her nap, Madeleine had had a vivid dream. The kind where, the first moments before stirring, the mind hasn't quite made the difference with reality. In the dream, Madeleine was in the parental house in New Jersey, standing in the bare living room except for a wicker chest of drawers. In her hand was a doll-sized replica of her Uncle Pierre and cousin Margot. Madeleine placed the dolls in the very first drawer and after closing it began stabbing the drawer violently with a large kitchen knife she held in her left hand. Having completed that task, she had to get rid of any evidence by setting the entire house on fire. Spreading gasoline and lighting a match, she watched from the outside as flames engulfed her childhood home. Suddenly she was in an all-white bedroom. There was a bed with no sheets or pillowcases, only a white blanket on top of the mattress. Under the blanket lay her distant cousin Jamie, shirtless. As she turned away from him to sit down on the side of the bed she considered the fact that she would have to live with the secret of having killed her uncle and cousin. And with no regret or questioning, she laid her head on the pillow and went to sleep only to awaken with a strange sense of accomplishment. It was a fleeting moment which disappeared as soon as she heard Detective Willoughby's voice coming from the living room where she'd sat a few hours ago. She rose silently, straining to hear the conversation. Barefoot on the carpet, her toes instinctively spread onto the lush material while she listened. She discreetly pulled back the paisley curtain from the glass doors so a sliver of the next room appeared. On the couch sat Aunt Evelyn and Uncle Pierre with the detective across from them, his back to Madeleine.

". . . such a shock. When Madeleine first told us about the suicide, I was surprised. Weren't you, *chérie*," her uncle asked, turning to his wife. Aunt Evelyn nodded in agreement. "She spent the weekend with us and she was a beautiful and interesting girl. Not an ounce of sadness about her. She had slipped into their group of friends perfectly. Like she was the missing link," she continued.

"Did she mention anything to you about being scared of family, friends, lovers . . . ," the detective asked, his eyes resting on Pierre Rousseau. Innocently, glancing at his wife. "Did she mention anything to you? I didn't pick up on anything except for her joy of life and her singing. This could be a crime of passion, perhaps an ex-lover?"

"Perhaps. Or a recent lover," Willoughby replied.

"Pierre, she was not that kind of young lady. She was extremely proper, detective. From a lovely Southern family," corrected Aunt Evelyn.

"For the moment we really can't say. All we know, is it was a homicide disguised as a suicide. Therefore, anything is possible," Detective Willoughby finished. He knew better than to ask this powerful man any questions in front of his wife. Making enemies was collateral damage in this work, making rich and powerful enemies was stupid.

Aunt Evelyn wiped away a tear. "Madeleine could have been in the room and, I just can't bear the thought of . . ." and her voice broke. This was the perfect time to step in. Madeleine slipped into the Tahitian robe her aunt had laid out, opening the neckline so as reveal part of her cleavage, as if unintentional. Smoothing her hair, she pinched her cheeks and bit her lips to redden both.

Stepping out of the bedroom, Madeleine rubbed her eyes, much like a child after a long sleep. Aunt Evelyn quickly dried her face and stood, reaching out for Madeleine to sit next to her. The detective turned to watch the young woman walking in, her feet bare and with an irritating nonchalance.

"Darling, this is Detective Willoughby, he's here to ask us questions about your friend . . ." Aunt Evelyn hurriedly explained. "I thought you would rest longer, I didn't want you to have to face questions right now."

Madeleine looked straight at the detective and thought she detected a slight side smile, hinting at a dimple.

"It's all right, we've met before, isn't that right, detective?" Madeleine asked as she sat down and leaned over, reaching for the tea.

"We certainly have," Willoughby replied. Madeleine poured the warm drink into a cup and sat back, not in the least bit compelled to ease the discomfort beginning to engulf the room.

"Detective, let us know if there is anything we can do for you. My wife and I are here throughout the weekend, maybe longer depending on what Madeleine chooses to do," Uncle Pierre explained, cutting the conversation short.

"Thank you, Mr. Rousseau. I have what I need for the moment. I'll be in touch."

Detective Willoughby stood but before leaving, he leaned over to take his cup of tea and finish it. "Never had smokey tea before. Very unexpected."

"It's Madeleine's favorite, she likes anything smokey," her aunt replied.

He looked straight at Madeleine as he finished his cup. The three Rousseaus stood, accompanying their guest to the front entrance of the suite. The detective slipped an arm in the sleeve of his grey coat. In the presence of such people, he was proud of his elegant attire, as if he nearly belonged. Uncle Pierre opened the door and put his hand out.

Willoughby took it firmly and nodded back to the ladies, hat in hand.

"I may have more questions for you as the case moves forward, if that is all right," he stated.

"Absolutely. We are entirely at your disposal. Thank you, detective for all of your help in this," Uncle Pierre said while patting him on the back, in the unwittingly condescending manner rich people could have. Madeleine reached out for Willoughby's arm.

"But, detective, do you think the campus is safe? What if he returns?" Her grip tightened.

"I have put men all around the school. I doubt anyone could get by without being seen," he answered reassuringly. Madeleine smiled, then nodded, as if in agreement with the statement. As he put on his hat and walked into the hall, he turned back:

"Then again, Miss Rousseau, who is to say the killer was a man?"

Chapter 27

Later that afternoon, Madeleine opted for a stroll through town to clear her head before heading back to campus. Aunt Evelyn and Uncle Pierre had decided to stay two more days after heavy convincing on her part for them to leave. She had argued that despite the sadness and fear, she had to move forward, that's what Rose would have wanted. And with the promise of law enforcement on campus, she was sure to be safe.

The day was cool, with only the sun warming Madeleine's face. Main Street had but a few cars passing by. In front of the grocery store, a young man was painting the sign. The top of the ladder wasn't properly snapped into place. How long would it be before he placed his foot on the last step, knocking the whole thing off balance with his bodyweight? Madeleine crossed the street, so as to avoid a falling man she'd have to help, and found herself in front of the red door of the OK Café. The small metal bell jingled as she entered. Only a few customers were sitting in the booths. Madeleine slid onto one of the cherry red vinyl-covered stools along the bar. The waitress came out of the swinging kitchen doors with a couple of breakfast plates balanced on one arm and a pot of hot coffee in her other hand. Wearing a light blue apron and matching head piece, she laid the plates packed with steaming pancakes, eggs over easy, crispy bacon, and golden hash browns in front of an elderly couple. As soon as she turned around, the couple switched their plates. The name embroidered on the shirt read "Peggy" and every effort she made was accompanied by heavy sighing. Madeleine examined the food lodged between the counter and the steel lining running along its side, wishing someone would use a toothpick to liberate the years of encrusted crumbs stuffed there.

Peggy impatiently stood across from her, hand on hip, annoyed Madeleine hadn't uttered a word.

"You gonna order something," she snapped, peering above her glasses.

Madeleine smiled. Not at her but at the thought that if Beardsmith was sleeping with the other waitress here, maybe he was sleeping with Peggy too.

"I'll have six muffins to go. An assortment. You decide which ones, I don't care," she stated.

The waitress frowned, not used to being asked to make decisions, but also not wanting to prolong their exchange either. She mumbled under her breath while placing muffins in the paper bag. Peggy's vocal agitation reminded Madeleine she'd have to face Janet later. Again with the questions, the overly helpful suggestions and would she want to change rooms now that the police were done inspecting the "crime" scene. Already annoyed, Madeleine left the money on the counter, taking the bag Peggy had purposely left just out of reach.

The newspaper stand was open and Madeleine stopped to buy the local paper. The burly old man, with a white mustache barely acknowledged her presence, only looking at the palm of his hand to count the coins. On the front page of the *Poughkeepsie Daily Eagle* was the article about Rose's suicide turned murder. Madeleine skimmed it. The killer was still at large, the sheriff was considering a curfew, not only for the school but for the whole town. Detective Willoughby was quoted in the paper:

"The police department will not rest until the murderer is found. I will make it my own personal business to see to it that they end up behind bars."

She easily imagined him saying something like that. He exuded a kind of confidence that one could find attractive. He wasn't particularly handsome, but he had strong wide hands, she had noticed. The article gave no additional information than what had become common knowledge on campus. Dumping the paper in the nearest public wastebasket, she headed down toward Fulton Avenue where a crowd had formed around the painter and his rickety ladder. He had fallen, badly, according to his cries. Madeleine passed by without slowing down, the bag of muffins in hand. Taking the scenic route back to campus, she strolled down Professor Beardsmith's street. As she approached his home, an unfamiliar car was parked along the sidewalk.

Madeleine slowed her pace, hoping to catch a glimpse of the professor's guest through the window. She suspected it might be the detective but wasn't sure. She had never seen him driving. As Madeleine approached the dark vehicle, she saw on the dashboard a piece of cardboard with POLICE written on it. On the front seat she saw some files and a brown paper bag with a grease stain. Did the detective have a lovely wife who packed his lunch every morning? Sure seemed that way. Madeleine looked back at the house, betting on her instinct.

By the time Detective Willoughby left the professor's home, he still hadn't managed to shake the unsettled feeling of the morning. The previous excitement about freedom had completely vanished. Now the case was complicated, and his mother and Lacey were sources of anguish. It was one of those days that had started off wrong and had not gotten better the way an optimist, of which he was not, might have hoped. Ever since the case had turned into a homicide, Willoughby had also considered the professor a potential suspect. He had no witness for his alibi since he was home alone. Although in his defense, no one saw him on campus either. The day of the murder he did not mention he had been with anyone yet there were dirty glasses with lipstick in the sink. When he had asked Beardsmith if on the day before the murder, had he seen or been with anyone in his home, he'd replied no. So, either the man did his dishes once a week or he was lying. But that was no solid proof; only casting a doubt on the veracity of his word. Madeleine Rousseau was another troublesome one. She and one of her friends said they were together in the library and then in a room on the other end of the hall. What if the two of them had done it? It could have been an accident they then attempted to cover up as a suicide. They had been the first two to discover the body. And why did the Rousseau girl want to sleep in the same room where a friend had died, unless she needed to hide evidence. But Willoughby was unsure about being able to pressure her into confessing anything. She had carefully avoided the few traps he had meticulously laid out. She was either naive and innocent or calculating and guilty. If the latter was the case, her every move was perfectly prepared. Her friend, Phyllis Burrows on the other hand, was a different story. A classic goodie-two shoes, as her school records showed. She was probably one of those who'd want a career. Dating certainly was not going to be a distraction given her looks.

There had been no one in the rooms adjacent to the murder scene as a meeting was being held at Main Hall about the work in the dorms over winter break. Had it been a random attack or had the murderer chosen Rose? Why bother staging it as a suicide? The staging is what led Willoughby to narrow his list to someone who knew Rose. With such few clues he needed to question the Burrows girl again and go over all of the photos, the statements, and the whereabouts on the timeline. He must have overlooked a small detail which could unravel the entire case. Willoughby checked the time, wondering if he should pay the nerdy girl a surprise visit to see if he might crack that nut. It was quarter 'til noon and hunger had manifested itself while he was still with the professor in a low rumble he hoped had gone unheard. As he'd walked out this morning, his mother had shoved a packed lunch in his hand. The gesture was both touching and irritating. This is how the unsettled day had begun. If he did not eat the lunch, the guilt would eat him. Still in his thoughts, he advanced down the cement walkway to the parked police car he'd taken this morning. The leaves had not been raked in the front yard. Willoughby was beginning to despise this lazy intellectual of a professor who was hiding something. He surely entertained relationships with his students. What else would compel a man to come and teach at an all-women's school? The entire class was probably entranced every time he peered out over his glasses, letting a strand of his thick dark hair fall across his forehead, the way it had when they'd spoken a few minutes ago.

Willoughby took a deep breath and put everything out his mind for the moment. Pleased with having taken the packed lunch in the end, he looked forward to some time to mull things over. While reaching into his pockets for the keys, something caught his eye on the roof of the car. An unidentifiable object. As he approached, the shape of a muffin came into sight, laid on a paper napkin. In the light layer of dust on the car, someone had used their finger to write "For Det. W." Despite himself, the corner of his mouth crept up. He couldn't be sure as to who left it but deep down, where he never liked to linger, there was an inkling of joy, a tiny bit of recognition for the small action responsible for the only smile of his day.

Detective Willoughby walked around the brick building referred to on campus as Strong House. On the right side of the building were the metal bars serving as a permanent access to the roof without having to enter into the building. The ladder was also reachable by the window on the top floor, the one that led onto the main hallway, next to Rose's room. The killer could have escaped through there. It was in plain sight, during the afternoon, quite a risk to take getting caught. After his series of questioning, he had drawn the conclusion there was a period of time in the afternoon of the murder with minimal movement in and around the building. The killer could have strangled Rose Suggs and then crawled out of the window without having been seen. Although an unknown man would have drawn more attention than a professor or another student . . .

Willoughby decided to open his lunch and eat it on a bench as he watched the comings and goings of students, wondering how women had the capacity to speak for hours on end. Lacey was like that, she maintained entire conversations with few interjections on his part. Well she *had*, when they were still a couple. Which reminded him, he put his hand in his pocket and pulled out a letter postmarked from

New York City. It was a letter from Lacey he had received two days ago but hadn't opened yet. It was probably like all of the other ones she wrote him about how they may be happier apart and in the last one, she had spoken of divorce. Willoughby had taken all of the feelings which had surfaced and mentally stuffed them in box he set aside, in the back of his heart, never to be unearthed or dealt with. That was how one survived this world. There was already another box labeled with his father's name and all of the emotions tied to him. He'd just put Lacey's right next to it. Come to think of it, she had probably hired a lawyer and was letting him know who it was. He felt a pit grow in his stomach and put his tomato and cheese sandwich, his favorite when he was a child, down on the waxed paper laying open on the graying wooden bench. Arthur knew there was no sense in trying to focus on anything else before reading the letter. He'd made the mistake of thinking about it and now it was too late. Like when he woke up in the night having to urinate, surely there was no way to get back to sleep before relieving himself. He opened it carefully, so as to not tear the name she had written on the back, "Lacey Willoughby." At least she still used his name. As he briefly scanned the letter, a frown crossed his face. He had to start again because he hadn't expected certain words to jump out at him:

"*I'm sorry, fixing things, together again, mistake, our history . . . .*"

As Arthur Willoughby read the letter his estranged wife had written him, his astonishment grew. She wanted him to come back to New York and if he did, they would make it work. His heart was racing. If he wrapped up this case, and by wrapping he meant *solving* then the department would have to accept a request to return to New York. Arthur could hear his mother's excitement at the idea. She might even forgive Lacey as long as it meant she no longer had to care for her son. He wondered what had brought on this change of heart. Lacey vaguely gave an explanation by saying she had done a lot of thinking. What about, she did not elaborate. But finally she had come to her senses and they would go back to their life, a normal life. Willoughby let out a sigh of relief. But strangely, the release he expected from it had not come. He took another deep breath and exhaled loudly. The pit which had formed was still there. Perhaps it was too much to absorb all at once and he would feel better later. What a strange day it had been. As he picked up his sandwich again he heard a voice coming from behind.

"Are you all right, detective? I thought you had taken ill there for a moment."

Willoughby turned to see Madeleine Rousseau walking towards him, gorgeous as ever, a smooth leather suitcase in her left hand. The thickly veiled sun was behind her, making it hard to distinguish her features accurately but he was familiar with them. He had spent the better half of the interview with her family, analyzing every detail about Madeleine's physique and behavior.

"I'm fine, Miss Rousseau. Just having a bite to eat before I continue working on the case. I feel I am getting closer and closer to the murderer," he said, staring through squinting eyes.

"That must satisfy your sense of purpose," she said approaching the bench. Willoughby folded Lacey's letter back quickly, placing it in his pocket. Madeleine had walked around to face him and was now standing directly in front of the detective. Arthur examined the intriguing person before him, her mismatched eyes and coy smile. The white bread sandwich, in his hand again, had but two bites missing.

"I didn't think you would still be hungry after the muffin," she said and with that, gave him a wink and walked into the dormitory where her roommate had been murdered.

In the mailroom, the small door to Rose's mailbox had been forced open and left agape by the police. Madeleine inspected it briefly. It was empty while in hers she found a message left by Aunt Evelyn concerning dinner.

She was to be ready at 6:30 p.m. at the main gate. Aunt Evelyn did not want her walking around in the evening while there was a killer on the loose. As she went up the stairs, she was debating what to wear for dinner, settling on the emerald dress from Paris. It was not typically mourning-like but worked well with her coloring. She'd pair it with the green and black silk scarf to tie it all in until she remembered it had ended up around Rose's neck. It was probably stuffed away in an evidence envelope on the desk of a careless police officer, next to a sticky donut and an old, abandoned cup of coffee.

Passing Phyllis and Joanie's room, Madeleine stopped in briefly.

"Good afternoon, ladies," she said. "I'm going to sleep at the hotel with my aunt and uncle tonight. I came by to get a few things."

Phyllis had turned around at the sound of the familiar voice. Her friend was always attractive but today she was mesmerizing. Embarrassed to be caught staring, she nodded and dropped her eyes, not wanting to also betray the disappointment of sleeping alone tonight.

"I'll go! Let me pack for you, I know exactly what you like," Joanie offered and before Madeleine could argue, she was out the door.

Joanie was an over-doer in times like these. As she ran down the hall to Madeleine's room, she thought of Stuart, the only boy she'd had a date with. He wasn't the tall, athletic, confident type but she really liked him. Stuart Haven was kind. And he was also caring. Joanie couldn't believe her luck. On their first date, he had taken her to the OK Cafe in town for a milkshake. He had opened the door, made sure she was comfortably seated. He had even asked if she wanted to try his chocolate shake. Joanie didn't like chocolate shakes but, to seem a little risqué, she accepted solely to put her mouth where his had been. Their first date had ended with a kiss on the cheek, making her blush from head to toe. Their second date, he had asked to hold hands while they strolled. Getting past the fear of sweaty and clammy palms, she'd let his fingers slowly interlace with hers, sending a warm sensation in her body she interpreted as a sign to marry Stuart.

Rose was the only one who'd known about him. With Madeleine's teasing being particularly sharp at times, Joanie had kept her big news a secret. And now given the situation, it was too superfluous. There was no right time to bring up this detail. Except for the fact that the afternoon Rose was murdered, Joanie had told the girls she would attend the meeting about the dormitory works and report back. Instead, Stuart had taken her on a small rowboat along the river. In time to catch the end of the meeting, she'd noted the important information to report back.

She'd begged Detective Willoughby not to reveal to the girls she was out with Stuart, fearing they might never trust her again. Joanie also tried to warn Stuart, leaving a message for him at school. But he had not answered. Surely, he wouldn't want to be tied to any woman whose friend had been murdered while she was off frolicking with him. The only part she hadn't mentioned to the detective was she could have sworn to have seen Madeleine heading into Strong House while walking back with Stuart, although she and Phyllis said they hadn't moved from the library then. But it was a minor detail. What was important was she had lied to the girls and perhaps ruined her chances of marriage with Stuart. All this pent up anguish had Joanie in overdrive.

While waiting for bags to be packed, Madeleine walked over to Phyllis's desk, who rose and pushed her glasses back up her nose to see more clearly.

"How are you, Madeleine? How are your aunt and uncle," Phyllis asked with concern. Madeleine had no desire to speak anymore. Every word that came out of her mouth felt like a drain of her focus and intelligence. She had to keep everything inside in order to control the situation. That was also why she had accepted Aunt Evelyn's invitation to sleep at the hotel. With more time, she'd evaluate the possibilities and choose the best road to her success. Meanwhile, she mustn't lose the trusting relationship with Phyllis who was staring at her like an admiring child. So, instead of speaking, she opened her arms and Phyllis quickly walked over to hug Madeleine's waist tightly, their bosoms pressing against one another. Phyllis wanted to melt into her friend.

Later that night while bathing, Phyllis recalled holding Madeleine so close. But before she could get any further in the agreeable memory, an uncomfortable and latent thought arose: their alibi. At first,

Phyllis hadn't really thought much of it because they'd believed Rose had hung herself. But the real truth was she was not with Madeleine all afternoon, the time during which Rose had been killed. She had previously refused to think any more about it because exploring the possibility, even for a faint moment, made her ill. Every time the idea flashed across her mind, her stomach tightened. It couldn't be. It was impossible. Surely, Madeleine was fiercely independent, and one might even go so far as to say unpredictable, but no one could imagine she might properly strangle a person. But here and now, alone in the bathroom, as Phyllis was letting water run down her face, her eyes closed, she entertained the thought for more than a fleeting second. What if Madeleine had killed Rose? She had acted so incredibly shocked but also very organized about what should be said and not said when the police arrived. If there was anyone Phyllis knew capable of doing it, it was Madeleine. But she would take that to the grave. Like Madeleine said, if she revealed the truth to the detective, she too would be suspended from Vassar, the summer internship at the State Department would be given to someone else, and her entire predestined fate upended by the truth. A truth bringing nothing but mayhem and chaos to her own life. If the detective did his work well, the murderer would be discovered. Torn between wanting justice to be served and prioritizing her future, Phyllis tightened the white ceramic levers to stop the flow of water as well as any remaining hesitation about keeping silent.

Chapter 28

There were not many places in which to dine in town and Uncle Pierre had settled on Carver's, a newer establishment, catering to special occasions for the local population. On its red awning, the owner's last name was written in gold cursive letters hoping to add a touch of refined elegance in the small New York town. It reminded him of the typical French brasseries, although by no means would he consider those elegant. Uncle Pierre walked in first as was customary in a restaurant to ensure it was a suitable place for his wife and niece to enter. Once upon a time, Madeleine had been impressed that her seemingly relaxed and casual uncle held on to such old-fashioned etiquette. Now she found it ridiculous.

"Hello, young man," Uncle Pierre said insistently, not having been greeted to his liking.

"Hello. Do you have a reservation," the host asked with such disinvolture, Madeleine sensed her uncle's frustration grow by the second. The young man had none of the formality or respect Uncle Pierre desired. The vaguely ironed white shirt with the first button undone behind his tie was a sincere indication he would have liked to have been anywhere else on a Saturday night than working at the nicest restaurant in town.

"We do. It's Rousseau. And we'll take the table over there in the corner," Uncle Pierre said, marching in a determined fashion to his preferred seating. The young man, not interested in arguing, unenthusiastically grabbed three menus from under the stand. Uncle Pierre shook his head in disapproval and Aunt Evelyn squeezed his hand to remind her husband to ease up as she passed him to their table.

Seeking the service of a proper maitre'd, he'd instead encountered ungrateful disinterest.

The dining room was original to say the least: an odd mixture of classic hunting scene paintings and contemporary portraits hung on dark colored walls. Had it not been for the chimney and its lovely small fire burning, the space would have felt oppressive. Seated between her aunt and uncle, Madeleine scanned the room while the host placed the menus on the table.

"He should know you give the menus in hand. Pffff," Uncle Pierre continued pouting.

"I didn't think so many people would be here at this hour," Aunt Evelyn said, knowing her husband would inevitably go on a tirade about how Americans ate so early and no one in France dined at such a time, and so on and so forth as he had innumerable times. He took the bait and the comparison between the two countries began, leaving the ladies time to look over the menu carefully. She glanced at her niece, concerned about the girl's well-being. Evelyn hadn't even wanted to go out for dinner but Pierre insisted it might be good for Madeleine to have a change of scenery.

"I'm not sure I'm really hungry," she said looking up at Aunt Evelyn after Uncle Pierre had finished the lengthy comparison on socially accepted behaviors.

"Oh, darling, you need to eat something. You're already too thin as it is. What about a tomato soup? Or here, look, a clam chowder. That might be nice and filling," Aunt Evelyn suggested as she perused the menu. She was always so concerned with how much Madeleine was ingesting. Thin people made her worry, they were frail and weak.

"I'm just not sure I can keep anything down. I haven't really been able to eat since . . . ," Madeleine's voice trailed off. Her aunt leaned over, leaving a trail of powdery perfume transporting Madeleine back to being tucked in bed with Margot while Aunt Evelyn leaned over, caressing their cheeks to bid them goodnight before going out and attending another charity or gala dinner, filling their extraordinary evenings. Madeleine had kept her eyes shut for too long reliving the moment, purposely worrying her aunt.

"Darling, are you ill? Should we leave? Oh Pierre, I told you this wasn't a good idea, we should have had dinner brought to the room," Aunt Evelyn exclaimed, convinced she should have trusted her maternal instinct.

"Chérie, how was I supposed to know. I thought it would do Madeleine good to step out, see other people. What is it that you want to do now," he replied, frustrated.

"Take Madeleine back to the room and I will order everything here and ask for it to be delivered. Go on now, don't make her wait," Aunt Evelyn gestured for them to leave. She had taken the commanding voice usually reserved for organizing the help around the house when she was throwing one of her large receptions. On occasion, she had to use it with her husband when he acted defeated.

Outside, dusk seemed to have disappeared more quickly than usual, engulfed into the night. Madeleine wished for a time when everything was less complicated, when being called in for dinner was the greatest constraint of life. She wanted the carefree instants of her youth, before Margot died, before it all changed and she had to fend for herself. Now she felt tired, tired of forecasting in order to win. She let out a heavy sigh before reluctantly accepting there was no turning back now. Uncle Pierre slipped Madeleine's arm under his as they walked on the street, a few blocks to the hotel. The light from the streetlamps gave the mist a golden glow. While her uncle was reciting a poem in his native tongue, Madeleine dove right in.

"Uncle Pierre?"

"What is it, *chérie*?" He always used the French endearment term, pronouncing it in perfect French before switching back to English. His "r" rolled deep in the back of his throat and he marveled at any American able to imitate the guttural exercise.

"You know how I really want to go live in Paris . . . ," she began slowly.

He interrupted her instantly. "Tonight is not the night for this discussion at all. You are unwell, too many emotions have come to shake you up. We cannot make any rash decisions. Besides, your aunt could not survive having you so far away. You are like our daughter. Our other daughter," he exclaimed.

But Uncle Pierre hadn't looked at Madeleine's face; he hadn't seen the expression of determination drawn over it. Nothing or no one would be able to keep her from leaving this city, this country, this family, this man.

Chapter 29

The conversation with the chief had not gone as smoothly as Willoughby had hoped. After having read Lacey's letter and the initial excitement it had provoked, he'd come back to reality and wondered if she had been left by the last fellow. Lacey preached a lot about independence but when it came down to it, she really wasn't capable of much on her own.

Chief Corbett had convened him to get firsthand information on the case of the murdered student. Local gossip had not ceased, an article about a killer on the loose in a college town had been in the paper, and it wouldn't be long before a national one got wind of the scandal. With rumors spreading like wildfire, he wanted a grasp of the situation with as many facts as possible.

"What in God's name do you need to catch this man, detective," Corbett barked at his head detective. He was a stout man whose bald head nearly always had a few beads of sweat, even on winter mornings. It was odd since hair was supposed to keep one warm and the chief had none, Willoughby thought.

"Sir, I have my best men on it and I have my suspicions . . . ," he explained, instantly regretting what he'd said. Their relationship had gotten off to a rocky start from the beginning when he'd moved to Poughkeepsie and had never improved since.

He never should have mentioned to the chief a suspect based on approximate circumstances and a gut feeling. Police investigation was a proof in the pudding kind of work and Willoughby had no dessert to bring to this table. Without a satisfactory answer, Corbett became even more infuriated.

"So, who is it? I need evidence, facts, and a murderer! I don't give a rat's ass about your damn suspicions, son. I suggest you take your big city instincts and stuff 'em where the sun don't shine." His voice dropped to a threatening whisper which, despite his lacking height, made him truly menacing. "You get me someone to pin this murder on or else it is your ass on the line. Do I make myself clear? Can you go and do that now? Get out of my office," he continued. Willoughby, who hadn't bat an eyelash during the rant, sighed heavily, nodding his head before walking out of the chief's office without a word. There was no sense in trying to defend himself. He knew the chief needed to blow some steam. Frances had told him Corbett had gotten a call from the commissioner. The chief was now in the hot seat and didn't like it. He was prepared to come down hard on everyone, especially on a city slicker he never particularly appreciated.

Willoughby headed down the hall, his colleagues pretending they hadn't heard the scolding that had not been contained by the flimsy glass and wood door.

"Detective Willoughby!"

One of the younger officers called out but he was intent on stepping outside before speaking to anyone else. Heading toward the exit, he pulled out a cigarette and placed it between his lips, while looking for the lighter in his jacket pocket. He held the filter tight on the other side of his mouth while bringing the flame of the gold Dunhill lighter close. It had once belonged to his father, though he wasn't sure how he had gotten it. His mother would probably know but speaking of her deceased husband brought on a slew of despair, from which she often took days to recover. The lighter was probably the most valuable object Willoughby owned, which wasn't saying much about his financial standing in the world. But he loved rubbing its miniature carved squares with his thumb, once he had mechanically closed the top back with his index finger, debating what Pops might have done with this case. He inhaled, filling his lungs, letting the smooth smoke graze the back of his throat. A faint drizzle started. He blew the smoke upward and watched the white cloud rise and dissolve, wishing his problems did the same. Willoughby checked his watch and instead of returning into the station, opted to head back to the murder scene, hoping to catch Rose's parents. They had been scheduled to come in for questioning at the station the next day but Willoughby was hoping to meet them in a more informal setting. He took another long drag from his cigarette, enjoying the crackling sound of the burning paper and threw the rest of it in the gutter. He didn't have much time.

Willoughby had been right. As he walked into Rose and Madeleine's dorm room, the victim's parents were inside. One side of the room looked bare, as if waiting for a new arrival at the beginning of the semester. How would they ever get another pair of girls to stay here, he wondered. The mother was seated on the chair in front of the desk, not far from where Rose's body had been hanging. Her eyes were glassy and her entire body deflated, wrung dry of any emotion. Her face was as pale as the blonde of her hair. She wasn't very much older than Willoughby but the horrendous heartbreak had rendered her aged and empty.

"Detective Willoughby, we spoke on the phone. Again, I am deeply sorry for your loss," he mumbled awkwardly. As much as he had to deal with death, giving condolences made him extremely uncomfortable for a reason he couldn't explain. He was afraid of provoking feelings in another person, reminding them of their loss. If only the pain this woman felt would ever escape her.

"Thank you," she said mechanically extending her hand as a faint smile drew across her lips, her eyelids still heavy with tears. Mrs. Suggs responded politely but remained understandably disconnected. Even the greatest loss did not wipe away the proper upbringing. Willoughby correctly guessed she had been given medication to calm her nerves, the predecessor to what would later be known as "mother's little helper." He recognized the vapid stare from a neighbor whose baby had died on their floor when he was about ten or eleven years old. Arthur had asked his mother if the woman was dead and she had replied the woman was surely dead on the inside.

Rose's father kept one hand on his wife's shoulder as he shook Willoughby's with the other.

"We didn't expect to see you here, detective," Mr. Suggs explained. He was a tall and broad man, with a melodious, soothing southern drawl. Willoughby was immediately charmed. Distraught by the death of his daughter, tears welled up in his eyes. He did not bother to wipe them away, he stood there visibly bearing his sorrow. Willoughby wasn't sure about presenting his condolences again, so he moved on.

"I was passing by and wanted to come and see if there was anything I overlooked. Is there anyone Rose mentioned to you, a new friend, an interesting encounter, anything at all," he asked.

Though sympathetic to Mrs. Suggs, he knew she would be of no use to him until perhaps the next day and even then, he wasn't sure she'd be able to muster coherent phrases. His surprise visit had not granted him the insight he'd initially hoped for.

"Nothing comes to mind. She'd only spoken of how much she enjoyed the school and well, yes her new friends and her roommate. Besides, she wasn't telling us the truth. We had no idea she'd gone to New York with them," Mr. Suggs replied. His wife let out a faint sob as a continuous stream of tears ran down her face.

"Was there anything missing from Rose's things? Any jewelry, any valuables," he pressed gently, his voice trailing.

"No, not to my knowledge," Mr. Suggs sighed.

"Rose always wore my mother, her grandmother's gold chain. It's not there and it wasn't on the list we were shown with . . . the rest of her things," Mrs. Suggs mustered, each word more painful than the last.

There had been no chain around the victim's neck, unless someone had ripped it off or it had fallen during the struggle.

"Could that be why he killed her, detective?" Mr. Suggs inquired eagerly, barely masking incomprehension. The sentiment of sorrow was accompanied by a side of determination and rage.

"We can never be sure. But I am looking into all possibilities to try to discover the identity of the killer," he stated flatly. He never wanted to give hope when, for the time being, none existed. If the murderer had kept the chain or pawned it, then perhaps. He'd have a drawing of it done and check the local spots.

Before Willoughby formulated an excuse to leave, Samuel Suggs guided the detective over to the other side of the room, away from his ghost of a wife. Standing next to Madeleine's bed, her closet still open from Joanie's packing, Willoughby smelt a hint of her perfume. He had noticed it again at the hotel. The victim's father stood uncomfortably close.

"Detective, my wife and I will not rest until the person who did this to my daughter has been taken care of. If that means behind bars or anything else. I am willing to go above and beyond to help with your investigation," he whispered heavily, his tight grip on Willoughby's shoulder.

The distress in his voice was heartbreaking.

"Sir, I can assure you, we are leaving no stone unturned, and I have every one of my men working around the clock. Unfortunately, with no eye witness or evidence, there is nothing substantial to work with here. But we will continue the investigation, I can promise you that much," Willoughby answered, trying to be as compassionate as possible to a broken father's plea.

"Listen, detective, I am not from around here, but I know how the world works. Soon enough, with no one to point to, the case will lose momentum and it'll be put away as an unsolved murder," Suggs moved closer to Willoughby. "I am willing to do anything to find this man. You hear me? Anything."

Willoughby eyed him quizzically, unsure of where Suggs was going. And as if he had asked the question aloud, Rose's father answered.

"I am willing to put you on my own payroll to find this person. I don't care how long it takes or what you have to do. I want him found. If it is the last thing I do on this earth. I'm asking you first because of your familiarity with the case but if you are not interested I will hire a private investigator to do the job. And trust me, I can make it worth your while, better than any salary at the police department," he explained, easing his hold on the detective.

Willoughby was never one to take advantage of people. Here was a wealthy father making a desperate appeal. As he quickly toyed with the idea in his mind, finally the sense of liberation he'd been seeking all day washed over him. The pit in his stomach magically disappeared. The police department was the only stable thing in his life. That and his mother. But if he wanted to return to New York, he would do it in style. And style required money. This opportunity would give him the additional finances necessary to comfortably move back to a better and bigger apartment in New York, get a brand new car, giving him and Lacey a new beginning . . .

"Of course, I'll leave you time to think it over, detective. My wife and I will be departing tomorrow after our appointment with you, feel free to let me know then. Also, if you agree, I will give you the check and every week thereafter and finally a large lump sum when you find the culprit," Mr. Suggs said looking back. "Now I must get her back to the hotel."

"Very well, sir. Thank you for the offer and for your trust in me. I will definitely consider your proposition with the utmost attention," Willoughby answered.

"Trust me when I say I really will make it worth your while," Mr. Suggs repeated. He was used to having his money speak for him. Taking his wife by the arm, ever so gently, as if holding a wounded bird, Mrs. Suggs gently raised her other hand to bid the detective goodbye.

"Goodbye, ma'am. I'll . . . I'll see you tomorrow," Willoughby blurted.

Finally, he was alone at the scene of the crime. Willoughby looked around the room. All of Rose's belongings that weren't at the station were in the open suitcases the Suggs had left on the bed. Surely, they would send for them in the morning. Madeleine Rousseau's side of the room had not yet been emptied. The officers had gone through it all. Was there anything they had missed? Willoughby got down on all fours to look on the floor, examining each interstice of the hardwood floors. By the desk, underneath the chair, a sparkle caught his eye. There lay a piece of a broken chain. He carefully pulled it out using the tip of the pen he always kept in his pocket. This was exactly why he couldn't count on anyone at the precinct to do the work properly. The chain might have snapped during the struggle but it was not helpful. The detective pulled out his notepad to jot it down. It seemed unimportant at this very moment, yet his years of experience taught him to never underestimate any piece of the puzzle. As he flipped through the pages, he smiled at the precious notes, the ones no one was privy, too. That is how he worked and despite the number of complaints from various chiefs, he never overshared information about a case unless it was completely necessary. No one else suspected Madeleine Rivers-Rousseau. And he wanted to find cold, hard proof to show them.

Willoughby stepped over to Madeleine's closet and saw the yellow Angora sweater that had tickled more than his fancy last time he was in the room. He smiled to himself. The proposition Suggs had made was a good one. The more he thought about it, the more he felt a world of possibility opening up. He reached out and grazed Madeleine's sweater with the tip of his fingers. The girl had something to hide, he sensed it. She knew more than she let on and his sole mission was to discover what it was and why. Willoughby's mind was already made up concerning his own future, now all he needed to do was close the case.

Chapter 30

Willoughby's conclusion was that the murderer knew the victim and was able to approach her all the while going unnoticed into an all-women's dormitory. Lighting a cigarette at his desk, Frances got up shaking her head. She disliked the smell of smoke, repeatedly complaining it lodged itself in her freshly styled hair.

"Did you see what Stevens left for you? There, in the folder," she motioned to the corner of his desk. Lost in thought about the case, Willoughby hadn't seen a report left by one of the officers.

"Thanks, Frances. Don't know what I'd do without you," he replied, opening the file.

On the day of the murder, one of the janitors had left after his shift and had not returned. Turns out the man, a certain Marion Ward, had had a stomach flu and had been away for a few days. His alibi having been confirmed by his cousin, Mr. Ward had gone on to reveal he had also seen a few girls, perhaps even Madeleine Rousseau, going into Strong House. He thought he'd recognized her while trimming the hedges because not long ago, she'd inquired about a lost gold pen. The janitor said he'd wanted to ask if she had ever found it but being too far away to hear him, he hadn't wanted to scare her by yelling. It was probably around four in the afternoon as he got off at five and went straight home afterwards to his cousin's house, already feeling queasy. In Stevens's observations, he'd noted the janitor's long hesitation until admitting he'd thought he'd seen a girl climb out of the building's side window and down the exterior ladder, before immediately retracting his statement, unwilling to admit if he could identify the person or not. Willoughby slammed his fist on the table with frustration.

Those in the background often had the most interesting perspective on the events of the main stage. If only he'd conducted the interview, the man wouldn't have taken back his testimony. No one put in as much effort as he did. That or they simply weren't as intelligent. On this case particularly, he had been obliged to include every single officer in the investigation as the chief continued breathing down his neck. A suicide-turned-murder at an affluent women's college had all sorts of elected officials fired up. Stevens last words on the page were: "Ward is genuinely sorry for the girl who died but he had nothing to add, got up, and left the room." Willoughby would have pressured the janitor. His "convincing" had crossed a few moral lines in the past, but it was always for the greater good.

He blew the smoke from his cigarette straight up and watched it billow and spread across the ceiling. He took a sip of the now lukewarm coffee thinking about how the offer made by Suggs to hunt down his daughter's killer had to be answered. The temptation of leaving the incompetence of his colleagues behind, rekindling the relationship with Lacey, beginning a new chapter, it was all within reach. Whether he chose to stay with the police or not, he needed to speak to the janitor soon. Every word counted, every piece of information at this point was vital. Willoughby needed to be face-to-face with the man to establish whether or not he may be able to identify the girl crawling out of the side of Strong House. He'd offer Mr. Ward anything in order to get the truth: protection, money, a new job. Whether or not he could deliver on those promises was not of interest. All he needed was for the janitor to identify the person using the exterior ladder as Madeleine Rousseau. The start of a different life glimmered on the horizon.

With an hour to spare before the encounter, Willoughby sat at the coffee shop with Marion Ward's police record Frances had brought up from the basement files. He had strategically organized for the initial meeting to take place on campus, at the janitor's office so as to maintain a casualness to their conversation. Having him come down to the station was out of the question. There was no need to scare the man. He opened the folder to see Ward had served in the war, had a few prior run ins with the law for petty theft and other "light" misdemeanors, as his mother liked to call them.

Peggy, the large bosomed waitress, walked over with a steaming coffee in hand. He had never understood why people wanted their coffees piping hot. What purpose did it serve? Did they want to scald their tongues or did they enjoy taking sips loudly. Ridiculous, he thought, shrugging his shoulders.

"Detective," Peggy greeted him as she put the cup on the table. Willoughby usually came in the morning and was surprised to see her working the afternoon shift.

"Hello, Peggy. How do you do?"

A familiarity had grown over the years between them and without asking, she always brought a cup of coffee. Though he wasn't particularly keen on having caffeine this late in the afternoon for fear of not falling asleep but since Peggy was never particularly pleasant, he also never wanted to ruffle her feathers.

"Anything else for you," she asked, hand on her hip, as if awaiting his answer for the last ten minutes. She had been standing there a few seconds. Her impatience made him anxious.

"You know what, a slice of cake or pie might be nice. What do you have back there," Willoughby asked. He wanted his bill to be big enough to justify the extra cash he was intent on leaving, he liked being labeled a generous tipper.

"Apple pie, cobbler, chocolate cake, banana cream pie . . . and then we got muffins and cookies. What's going to hit the spot, detective," Peggy asked, never cracking a smile. She sighed, waiting for a reply.

"How's the banana cream pie," Willoughby probed, trying to engage her in conversation. It was all but impossible. Peggy didn't care to interact more than necessary. She walked away to the dessert counter and pulled out an aluminum tin with a smooth, white mountain of whipped cream on it. Willoughby had begun salivating at the vision when the bell above the door chimed. He turned away from Peggy and the pie she was slicing to see Madeleine Rivers-Rousseau.

"Miss Rousseau," he called to her from his table.

Madeleine turned and waved to him. She had pulled her hair back into a high ponytail giving herself a youthful, innocent look. The eyeliner she had stolen from Aunt Evelyn's makeup bag accentuated the almond shape of her peculiar eyes.

"Detective. How do you do," she courteously said, nearing his table. He indicated for her to have a seat. Hiding her reluctance behind a charming smile she slid into the booth, across from Willoughby.

Peggy moseyed her way back to the table with a heaping serving of the banana cream pie. She looked at Madeleine, vaguely remembering her face but no interest in making it known.

"What'll it be," Peggy demanded with usual curtness.,

"Oh, I won't be staying long, thank you," Madeleine answered quickly without taking her eyes off Willoughby.

"You are more than welcome to a bite, Miss Rousseau, as you can see there's plenty here for two," he replied pushing the pie and a spoon towards her.

Peggy walked off quickly, uninterested in the exchange happening at table four. The clock above the door showed quarter past two, giving her enough time for a cigarette out back before her next shift started. The pack was in her apron with a book of matches. She stepped out, leaving the door ajar to see if anyone walked in.

Madeleine plunged into the multiple layers of the pie. Willoughby watched her precision, not lowering his stare as she opened her mouth wide to engulf the creamy bite, noting her every move.

"Mmmmm, it's delicious. You should really have a taste. Now, detective, were you sitting here in hopes of watching me eat pie," Madeleine asked, preparing another spoonful. Her use of tactical flirtation would not deter him from discovering the truth. His determination to corner the young woman was stronger than her powers of seduction.

"No, I didn't ask you here to watch you eat pie, though it is quite a sight," he replied. Two can play this game, he thought.

Madeleine batted her eyelashes mockingly. Willoughby let out an unintentional chuckle at her forced demeanor before resetting himself.

"Miss Rousseau or shall I call you Rivers, I never know . . . ," his voice trailing. Madeleine flinched. He had struck a nerve. She did not like to be reminded of her parents, of her other self. When she crossed the Atlantic, no one would know about Madeleine Rivers.

"Go on," she said, not acknowledging the questioning of her last name.

"Well, it is important how to address you. Are you Madeleine Rivers or Madeleine Rousseau? Are there two of you? A nice one and a naughty one? Like a Miss Jekyll and Mademoiselle Hyde?" He paused. "It seems your eyes couldn't agree on being the same, so maybe you wanted to be two different people too."

Madeleine sought comfort in the layers of banana and soft vanilla wafers but an uneasy feeling came over her; she did not like where the conversation was heading.

"Did you ask me here to expose a hypothesis on my personality, detective? I assure you, there's only ever been one of me," she said, licking the spoon and placing it back onto the side of the plate. "Seems I ate most of your pie. Let me pay for it," Madeleine offered, reaching into her purse and pulling out an expensive leather wallet. She wanted to remind him he was but a small town detective who should know his place. Placing a twenty dollar bill on the table, she pushed it across the table.

"Do you think that will cover it?"

Willoughby ignored the irritating gesture.

"I'd like you to come down to the precinct on Monday," he examined her face intently.

"On Monday? Why is that? Haven't I answered all of your questions already," Madeleine asked, wide-eyed.

"There is something I need to show you," he lied, preemptively relying on what the janitor would reveal. Intimidation would be easier on his turf.

"Exactly what is it that you want to show me?"

"I cannot imagine you'd refuse to help the police find your friend's murderer?"

"Of course not, detective. What an appalling image you have of me if you assume I wouldn't do everything to help."

Madeleine's eyes had grown darker and her brow furrowed. He'd successfully provoked the young woman.

"I am not interested in an image. Ninety percent of the killings I've worked on, the murderer is a person close to the victim. I am simply asking you to help me paint a better picture of your friend and room-mate to find who killed her, Miss . . ." He spoke with utter calmness that countered with Madeleine's growing angst. Her palms grew moist.

"Call me Madeleine," she said. "I cannot imagine a detective from Poughkeepsie needs the help of a college girl to solve a case but here's what I can tell you. There are several people whose motivations for getting rid of Rose might be of interest. Think about it, detective: Professor Beardsmith, for example, was having an affair with Rose. Perhaps he had found out that Rose had gotten pregnant last year by a professor back in Georgia and wanted to end things but she had threatened to reveal everything to the school if she spoke. A murder to save his career? Or maybe my dear friend, Phyllis, got very envious that Rose was getting too close to me and in a fit of jealousy, strangled my roommate to death. She's like a sneaky little mouse, no one would suspect her, no one would notice her. We were in the library together, but she could have gone and done it while I was in the basement collecting the reference books I needed. I was gone for a while, you know. I couldn't say for sure how long. The list goes on. You know behind that sweet face, Rose hadn't only made friends. Was that helpful enough, detective?"

He watched carefully without saying a word as Madeleine wiped her mouth with the paper napkin Peggy had placed under the spoon.

"I must leave you now, I've got to finish packing," Madeleine said as she closed her purse and placed both hands on the table.

"Where are you off to? You aren't leaving town are you?" Willoughby asked, trying to sound threatening.

"When I do, detective, I promise to let you know." Madeleine rose from the table and Willoughby did the same, putting his hand out to shake hers. Madeleine looked at it and then back at him, discreetly wiping her palm along the side of her skirt.

"I'll come by the station on Monday, so you can show me what you like," she said, slipping her hand in his.

"One last thing, Miss Rivers. Your cousin Margot, Margot Rousseau, died falling out of a window is that right?" he asked, still holding her hand tightly. "Was it a suicide?" he pushed.

"An accident," she answered, not flinching this time.

"Seems like you are a dangerous person to know. People keep dying around you," Willoughby knew this was going too far, but he couldn't help himself. The thought of the money he was going to make with Suggs was making him careless.

Madeleine leaned in, slightly pressing her shapely chest to him. She could feel his warm breath on her cheek.

"People should learn to be more careful, detective. *Au revoir*,"[8] she whispered.

Peggy watched through the window, cigarette in hand, as the odd couple pulled away from one another, wondering what strange pact had been sealed before her eyes.

---

8 Goodbye

Chapter 31

On the fateful afternoon of the murder, while still at the professor's house, Madeleine had caught a glimpse of a file titled "Paris Summer 1960 Exchange." When the professor went to the restroom, she discreetly opened it to find the final list of students. Next to the junior candidate line the name written was not hers. Instead, it read "Rose Suggs," in Beardsmith's familiar handwriting. Madeleine had rushed out of the house, not bothering to slam the door. Fuming, she'd walked briskly from the professor's house back to campus, her small feet determined to get to the next destination with gusto. She had to talk to Rose and get her to refuse the exchange. How did she think she was possibly going to steal Madeleine's spot in the first place? She had gotten so close to the goal, Rose imagined she could come in and take all of this away? Madeleine would reason with her and all would be back to normal. Running past Main House, she'd stopped by the library. Phyllis was at their usual table but no Rose.

"Are you here alone," she'd asked. Phyllis had started to make room for Madeleine to sit down.

"Yes, Joanie is at the meeting and I don't know where Rose is," she had answered.

"I'll be right back, I forgot my notebook," Madeleine had pretexted and left abruptly before Phyllis had a chance to say anything else.

Madeleine had run up the two flights of stairs in the quasi-empty Strong House. The information meeting about the remodeling next semester had advertised muffins, cookies, and cold beverages, a surefire way to ensure attendance. Joanie had promised to report back any relevant information.

As she'd walked silently down the hall to the room, various approaches to force Rose to back out of the offer came to mind. Firstly, Madeleine knew Rose had been flirting with the professor. She wasn't entirely sure what had happened, but it wouldn't be hard to guess once she came face to face with Rose. People were far easier to read than they imagined themselves to be. So that was one possibility. She could also use her former Agnes Scott lover and father of her child to break Rose down. Shame was a good way to manipulate, although Rose did not seem very sensitive to it. Madeleine had decided to improvise.

Rose had been sitting on her bed and jumped up, holding a letter she'd been reading as Madeleine barged in.

"Maddie!" Curious about the serious expression on her friend's face, she'd asked "Are you all right?"

"Of course. How are you?" she'd replied in a monotonous tone. Rose had placed the letter face down on her desk and walked toward Madeleine.

"I'm over the moon, I must tell you. It's a secret but I spoke to Professor Beardsmith and he is going to make sure I get the Paris summer exchange spot! He told me not to tell anyone yet but . . .—Can you believe it? I'm sure my parents will let me if it is through the school. This is my only chance! I am going to sing and study and '*parler français*,"[9] Rose had exclaimed with an enthusiasm worthy of a child on Christmas morning. She had become so gauche and loud, entirely unsophisticated, Madeleine thought. If she landed in Paris, she would stick out like a sore thumb. Immediately upon arrival at Orly airport would she offend the French with her idiotic, wide-eyed stare.

The more Madeleine had listened to Rose's monologue, the more she'd wanted to silence her forever. Madeleine had thought she was going to convince Rose to drop the Paris trip or shame her out of wanting to go. But, face to face with the current enemy, she'd lost the will and patience to unravel Rose's reasons. She had only wanted it to come to an end right there and then. It had been the same feeling when she had had her last fight with Margot and her cousin wasn't

---

9   speak French

listening to her. Madeleine didn't want another word muttered, another idea evoked. She had watched Rose walk around the room, deciding what to pack for a trip taking place in nine months. It was then Rose had unknowingly made the gravest mistake of her life. She had reached into Madeleine's closet, in an overly familiar fashion, and pulled the long silk scarf Uncle Pierre had given her, the one she'd previously been allowed to borrow multiple times. She'd wrapped it around her neck, pretending to smoke a cigarette, and with a French accent, addressed Madeleine.

"*Ma chérie*, do you want *un verre de vin avec moi*?"[10]

She'd laughed at herself and pranced around, posing in what she imagined to be elegant stances, blowing imaginary smoke all around. Madeleine had leaned against the desk, pretending to admire the show while discreetly turning over the letter Rose had quickly hidden. The paper was thick and as soon as she'd seen the penmanship, her heart had dropped. At the very bottom of the letter it was signed "Pierre."

> "*Chère Rose,*
> *. . . like a ray of unexpected sunshine on these cloudy years . . . Consider the invitation . . . an empty apartment in Paris . . . a beautiful young woman like yourself to give it some life . . . may show you around the old city of lights. My dear . . . am eternally grateful . . . next time we meet . . . Until then, douce Rose, do take the greatest care of yourself.*
>
> *Pierre*"

Madeleine's hand had begun to tremble. Her head had felt weighted and her breathing sped up. The bottled up rage and jealousy from the New York trip had filled her instantly. What was this apartment in Paris Uncle Pierre was referring to? When they had gone with Aunt Evelyn, they'd stayed at l'Hotel de Crillon. He certainly hadn't mentioned any sort of residence he still had. Next summer they would holiday in

---

10   My darling, do you want a glass of wine with me?

Egypt and she had of course been invited to join them. Uncle Pierre had scoffed at the idea of returning to Paris when the rest of the world awaited to be discovered. Yet here he was offering the city of Paris on a silver platter to a girl he had only just met. She *knew* something had happened between the two of them. They had exchanged more than glances. She had seen Rose turn on her charm, playing the damsel in distress, infuriating Madeleine. Why had Uncle Pierre been prepared to offer everything to a woman he barely even knew? They had no familial bond, no history together, where was all of this coming from? Had Madeleine underestimated the attraction of novel attention from a young and impressionable girl on a middle-aged man? Uncle Pierre was prepared to have a whirlwind adventure with her roommate of all people? The image of Uncle Pierre putting out his arm for Rose had come rushing back, he was enamored by the simpleton while she, batting her eyelashes like an ingenue in awe of the man to seduce him; like a moth to a flame.

As Rose had continued galavanting around the room and finally broke into the extraordinarily sultry rendition of "La Vie en Rose", exactly like she had at Club 82 in New York. Hatred and vile visions of this ridiculous excuse of a girl had filled Madeleine. She had not come this far to see her future wrecked. As Rose had continued spinning around the room like a dreidel, every word she'd uttered infuriated her roommate more and more. Rose had come closer, reaching out her hands to make Madeleine dance.

"Come on Madeleine, don't be a grump! Are you going to pout all day? Let's sneak out tonight and celebrate!"

As she'd gotten closer, Madeleine had closed her eyes trying to subdue every bit of rage gathering inside. But when she'd opened them again, the tipping point had been reached. She'd playfully whirled Rose around and snatched the ends of the silk scarf in either hand behind Rose's back. Nothing or no one had ever held on to anything with more determination. Madeleine had pulled each side apart so it wrapped itself tightly around Rose's neck. Immediately, she'd stopped dancing and tried to pivot to make eye contact. Her half smile had only taken a few seconds to disappear as the joke was no longer amusing. She'd brought her hands up to her neck, trying to slip a finger between her throat and the soft, smooth silk, desperate to tear the scarf off, but Madeleine had already tightened her grip. Rose's arms had flailed as she became more agitated. And with what felt like extraordinary force, Madeleine had suddenly yanked the two ends of the scarf apart in one audible snap, like a magician pulling the tablecloth out from under a beautifully set table. She'd felt a collapse in Rose's throat. The struggle had died down and Rose slid to the ground. It had been easier than she could have imagined. Or maybe Rose had known it was her time to go and did not put up a real fight. In a way, she *had* brought it upon herself. Standing over the body, Madeleine had scanned the room, her eyes falling upon the pipe running from the front door along the wall, probably less than six feet off the ground.

After the difficulty of properly attaching the body to resemble a suicide, she had checked everything was in perfect disorder, including the knocked-over chair Rose would have used to get up to the pipe. Grabbing the letter from Uncle Pierre off the bed, she had torn it in half and stuffed it in her pocket. Satisfied with the display, she had quietly peered out of the room. There wasn't a soul in the hallway. She had closed the door silently and turned to head down the stairs until she'd heard voices coming from the stairwell. Not yet prepared to fake the discovery of her dead roommate, she had had to find another way out. On the right was the window Janet was always asking the girls to keep closed since it created a draft, making the doors slam shut. It was open and as she'd glanced down, she'd seen the spaced metal bars leading to the ground.

Chapter 32

Every time Willoughby stepped on the Vassar campus, it was like an ant farm, constantly bustling with activity. In every direction appeared an ideal snapshot for an advertisement pamphlet presenting the college experience as picturesque and refined. On the brochures Willoughby had seen in the main office, one couldn't read the despair, the jealousy, the anguish, the hatred, which had pushed someone to murder a girl from Georgia. All sorts of rumors were circulating at the school, including the one where only pretty girls were at risk of being murdered by the uncaught killer. Though the idea might initially have sounded ridiculous, Willoughby found there could be truth to the reasoning. Was it not conceivable for lesser attractive or simply jealous women to want to take revenge on a prettier, happier, better dressed girl? If it were the case, his list of suspects was extensive.

As Willoughby walked to the end of the hallway, down the stairs and to the basement where the janitorial office was, he did not go unseen. He was averagely pleasing to the eye but in a women's college, it was enough to make an impression.

The janitor was not looking forward to meeting with the head detective on the case. He now intensely regretted having said anything at all to the officer with the very blue eyes, but the murder had shaken him quite a bit. It's not that he hadn't seen his fair share of dead and decapitated bodies in the war. The smell of death, of burnt skin and torn flesh was seared in his memory and continued to haunt his nights. He often woke up drenched in sweat, while during the day any unexpected loud noise sent a wave of panic through his body. But since getting hired at Vassar nine years ago, Marion Ward functioned by solely focusing on the janitorial duties, which required minimal interaction, finding solace in mundane repetition. Tackling only the task at hand instead of letting the mind wander, meant less nightmares and more peace overall. So, with every mopping motion from left to right, the individual strands of twisted cotton slid across the smooth stone floors, cleansing it. The same way he wanted to cleanse his memory from the time in France, in the trenches, fighting to defend people he had never met, risking his life for a country that wasn't his. Today, he'd lost faith anyone would ever do the same in return. The aftermath of war left more than physical scars. Since his return nearly fifteen years ago, he'd kept out of trouble. None of the students at Vassar ever thought to consider the man picking up after their meals, the one ensuring their classrooms were tidy had also spent a part of his life ensuring their freedom and the freedom of this country. He wasn't interested in recognition. Quite the contrary, he wanted to blend into the background, never jeopardizing the stability earned. His cousin Joe, who had welcomed him into his home when he'd been down and out, had also shared his friends. Now they were a solid group of musicians who played cards together. It was the only luxury and outing he afforded himself. Looking around the office, he gathered the sheet music spread on the desk and meticulously placed it in the correct order, then in the top right drawer, not wanting to supply the detective with extra insight. He wanted to be as uninteresting and nondescript as possible. Joe had already yelled about having spoken to the cops at all. So, Marion prepared to be vague during the questioning even if he knew the exact time Madeleine Rousseau had gone in and out of the building. It was if it had never happened.

Chapter 33

The Poughkeepsie Police Department was housed in the back of the Town Hall, alongside the headquarters of the Highway Department. The town was developing as was its small police force but had yet to outgrow the designated area behind the stout stone building. A vague entrance had been arranged with a few trees planted to make the rear location more notable; an attempt to inspire the respect of the offices it held. Despite the mid-morning hour, it all seemed very still: no cars were passing, no mother walking past holding the small hand of a child, no bird heard singing in a tree; it seemed the world had stopped. In the moment Madeleine was heading toward the entrance, she smoothed the front of the dark green coat she reserved only for special occasions. It was made of the finest silk blend, a softness comparable to the grazing of a raspberry on one's lips. The evergreen shade complemented her coloring, while the style accentuated her narrow shoulders perfectly, tying tightly at the waist. It made her feel in control and powerful, which she needed to face Detective Willoughby. He thought himself so ingenious. But he did not know who he was up against. She hoped to have outsmarted Willoughby but wasn't so sure after his request for her to come to the precinct on Monday. Madeleine was certain neither the professor nor Phyllis would risk their own futures to set the record straight, but she was afraid there may have been a forgotten weak link along the way. Nervous about being there, she knew it would draw more attention if she ignored the request. Instead, she opted to show up unannounced on a Friday morning, on her own terms, as if it was the most natural thing to do between two errands in town. Madeleine pushed through the front door and stepped into a stuffy room, a narrow desk off to the right. An elderly woman was sitting pulling various pieces of paper from a large envelope and showing them to the officer.

"Mrs. Harper, this is not the registration certificate. That's what we'll need to take care of the fine."

"Dear, this is all I have. I didn't get a registration certificate. They must not have given me one so I will never find it."

The woman opened and closed the clasp of her purse nervously. The officer spoke in a calm and reassuring voice, surprising for his robust appearance.

"Why don't I get one of the fellows to come by later this week and help you look for it? There's no hurry to have this done right now you know?"

The woman nodded, reassured as one of the sheets slipped from her lap onto the floor. Madeleine knelt to pick it up while two police officers walked by to step outside. She recognized one of them from the day they had barged into her bedroom on campus.

"Thank you, you are such a kind young lady," Mrs. Harper said, tucking the sheet into the envelope as she stiffly rose from the chair.

"Why don't I help you out," Madeleine offered. The man smiled, appreciative of the gesture.

"Why, aren't you a dear. I'll be waiting for one of your men, Andy." She slipped an arm through Madeleine's for stability. The door to the exterior opened, revealing an animated conversation between the two officers.

"I can't stand the guy. He thinks because he's from the city, he's seen it all. Well, you know what, I'm sorry for the girl's parents who came all the way from Georgia but this case ain't getting solved and I'm glad." He took a long drag from his cigarette. "You know he won't share ANY information?"

"My car is right over there," the old woman said, interrupting Madeleine's eavesdropping and pointing to a blue and white Ford Skyliner in the parking lot surrounded solely by police vehicles.

"Walter bought it right before he died. I don't have the heart to sell it," she lamented. Madeleine patted her hand in compassion, straining to finish listening to the conversation between the two men.

"He told the captain he was closing in on a suspect. He's going to New York this afternoon and by Monday, it was going to be in the bag," the blonde one said.

The first officer laughed, lighting another cigarette with the butt of the first one.

"I'd like to see that. You think a janitor with a record is going to talk? How much you wanna bet it's a bust? I'll put five on it."

"That's a lot money. I don't know. Willoughby may be a cube, but I've asked around. You can count on one hand the number of cases he hasn't solved. No matter what it cost him."

"Even his wife," the one smoking replied and their laughter exploded like gaggles of geese. He went into a coughing fit, as if his lungs were trying to escape his body.

Madeleine froze.

"What's the matter, dear? You've gone all pale," Mrs. Harper asked, pressing her fingers deeper into Madeleine's arm.

Willoughby was going to present his main suspect at the beginning of next week. It was her name he'd give the chief of police, she was sure of it. Why was he going to New York? To speak with Uncle Pierre and Aunt Evelyn? To warn them about her arrest, her guilt? This absolutely could not happen. She had to find a way to stop him. Had he some personal vendetta in solving this case?

"This is a lovely coat dear. You mustn't get it wet, it would damage it you know. It may rain, why don't I give you a ride?"

Madeleine forced a smile as her mind raced. She had to speak with the detective again. But not here at the station. She had to find him elsewhere.

"Thank you, I'm fine. It was lovely to meet you, Mrs. Harper. Drive safely."

The police officers finally saw the attractive young woman standing nearby and nudged each other before lowering their voices. But before they had a chance to flirtatiously ask if they might be of service, she had spun around, in the direction of the center of town.

Chapter 34

The train was slowly pulling into Penn Station. Willoughby was not the type to hurriedly stand during the final approach, hoping to be one of the first to get off. Certain passengers might be in a rush to get to an appointment, but it seemed most were wanting to get out before their neighbor for no particular reason other than pure impatience. He placed the grey fedora on his head and waited for the train to come to a complete stop before rising and grabbing the small black leather suitcase he had packed for the weekend. Lacey would be surprised to see him. He had not replied to the letter. After having read it, he had gone through an array of emotions. Once the initial shock had worn off came the questioning, then the anger, followed by a rage he nearly did not surpass. Finally, with the offer Suggs had proposed, he let himself be seduced by the idea of a more comfortable life and recapturing the stability of being in a marriage. It certainly outweighed the lonely nights, the snickering remarks, the never-ending questioning if he would die alone. Going back to the reassuring relationship meant prioritizing a sense of familiarity more so than amorous love. If so, what was wrong with that? All he had to do was be sure to never again think about another man touching Lacey and all would be forgiven.

As he was placing his foot down on the metal step to exit the train, a young boy, dressed in raggedy clothes, pushed past him violently. Losing his balance, Willoughby's leg began to slip down the gap between the train and the platform. Instinctually he reached out for the metal handle on the door but missed it by an inch. He felt no ground under his foot as his other leg began to buckle with gravity and the fear of the pain about to occur paralyzed him. But a large hand suddenly grabbed the back of his coat, abruptly halting his fall.

"Catch him! Catch the kid!"

The train conductor, a heavy-set man with a big mustache, had come plowing out of the train, and had caught Willoughby at the last moment. The kid had been swallowed up by the sea of people headed to the staircase at the end of the platform.

"Are you all right, sir?"

"I'm fine, thank you. Nice catch," Willoughby said, his heart racing. He took a minute to stand to the side and gather himself and his thoughts. After a few moments, he laughed at the thought of having been taken out by a child thief. It would not have made for a grand entrance back into Lacey's life had she had to pick him up from the hospital instead of surprising her at home with the flowers he intended to buy. Making his way down the platform amidst the crowd again, he looked forward to the station's grandiose waiting hall. It was such an extraordinary place. Willoughby liked to stand under the gigantic clock hanging from the ceiling and look up at it, letting a kind of reverse vertigo creep in. He found it a helpful reminder of the insignificance of human beings on the planet. Like small ants crawling around on the Earth, rarely looking elsewhere than right in front of them. Now he never liked to stay too long in that state of mind, distancing himself from life. The job he held was ground in reality of human behavior and usually the darkest forms of it. But today, he had no time for such distractions. Still caught in the flow of travelers, the hustle and bustle of people politely trying to run each other over got to be too much, especially after his close call. He safely made his way all the way on the other side of the platform, where the tracks lay bare awaiting the 12:18 train from Philadelphia. In the far distance, it had appeared, coming into the station, so Willoughby quickened his step before everyone from those northbound carriages would encumber his way. Since living in Poughkeepsie, he'd forgotten how people in the city did not mind physical contact with other bodies as they pressed on, bumping shoulders, accidentally knocking hands, being pushed up against one another. It had been a long moment since he had been pressed up against anyone, with or without clothes on. In the back of his mind, he wondered if when Lacey opened the door, he would feel an excitement urging him to take her directly into the bedroom. Would they need to talk, or could they do that after having found each other again? Willoughby was deeply lost in thought about calculating the number of weeks it would be before he could properly move back to New York and give his marriage another chance. The train from Pennsylvania steadily rolled into the station behind him as he paid it no mind.

The janitor's testimony was essential to the case, which is why he had promised him an immunity which, in reality, he couldn't ensure. He expected Captain Corbett to refuse it but Willoughby absolutely needed him to go on record Monday about having recognized Madeleine Rousseau walking into Strong House and soon after, down the side of the building. He didn't care if the janitor lost this job or anything else for that matter. Convinced a written deposition from Marion Ward along with circumstantial evidence would be sufficient to break the girl and obtain a confession, he felt the end was near. He would be given sole credit for solving the case. And that's how he would get himself back to the city on his own terms, with the recognition of closing the town's most important case and a grand reward from Suggs. Thanks to a local investigative journalist who had written an in-depth article about the murder, it had also gotten coverage on the state level. He had surely convinced someone on the force to speak for the details of the crime scene were much too specific. This comforted Willoughby in his decision to keep his discoveries, suspicions, and evidence to himself before he needed to use them.

Filled with the burgeoning thrill of solving the case, and the first of several checks to come from Samuel Suggs burning a hole in his pocket, Willoughby migrated closer to the edge of the platform.

While still deep in thought about his future recognition, a powerful push came from behind his right shoulder. Again, he thought. He really wasn't used to being in the city anymore. As he lost his balance, he tried to grab onto anything, a pole, a person but this time there was nothing. What felt like a slow, incredulous fall ended abruptly as he landed heavily onto the tracks, in front of the oncoming train. A terrible screech echoed throughout the station as the conductor desperately tried to halt the engine, but it was too late. Before Willoughby's body was crushed and dismembered by the metal wheels, he saw there on the platform, the back of young woman walking away, with perfectly curled dark brown hair, wearing an evergreen silk overcoat tied tightly at the waist, which she wore for special occasions. And while everyone on the platform turned as they heard the detective's bloodcurdling scream, Madeleine pressed on, filled with a sense of relief and burgeoning thrill about her own future.

Chapter 35

Phyllis had returned from Christmas vacation the day before classes were to start. She usually liked to arrive a few days prior but her parents had insisted she stay as long as possible. In the end, she didn't mind for Madeleine would not be returning. So much had happened last year that her aunt and uncle had insisted she move to New York. As Phyllis passed Main House, suitcase in hand, the air was cold and crisp and her heart heavy. She wore the delicious leather gloves gifted by Madeleine a few months back. It seemed like an eternity ago, when everything was simple. Before New York, before Rose, before the detective . . . before it all. As she walked up the front steps to the main entrance of the dormitory, Phyllis sighed. She would focus on her studies but she longed for Madeleine's presence, for the friendship between the three girls, well four. Rose's case had been left unsolved after the detective had died in New York. Phyllis had wondered if he'd fallen or . . .

"Phyllis! Phyllis darling!"

She turned around to see Madeleine, her hair bouncing up and down with every step, waving a gloved hand.

"What are you doing here," she asked in complete dismay.

Madeleine threw her arms around Phyllis and held her close.

"I have been waiting for you all weekend! I wanted to surprise you."

"You've certainly succeeded. Are you visiting? Didn't you transfer to Columbia or . . ."

"Oh no! It took a bit of convincing for Uncle Pierre and Aunt Evelyn to let me return but here I am."

"For good?"

"For the spring semester. Then I'll be off to Paris for the summer of course since Professor Beardsmith had chosen me for the exchange," she exclaimed victoriously. "Shall we put your suitcase down and ask Joanie to join us for a late lunch?"

It all felt so very normal again. As if the chaos of the fall semester was already but a faint memory, ready to disappear like a fading watercolor. Had it even been real? As she watched Madeleine, she too wanted to forget, pretend nothing had happened, no doubts having ever existed, no friends lost. Although Phyllis was already pained at the idea of another separation in a few months, for the moment, this glorious friend was hers to keep.

Acknowledgements

I would like to express my deep gratitude to the following individuals who have contributed to the creation of this book:

To Lars Bill Lundholm for his everlasting encouragement and support, his words of wisdom, and helping me « paint it black ».

To my writer's group: Dennis Broe, Judith Chusid, and Dan Kavulish for their guidance, mentorship, and providing a supportive community of fellow writers for numerous years.

To my readers Gratiane de Montebello, Dennis Broe, Emmanuelle de Villepin, and Caroline Karim Kassar for their insightful feedback.

To Claude Clin for her precious anecdotes of Paris in the late 1950's.

To Marie Alani for her support, patience, and invaluable guidance in managing everything surrounding this book, including me.

To Anna Ogden-Smith, for her amazing creativity and aesthetic eye in designing a visually stunning cover for the book.

To Mark Schoenecker for agreeing to share his talent and producing original lettering for the cover.

To Shelley Oliver for meticulously proofreading the manuscript.

To Jaye Manus, for her expertise in formatting the book and making it visually appealing.

To all of my friends, for their continuous support.

All of the people mentioned above are extremely talented in their respective domains. I am lucky to count every single one, apart from one professional relationship, as a friend. They have been very generous in their time, support, and intellect so that this book could find its way into your hands. Thank you all.

Lastly, I would like to thank ALL of the readers and supporters of my work. Your enthusiasm and appreciation for my stories fuel my will to publish.

About the Author

MATHILDE MERLOT is a French-born, American-raised screen-writer and playwright whose work has been produced in Mexico, the US, and in Europe. She continues to share her time between L.A and Paris. *Death at Vassar* is her first novel and initial book of the Madeleine Rousseau Mysteries.

To learn more about the author, visit www.mathildemerlot.com

Printed in Great Britain
by Amazon

31954883R00158